Famous Leaders Among Women

JULIA WARD HOWE.

FAMOUS LEADERS AMONG WOMEN

BY

SARAH KNOWLES BOLTON

" Life is meant for work, not for pleasure "
PRINCESS ALICE, DAUGHTER OF QUEEN VICTORIA

Essay Index Reprint Series

WHITTEMORE LIBRARY
Framingham State College
Framingham, Massachusetts

BOOKS FOR LIBRARIES PRESS
FREEPORT, NEW YORK

First Published 1895
Reprinted 1972

Library of Congress Cataloging in Publication Data

Bolton, Sarah Knowles, 1841-1916.
  Famous leaders among women.

  (Essay index reprint series)
  Reprint of the 1895 ed.
  CONTENTS: Madame de Maintenon.--Catharine II. of
Russia.--Madame le Brun.--Dolly Madison. [etc.]
  1. Woman--Biography. I. Title.
CT3202.B6 1972   920.72   76-38745
ISBN 0-8369-2639-0

PRINTED IN THE UNITED STATES OF AMERICA
BY
NEW WORLD BOOK MANUFACTURING CO., INC.
HALLANDALE, FLORIDA 33009

TO

𝔐y 𝔗eachers

OF THE OLD

PRATT STREET SEMINARY, HARTFORD,
CONNECTICUT.

PREFACE.

PHILLIPS BROOKS said in an address before the Phillips Exeter Academy in 1893, " Since the noblest life on earth is always human life, the literature which deals with human life must always be the noblest literature. And since the individual human life must always have a distinctness and interest which cannot belong to any of the groups of human lives, biography must always have a charm which no other kind of history can rival. I believe fully that the intrinsic life of any human being is so interesting, that if it can be simply and sympathetically put in words, it will be legitimately interesting to other men." I trust that the lives here sketched may be found interesting.

Madame de Maintenon, with neither beauty nor youth, but with great intellectual power, was able to win and keep the love of a fickle king.

Catharine II. of Russia made a comparatively uncivilized country the Mecca of scholars and artists during her reign. She was fitly called the "Star of the North."

Louise Le Brun became the painter and friend of sovereigns, overcoming obstacles that would have disheartened most people.

Dolly Madison will always be remembered as one of the most lovely women ever in the White House.

Catherine Booth, the mother of the Salvation Army, unused to public speech, became the eloquent advocate of a wonderful movement.

Lucy Stone was the gentle leader in a great reform.

Lady Henry Somerset and Julia Ward Howe show how women of wealth and social position may give their lives to good work, if they feel a true sense of responsibility.

Queen Victoria's name will be illustrious through the centuries as that of a good woman, and a wise and able ruler. Cardinal Manning said in her Jubilee year, "Her home and her court are bright and spotless examples for all who reign, and a pattern for all people."

S. K. B.

CONTENTS.

	PAGE
MADAME DE MAINTENON	1
CATHARINE II. OF RUSSIA	55
MADAME LE BRUN	92
DOLLY MADISON	123
CATHERINE BOOTH	159
LUCY STONE	212
LADY HENRY SOMERSET	250
JULIA WARD HOWE	272
QUEEN VICTORIA	304

MADAME DE MAINTENON.

MADAME DE MAINTENON.

"No woman in modern times," says Dr. John Lord in his "Beacon Lights of History," "ever rose so high from a humble position, with the exception of Catherine I., wife of Peter the Great."

"During more than thirty years," says Imbert de Saint-Amand in his "Court of Louis XIV.," "she was to reign without a rival over the soul of the greatest of all kings; and it was not the monarch alone, but the monarchy, which was to incline respectfully before her. The whole court was at her feet, soliciting a word, a glance."

Again, he says of Madame de Maintenon, "Here we have a woman who, at fifty years of age, takes possession of a sovereign of forty-seven in all the prestige of victory and power; a woman who, with an ability that borders on witchery, supplants all the fairest, richest, and noblest young girls in the world, not one of whom would not have been proud to unite herself with the great king; a woman who, after having been several times reduced to poverty, becomes, next to Louis XIV., the most important personality in France."

Françoise d'Aubigné, the future Madame de Maintenon, was born Nov. 27, 1635, in a prison at Niort, one hundred and three leagues from Paris, where her father was confined for debt.

2 MADAME DE MAINTENON.

Constant d'Aubigné, the father, though a talented and handsome man, was a gambler; set up a mint to make false coin; murdered his wife in a fit of jealousy; was put in prison for his misdeeds; won the heart of a young girl, Jeanne, daughter of Pierre de Cardilhac, the governor of the fortress where he was confined, married her, and made her wretched till his death, twenty years afterward.

Jeanne was a Catholic, of a poor but noble family, while Constant was the son of the distinguished Théodore Agrippa d'Aubigné, one of the leaders of the Protestants in the Huguenot wars, an author, soldier, and man of property. He disinherited Constant for "being a destroyer of his family honor by his enormous crimes."

After various sojourns in prison, Constant was released in 1642, when he was fifty-seven years old; and with his young wife and three children, two boys and Françoise, then seven years of age, started for the West Indies. Some friends had obtained for him from a trading company to the American Isles, the governorship of the Marie-Galante Island. When he learned that only the native Caribs lived there, he determined to remain at Martinique, where he found employment. Here, as before, he borrowed money under false pretences, kept two dozen slaves about him, so as to appear wealthy, and died in 1647, leaving his family destitute.

Fortunately the mother possessed both courage and energy. She brought her children back to Paris, placed them with her husband's sister, Madame de Villette, and tried to support herself by needlework. The struggle was a hard one. She endeavored to pay some of her husband's debts, for which creditors were clamoring, while her own rooms were bare and comfortless.

She had not forgotten to instruct her children in the Catechism of the Romish Church, and to foster their love of reading. Françoise especially enjoyed Plutarch's "Lives." She taught them also to rise above circumstances. When their house at Martinique took fire, and Françoise was crying bitterly, Madame d'Aubigné, who thought only of saving her books, said, "What! is my daughter crying about a house?" The child was sobbing really because her doll was burning.

Charles, the brother of Françoise, had been placed as a page with a relative, Madame de Neuillant. This lady represented to the queen-mother, Anne of Austria, that Françoise, a Catholic girl, was being brought up as a Protestant, and asked her removal. The girl could not bear to leave her aunt, Madame de Villette, whom she devotedly loved, and accept the home of a stranger.

She did so; but her life with Madame de Neuillant was not an easy one. She and the daughter of the madame were dressed like peasants, and were obliged to tend geese and turkeys all day long, to see that they did not stray away.

Later, Françoise was placed in a convent; but having already embraced the Huguenot faith from the influence of her father and her aunt, Madame de Villette, and showing no prospect of a change of belief, the nuns sent her back to Madame de Neuillant, who returned her to her mother.

Poor, and weary with her struggles, the mother sent her to another convent, where the girl finally abjured her Protestant faith, and accepted Catholicism, stating, however, that she could never believe that her aunt, Madame de Villette, would be lost on account of her Protestant views.

At fifteen years of age Françoise was again with her mother in one small room in the Rue des Tournelles in Paris. Life presented no roseate picture for either of them. One brother was dead; and the mother doubtless thought him better off than to be alive, and experience their want and sorrow.

About this time a dramatic author and comic poet, Paul Scarron, desiring to learn something of Martinique, sent to Madame d'Aubigné for information. Not wishing to receive the writer in her poor abode, she went with her daughter to his home. Here the girl found many fashionable people who loved to gather with the witty poet, and was so ashamed at her short and shabby dress, that she burst into tears. The author, moved to pity by the girl's helplessness, offered her some money, which she courteously, but decidedly, refused.

Poor Madame d'Aubigné at last broke down in her struggle to earn a living, and went back to Niort to die, where she had given birth to Françoise in prison. Nothing but sorrow had resulted from her love of the worthless Constant d'Aubigné.

Françoise was homeless and penniless in the great city. Her aunt was dead, and she was obliged to look to Madame de Neuillant for protection.

The Abbé, Paul Scarron, had not forgotten the modest and sweet-mannered girl. He was an invalid from acute rheumatism, and used to compare his form to the letter Z. "His head," says Walter Bennett in his life of Madame de Maintenon, "was sunk between his shoulders, his legs bent under him; his knees served him for a writing-desk." He not inaptly called himself "an abridgment of human misery." Knowing how much the girl suffered with Madame de Neuillant, he resolved to offer her a choice between a convent and marriage. "If you wish to be a nun, I will pay your portion," he said. "If you like to marry, I have only a very moderate fortune, and a very ugly person to offer you. Whichever you choose, I shall only be too happy to have delivered you either from the tyranny of Madame de Neuillant or the artifices of courtiers."

She accepted his offer of marriage, though only seventeen, and he forty-two and a cripple for the past twelve years. She become his willing secretary and pupil; studied under him Latin, Italian, and Spanish, and presided with grace and tact at his literary gatherings. The most eminent men and women came to his home, — Madame de Sévigné, Mademoiselle de Scudéry, the Marquis de Coligny, the beautiful Ninon de l'Enclos, and others.

For eight years Françoise was the cheerful, devoted companion and the grateful wife of Scarron. "I shall not make her commit any follies," said the burlesque poet; "but I shall teach her a good many." Instead of this, Françoise, by her wise suggestions, taught him to avoid follies. Her modest conversation banished much coarse wit from his home. Unselfish, a good listener, simple in taste and manner, yet dignified, interested in the joys and sorrows of all about her, amiable, and very intelligent, she became a universal favorite.

Christina, Queen of Sweden, asked that Madame Scarron might be presented to her. She was so pleased with her, that she desired a friend to tell the poet that she " was not surprised that with the most charming woman in Paris for his wife, he was the happiest man in that fair city."

Having been obliged to give up his canonry of Mans at his marriage, and the income from his books being uncertain, Scarron and his wife were obliged to practise economy; but Françoise had been reared in the school of poverty, and she never murmured. Her allowance was five hundred francs per annum, and out of this sum she gave much in charity. The queen-mother, when she heard of the poet's marriage, had said, " What will Scarron do with Mademoiselle d'Aubigné; she will be the most useless piece of furniture in his house."

But Anne of Austria was mistaken. Françoise proved to be the one useful and blessed compensation in a life of pain and shadow. On his death-bed in October, 1660, at the age of fifty-one, Scarron said, "I could quit the world without regret, if I did not leave in it a wife I have so many reasons to love, who will have neither hope nor fortune to sustain her."

To Françoise he said, holding her hand, and thanking her for all her care, "I beg you to think of me sometimes. I leave you without fortune. Virtue never obtains its reward; still be always virtuous."

When Scarron was married, the notary asked him what settlement he proposed to make upon his wife. "Immortality," was the answer; and his words were destined to prove true.

After Scarron's death, his wife was offered a home

with different friends; but she declined all, and entered a convent, so as not to be dependent upon any one.

She was at this time an attractive woman of twenty-five. Mademoiselle de Scudéry said of her, "She was tall, and had a fine figure. . . . A smooth, beautiful skin, pretty chestnut hair, a well-shaped nose, a clean-cut mouth, a noble, sweet, modest expression, and, what made her beauty more striking, the finest eyes in the world. . . . Her mind was just suited to her beauty,— large, gentle, pleasant, and well-balanced. . . . Joining her good qualities to her beauty and wit, it must be owned that she was worthy of all the admiration she excited."

Madame Scarron said of herself, "Women like me because in society I occupy myself more with others than with myself; men follow me because I have beauty and the grace of youth. The feeling they have for me is more a general friendship than love. I do not wish to be loved by any one in particular, but by everybody. . . . To be well spoken of, to be singled out and approved by good people; for that was, in a way, my idol. For that I could have done or suffered anything." From childhood her true desires seemed to be these: "I wished to be esteemed," she said, "and to make myself a name was my chief aim. I was really what is called a good child; so much so that everybody loved me. When I was a little larger I lived in the convents; you know how much I was loved by my mistresses and my companions. I thought of nothing but obliging them, and making myself their servant from morning to night." Françoise would get up at night and iron the garments of the younger children, thus surprising and pleasing the sisters.

She was equally anxious for fame. The story is told of her, that when a child, and her mother was relating the exploits of her grandfather, Théodore d'Aubigné, so much esteemed by the King of Navarre, Henry IV., the little Françoise said, "And shall I be *nothing*, mother?"

"What should you like to be?" asked Madame d'Aubigné.

"Queen of Navarre!" was the ambitious answer.

A year after Scarron died, when it was known by some friends that his pension of two thousand livres was discontinued at his death, Anne of Austria was asked to continue it to his widow, which request she readily granted. For about five years, till the death of the queen-mother, Jan. 20, 1666, Madame Scarron lived in comparative ease and happiness. She dressed simply, almost always in soft wool, gave much time to the church and to the poor, and frequented the charming salons of Mesdames d'Albret, de Richelieu, de Sévigné, and a few others, where she met the most cultivated society in Paris; even, as was said, in her "glorious and undeniable poverty."

Having lost her pension by the death of Anne, Madame Scarron again retired to a convent, and devoted herself to study. Among her favorite books were the lives of St. Elizabeth, St. Louis, and Plutarch, which had so charmed her in her girlhood. Friends again asked for the renewal of her pension, but in vain. Colbert, the great minister of Louis XIV., managed the finances with rare ability, and tried to economize at every point.

The daughter of the Duke de Nemours, of the House

of Savoy, was about to marry the King of Portugal, and requested Madame Scarron to accompany her to Lisbon, as secretary and companion, with the prospect of an appointment as lady of honor. Although unwilling to leave France, she consented, as it had become a necessity to earn some money.

Among her friends was Madame de Thianges, the sister of the beautiful Madame de Montespan, lady of the queen's palace. Madame de Thianges introduced Madame Scarron to her beautiful sister, telling her that she was about to depart for Lisbon.

"That is a long way off," said Madame de Montespan. "You must remain here; d'Albret has spoken to me about you, and I know your *value*."

"I should much prefer," said Madame Scarron to herself, "that she knew *all my misery*. So I described it to her without humbling myself. She listened to me attentively, although she was at her toilet. I told her that my pension had been suppressed; that I had solicited M. Colbert in vain; that I was obliged to seek my living out of my own country. Madame de Montespan was much touched by my recital, and asked for the petition, which she promised to present to the king herself."

Madame de Montespan presented it, when Louis XIV. exclaimed, "What! the Widow Scarron again!"

"Sire," said his charming petitioner, "it is a long time since you have been spoken to on the subject, and it is surprising that your Majesty should not yet have listened to a woman whose ancestors were ruined in the service of yours."

Madame Scarron again received her pension, declined

10   MADAME DE MAINTENON.

the offer to Lisbon, and settled in a modest apartment in the Rue des Tournelles, where she had once lived with her mother. How improbable it then seemed that she would ever be the wife of Louis XIV.!

This "Grand Monarch," one of the most renowned kings of the world, was at this time, 1668, thirty years of age. His father, Louis XIII. was a weak, jealous man, "the most impotent of all the Bourbons," says Dr. Lord; married at fourteen to Anne, daughter of Philip III. of Spain, called by the French, Anne of Austria, a child of eleven. She was beautiful in person, haughty in manner, and, like her husband, governed for years by the unscrupulous minister of foreign affairs, Cardinal de Richelieu.

Nearly twenty-three years after their marriage their first child, Louis XIV., was born, to the great delight of the whole kingdom. The Pope sent clothes embroidered in silver and gold in two chests of red velvet, to the royal infant, with his blessing. Two years later a second son was born, Philip, Duke of Anjou.

When Louis was four and a half years old he was declared king, under the regency of his mother. He was taken to the bedside of his dying father, who, in the prime of life, at forty-two disliked to leave the world.

"What is your name, my child?" asked the father tenderly.

"Louis XIV.," replied the lad promptly.

"Not yet," said the king sadly; "but pray God that it may soon be so." He kissed the dauphin, as the king's eldest son was called in France, on both cheeks and brow, and expired, May 14, 1643.

Richelieu had at his death bequeathed his Cardinal

Palace, costing a million dollars, to the young king. The name was changed to Palais Royal, as it was thought unwise for the home of the king to bear the name of a subject. To this palace the boy king and his mother came when he was five years old.

At the age of fourteen, with great pomp and splendor, Louis XIV. was declared monarch of France. He was a handsome boy in his court dress almost covered with gold, sitting erect upon his magnificent cream-colored horse. When the people cried, "Long live the king!" the animal became frightened, and nearly threw his rider.

Covering his head before his uncovered Parliament, the young king said, "Gentlemen, I have attended my Parliament in order to inform you that, according to the law of my kingdom, I shall myself assume its government; and I trust that, by the goodness of God, it will be with piety and justice."

The self-possession and kingly manner of the lad greatly pleased the people, while his courtiers soon saw that he was not to be ruled, but to rule.

When Louis was about eighteen he became very much in love with Mary de Mancini, the niece of Cardinal Mazarin, then prime minister. She was a girl of great refinement of nature, very intellectual, and led the young king to read the best literature of France, and to study the Italian language for her sake. She loved him devotedly; and had Louis been allowed to marry her, his whole life would probably have been changed. For reasons of state, and to make peace between two countries almost constantly at war, Maria Theresa, daughter of Philip IV. of Spain, was chosen for Louis XIV., she

12 MADAME DE MAINTENON.

renouncing her claim to the Spanish throne in consideration of the promise of 500,000 crowns to France. Very little of this was ever paid. Both Louis and Mary de Mancini wept and tried to avoid the unwelcome fate which separated them, but in vain. Mary, heartbroken, married the rich Prince Colonna, and lived a most wretched life.

The marriage of Louis XIV. with his first cousin, Maria Theresa, was celebrated in the most magnificent manner. The Isle of Pheasants, a small Spanish island in the boundary river between France and Spain, was chosen as the place of meeting. A temporary palace was erected, with covered bridges leading to the mainland, where the articles of marriage were signed. Then the ceremony was pronounced on Spanish soil, and again on French, with the most elaborate etiquette.

The gentle and timid Maria Theresa, with blue eyes and light hair, wearing a royal mantle of violet-colored velvet with *fleur-de-lis* over a white satin dress, radiant with gems, was united to the handsome king, whom she afterwards seems really to have loved, and equally feared.

On Aug. 26, 1660, a gorgeous entrance was made into Paris. The queen was seated on an antique car wellnigh covered with gold, robed in great splendor. By her side rode the king of twenty-two years, attired in the richest velvet adorned with gems, at a cost of a million or more dollars. The houses along the streets were hung with garlands; the ground was covered with flowers and sweet-scented shrubs, the carriage wheels crushing out the delicious perfume as they passed. Paris was intoxicated with joy, and did not know that two royal hearts cared little for the gorgeous display.

Cardinal Mazarin, who had really ruled France for eighteen years, able but parsimonious, died March 9, 1661, leaving, says Miss Pardoe in her life of Louis XIV., two hundred million francs in the money of the present day. Fifteen millions of this was concealed in various places, and reverted to the king, as it was believed that Mazarin intended thus to replenish the exhausted treasury of his majesty.

As soon as the cardinal was dead, to the astonishment of France, Louis showed his real nature. Mazarin had said, "He set out rather late, but he will go farther than any one else. There is stuff enough in him to make four kings and an honest man."

Louis called his councillors together, and said, "I have summoned you . . . to tell you that it has pleased me hitherto to permit my affairs to be governed by the late cardinal; I shall in future be my own prime minister. You shall aid me with your counsels when I ask you for them. I request and order you . . . to sign nothing without my command."

"He had in himself," says Henri Martin in his "History of France," "a confidence that was, at this first epoch of his life, but a legitimate feeling of his strength and his future. There has, perhaps, never been a will superior to his in persistence and intensity. The effort of attention and labor which it was imagined he would not sustain three months, he sustained during fifty-four years."

Handsome in person, stately in manner, surrounded by a flattering court, with, as Martin says, "a thirst for glory and a passion for the great in all things," he began to build gorgeous palaces, to engage in wars, to find pleasure outside of his loveless marriage.

Maria Theresa, devoted to religion, with no love for the pomp of courts, a faithful wife and a devoted mother, deserved a better fate. Of her six children, three sons and three daughters, only one, the dauphin, survived. She did not weep at the loss of children only; she wept at the loss of love on the part of the king.

About a year after Louis's marriage, he met Mademoiselle de la Vallière, the daughter of a marquis, and a maid of honor to Henrietta, sister of Charles II. of England, and wife of Louis's brother Philip, then Duke of Orleans. She was seventeen years of age, with large blue eyes, flaxen hair, brilliant complexion, and timid, modest manners. The king seemed to her almost above mortals. She trembled when he spoke to her, and was grateful and honored by his slightest attention. The king was flattered by her homage, soon wrote to her daily, and in the end completely won her heart. He gave *fêtes,* ostensibly for Maria Theresa, but in reality for Louise de la Vallière. The queen wept in secret, but was powerless. Louise saw her anguish, repented of her wrong-doing, and fled to a convent, fainting on the stone pavement before it. The king was angry when the queen-mother, Anne, upbraided him with his lack of self-control. "It may be so that I do not know how to control myself, but I will at least prove that I know how to control those who offend me,' was the stern reply.

He immediately sought the convent, found the unhappy girl, brought her back to court, and made her a duchess. Of her three children, the eldest, a son, died; and the others, a daughter and son, were legitimatized by the king, as he was extremely fond of them.

After a time, when the inconstant king had found another affection, Louise was often in tears. She had lived quietly, idolizing the king and her children. When he saw her weeping, he said haughtily, " Let there be an end of this. I love you, and you know it. But I am not to be constrained."

Again Louise fled to a convent, and again Louis XIV. brought her back. As she took leave of the sister in charge of the convent, she said, " This is not a farewell; I shall assuredly return, and perhaps very soon."

For a year she lived at court; but her unhappiness brought on a well-nigh fatal illness. She gained the king's consent to retire to a Carmelite convent. Still beautiful, she bade farewell forever to her children; falling on her knees before the queen, she asked and received her forgiveness, and then exchanged her luxury for the narrow bed and fastings of a sincere penitent for thirty-six years.

The king did not entirely forget her, and wrote her when her brother died in 1676, — she was then only thirty-two, — that if he were good enough to see a Carmelite so pious as she, he would go in person to tell her of his sorrow for her loss. Sister Louise of Mercy, as she was called, had said that if the king came to see her, she would hide herself so effectually that he would not find her; and he never saw her again.

When her son died, Count de Vermandois, grand-admiral of France, a few years after her brother, she was much overcome, but did not weep, saying submissively, "It would ill become me to weep over the death of a son whose birth I have not yet ceased to mourn." She died at sixty-six, in 1710, in the arms of her daughter, the Princess de Conti, who was married to a nephew of the Great Condé, glad to leave a world where the mistakes of her girlhood had blighted her whole life.

There was a singular rumor in connection with Count de Vermandois, the son of Louise de la Vallière. It was said that he was the extraordinary character known as the "Man with the Iron Mask." On Nov. 19, 1703, there died in the Bastile a man whose face for twenty or thirty years had been covered with a mask, probably of black velvet, who was treated with the most profound respect by all attendants, who had every luxury of fine wearing-apparel, but who was to be immediately put to death if he ever announced his name. After his death the walls of his chamber were rubbed and whitewashed, and the tiles of the floor removed, that nothing might be hidden underneath. He had been taken to the Bastile in 1698 from St. Marguerite Isles, where he had been in prison for ten years. He was in the fort of Exilles, and at Pignerol in 1681.

Some persons believed that the Count de Vermandois, who was a dissipated man, had struck the dauphin; and, being the son of a king, for this offence was placed in prison for life, instead of being put to death. Others said it was Fouquet, a dishonest minister, whose extravagance had caused the displeasure of Louis. Others, that it was Count Hercule Antoine Mattioli, secretary of Charles IV., Duke of Mantua, who had sought to unite the Italian princes against Louis, and had deceived the French government.

Such imprisonment was against the laws of nations, and if known would perhaps have brought on a war. Others claimed that the person was General de Burloude, imprisoned for having raised the siege of Conti without permission, and that a letter from Louvois to Louis XIV. in cipher proves this. Henri Martin says the most popular opinion is that suggested by Voltaire, that the person was a natural son of Anne of Austria, and that Louis desired to save the royal honor by keeping it forever a secret. And the secret has been kept.

Meantime, Madame de Montespan, who had won the king away from Louise, was living with him in regal state. She was of a noble family (Athénaïs de Mortemar, also called Mademoiselle de Tonnay Charente), a haughty and radiant beauty, commanding, witty, of quick temper, ambitious, and fond of display, — a complete contrast to the gentle, loving Louise de la Vallière.

At the age of twenty-two she was married against her will to the Marquis de Montespan, of an illustrious family of Gascony. It is said that she entreated her husband to take her away from a corrupt court; but as soon as she saw that the king was pleased with her, she refused to leave it. Her husband came to Paris to demand her; but, failing to obtain her, returned to his home, put on deep mourning, hung the carriage entrance of his house with black, ordered a funeral service at the parish church, to which he invited the whole town, and mourned her as dead.

For thirteen years she was the queen of Louis XIV. in all save the name. Her robes were of the most magnificent kind. Madame de Sévigné wrote her daughter,

"Madame de Montespan was covered with diamonds the other day; no one could stand the lustre of such a divinity."

The king showered upon her pearls, sapphires, emeralds, and rubies. He gave her the beautiful château of Clagny, not far from Versailles. "You cannot imagine," wrote Madame de Sévigné, June 12, 1675, "what triumph she is in amongst her workmen, who number some twelve hundred; the palace of Apollo and the gardens of Armida are a slight description of it." Louis wrote his minister of finance, Colbert, "Madame de Montespan sends me word that you have acquitted yourself very well in what I commanded, and that you are always asking if she wants anything. Continue always to do so."

Madame de Montespan bore the king seven children, the eldest dying at three years of age, and the third, the Count de Vexin, at eleven. In 1675, under the influence of the noted preacher Bossuet, the king and Madame de Montespan promised to separate. But the promise was quickly broken. However, their life together was not a happy one. Their quarrels were frequent, and tears and reconciliations followed.

When Madame de Montespan's first children were born, she bethought herself of the young widow of the poet Scarron, for whom she had obtained the pension from the king, and sent for her to become governess. As the birth of the children was at first kept secret, Madame Scarron had a most difficult task. "Often I was standing on ladders," she writes, "doing the work of upholsterers and workmen, who might not be allowed to come into the house. . . . I often went on foot and disguised, seeking one nurse after another, or carrying linen or meat, etc., under my arm. I would often spend the whole night with one of the children who was ill in a little house outside Paris. Everybody saw how thin I became; but no one guessed the reason."

Madame Scarron was not happy in her life, though devotedly attached to the children, who, as they grew older, returned the love most ardently. She wrote to her confessor, "There is nothing so silly as to love to this excess a child that is not my own, whose lot I can never dispose of."

Madame de Montespan proved a hard mistress. Her temper was ungovernable; and she was constantly complaining to the king, who was not attracted to the dignified, plainly dressed governess, whom he called Madame de Montespan's "learned lady." Finally Madame Scarron begged to leave her position, but was not permitted to do so. Later, the king gave her two hundred thousand francs for her services, with which, adding forty thousand of her own savings, she bought the old property of Maintenon; and Françoise Scarron became Madame de Maintenon.

Again she wrote her confessor, "Sometimes I determine not to put so much energy into what I do, and to leave these children to their mother's management; then I scruple to offend God by this neglect, and I begin over again that care which increases my love."

One day when the king entered her apartment, he found her seated by the Duke du Maine, the second child of Madame de Montespan, holding his hand, as he was ill with fever, the Count de Vexin asleep on her lap, and her other hand fondling the little Mademoiselle de Nantes. "That woman knows how to love," said the king to himself. "It would be a pleasure to be loved by her."

Month by month the patience and good sense of Madame de Maintenon impressed the king in her favor. He enjoyed her conversation, and believed thoroughly in the uprightness of her life. Madame de Montespan, who had supplanted Louise de la Vallière, became jealous lest, after all, the king might love the "learned lady," three years his senior.

When the dauphin, the son of Louis by Maria Theresa, was married to Mary Anne, the daughter of the Elector of Bavaria, Louis determined to give her as a second lady-in-waiting, a woman of "unequivocal virtue and incorruptible fidelity." He naturally chose Madame de Maintenon, which gave great offence to Madame de Montespan. The latter told the dauphiness the details of the early life of Madame de Maintenon, and thus prejudiced her forever against the governess.

The birth of a son to the dauphiness in 1682, the Duke of Burgundy, grandson of Louis XIV., was cause for great rejoicing. Everybody kissed the hand of the king. The people were so excited that they burned even the flooring intended for the grand gallery. "Let them alone," said Louis, smiling; "we will have other flooring." The poor dauphiness longed for her German home; was never happy, and died when her third child was born, at the age of twenty-nine. She embraced her baby, repeating the line, "Ah, my son, how dear thy life has cost thy mother!"

Louis XIV. had tired of the imperious Madame de Montespan as he had of the loving Louise de la Vallière.

She threatened to enter a convent; but she did not go. The priests and Madame de Maintenon were urging upon Louis the necessity of living a moral life. Maria Theresa had grown fond of Madame de Maintenon. She said gratefully, "The king has never treated me with so much tenderness as since he listened to her."

The pious queen was not long to enjoy the returning tenderness of the king. After a brief illness she died, July 30, 1683. Handing Madame de Maintenon a superb ring from her finger, she said, with almost her latest breath, "Adieu, my very dear marchioness; to you I confide the happiness of the king."

She was placed in her coffin in the Hall of Peace at Versailles, hung with black. The king was much affected as he exclaimed, "Kind and forbearing friend, this is the first sorrow that you have caused me throughout twenty years!" "The court," writes Madame de Caylus, "was pained by his grief."

After the death of the queen, Madame de Maintenon would have left the palace; but Duke de la Rochefoucauld said earnestly, "This is not the time for you to be going, madame; in the state of grief in which the king now is, he will want you."

"God is punishing me," wrote Louis to Madame de Maintenon, "and I submit to his will. I have given that beautiful soul [the queen] only too much cause for complaint. Do not go away from us, dear Madame de Maintenon, for I need comfort. You can go when you are weary of telling me the truth."

"Sire, the queen is in no way to be pitied; she lived and died like a saint," wrote back Madame de Maintenon. "The certainty of her salvation is a great consolation. You have, sire, a friend in heaven who will implore God to pardon your sins, and ask the intercession of the just. May your Majesty feed upon these thoughts. Be as good a Christian, sire, as you are great as a king."

Louis, with all his faults, was not destitute of heart. When his mother, Anne of Austria, died in January, 1666, he fainted, and was borne senseless from the apartment. All night long he wept like a child.

In his memoirs, intended for the dauphin, he wrote, "My respect for her was not one of those constrained duties which are performed for the sake of decorum. The habit I had formed of having ordinarily the same dwelling and the same table with her, the assiduity with which I was seen to visit her several times every day, no matter how pressing my affairs might be, were not a law I had imposed on myself for reasons of state, but a sign of the pleasure I took in her company."

Now that the king was free to marry, it is probable that Madame de Montespan had hopes that at least for the sake of her children she might become the wife of the king. But she was doomed to bitter disappointment. Another woman was to more than fill her place, — a woman three years older than the king, a devoted Christian, of uncommon mind and remarkable judgment; not beautiful, but with a "face sparkling with intelligence," — a woman of prudence, refinement, dignity, and tact, whose advice was always worth receiving. This woman, born in prison and reared in poverty, was to hold for thirty years, as Lamartine says, "absolute domination over a great monarch."

"The fictions of romance," says Saint-Amand, "are

not nearly so prodigious as the realities of history; and when Madame de Maintenon at the age of fifty saw a king of forty-seven — and what a king! — come to offer to be her husband, she must have thought herself the plaything of a dream. The year when Louis XIV. espoused Scarron's widow was the apogee, the zenith of the royal star. . . . It was the epoch when, in face of his motionless enemies, he enlarged and fortified the frontiers of the realm, conquered Strasburg, bombarded Genoa and Algiers, finished the luxurious constructions of his splendid Versailles, was the terror of Europe and the idol of France." Brilliant offers of alliance with princes were made to Louis; but he refused them all. The Pope, Innocent XI., and others high in authority, were consulted as to the marriage with Madame de Maintenon, and all approved, though several advised secrecy, as the position of the king was so much above that of the subject.

At midnight, in 1684, — it is believed that June 12th was the date, — Louis XIV. and Françoise d'Aubigné were married by the Archbishop of Paris (Harlay), in the presence of Père La Chaise, confessor of the king, who said the mass; Bontemps, first *valet-de-chambre* to the king; and two marquises, de Louvois and de Montchevreuil, the former witnessing for the king, and the latter for Madame de Maintenon. The ceremony was performed in a private oratory of Versailles.

It is said that the king wished to make the marriage public, but was overruled by some of his advisers. Madame de Montespan, although she hated Madame de Maintenon for having the place she wished to occupy, says in her memoirs that the latter refused to have the marriage declared, "and by this wise and prudent conduct reconciled in time even those who had been the most hostile to the measure."

Beautiful apartments were provided for Madame de Maintenon at Versailles, close to those of the king. He gave her forty-eight thousand livres annually, besides a New Year's gift of twelve thousand livres. She continued to dress simply in soft wool, generally of a dead-leaf color, without gold embroidery so common in those days.

Madame de Montespan remained at court several years after the marriage of Madame de Maintenon; but the king showed her little attention. He had long wished her to depart; but, unhappy though she was, she loved the life of gayety. Finally, at the request of the king, after a stormy interview, she took her departure in 1691, living by turns at the abbey of Fontevrault, the château of Oiron, or at the convent of St. Joseph, which she had built, the site now occupied by the Ministry of War.

The last sixteen years of her life were spent in penitence. Her confessor made her write to her husband, beg his pardon, and submit to any commands he might make. The Duke of Saint Simon, in his memoirs, says that the Marquis de Montespan returned her word "that he wished in no way to interfere with her, or even to see her."

"Little by little," says Saint Simon, "she gave almost all she had to the poor. She worked for them several hours a day, making stout shirts and such things for them. . . . She unceasingly wore bracelets, garters, and a girdle, all armed with iron points, which oftentimes inflicted wounds upon her; and her tongue, formerly so dangerous, had also its peculiar penance imposed on it." At the hospital which she founded she often cared for the sick with her own hands.

She died at the baths of Bourbon, May 27, 1707, at three o'clock in the afternoon, at the age of sixty-six. Her body was sent to Poitiers, and placed in the family tomb, and her heart, in a leaden case, to the convent of La Flèche.

Her children, though they sincerely mourned for her, were forbidden to wear mourning; and the king, with no apparent feeling, went hunting. Madame de Maintenon, on the contrary, wept and withdrew herself for a time from the public gaze.

Madame de Maintenon tried to restrain Louis from his extravagance in building; but he loved glory, and felt that the eyes of the world were upon him. He determined years before to build a palace and gardens which should be the wonder of the age, and he succeeded. He selected the little village of Versailles, surrounded by a forest, where Louis XIII. had a small château. Lenôtre, the great landscape gardener, laid out the gardens; Jules Hardouin Mansart was the architect of the gorgeous palaces.

For the garden and grounds, says Henri Martin, "whole thickets were brought full-grown from the depths of the finest forests of France. . . . An innumerable nation of statues peopled the thickets and lawns, was mirrored in the waters, or rose from the bosom of the wave." Thirty-six thousand men and six thousand horses were at work month after month. It was attempted to bring water in an aqueduct thirty-one miles from Maintenon for the great fountains; but the soldiers who were employed died in such numbers that the plan was given up, and the water was brought from Marly, at a cost of four million francs.

Through twenty-five years the great buildings rose before the eyes of the delighted monarch, till a sum variously estimated from four hundred to one thousand million francs had been used. Madame de Maintenon wrote, "Men are indeed fools to give themselves so much trouble to embellish a spot where they have but a few days to dwell."

When reasoned with by Colbert, the minister of finance, Louis would reply with the old fallacious argument, used to the present day, when money is squandered, "The king gives alms in spending largely."

Martin justly remarks, " Doubtless, a government that *spends largely* for works adapted to increase the national wealth, and profitable to the mass of the citizens, really serves the interests of the poorer classes; but it is not the same with one which consumes much in expenses for luxuries, in unproductive expenses, and which thus puts into the hands of the few the money wrung from the sweat of the many."

Marly, another royal palace, cost Louis about fifty million francs. The amount spent by Louis, both in works of luxury and utility, Martin places at seven hundred million francs in the money of the present day.

Louis did, however, many grand things. His home for six or seven thousand old soldiers who had served the state, the Hotel des Invalides, finished in 1674, where Napolean I. now rests, does honor to his heart and his to memory.

He gathered into his court those distinguished in art, science or letters. Corneille, Molière, Boileau, Racine, and others, gave brilliance to the age. No such assemblages were known before or since. Not only were pensions granted, but the king gave his personal encouragement and favor. He commissioned his ambassadors to seek out men in all lands who were worthy of pensions or fine positions on account of talent.

The astronomer Hevelius of Dantzic, having lost his library in a fire, received from Louis a similar one. He built a home at Florence for the Italian astronomer, Viviani. He gave to French and foreign authors and artists, from 1664 to 1690, nearly two million livres in pensions. Whenever a man made some discovery in science, he was invited to reside in Paris. Huyghens, the celebrated astronomer, came over from Holland and remained fifteen years. He dedicated some of his greatest works to Louis XIV.

Journeys in the interest of knowledge were made all over the world by order of the French government. Art and architecture flourished. Ships were built through the influence of Colbert; two hundred and forty-three in thirteen years. Laws were improved in the Code Louis. Hospitals were established for the sick and the orphan poor. A tariff protected manufactures. Louis studied all departments; for he said with truth, "I am the state!"

Louis was the soul of politeness. Saint Simon says he never passed a woman of the humblest station even, without taking off his hat to her. He was never ironical in speech, but always gracious. "At all hours, in all places, in the most trifling circumstances of life," says Martin, "he was always king; a marvellous art of reigning, the secret of which he had found, and was to carry away with him. His affability never contradicted itself; he expressed interest and kindness to all."

Not content with great internal improvements for France, his ambition made him desire more territory. He feared the power of his neighbor Spain. As the dowry promised with his Spanish wife, Maria Theresa, had never been paid, after the death of her father, Philip IV., he determined to obtain some of the Spanish possessions in the Belgian provinces. This produced the "War of the Queen's Rights."

In 1667 Louis started for Flanders with an army of 125,000 men, the whole under the command of Turenne. Several towns were easily conquered, and Louis brought the queen and her court with great display to show them their new subjects. Lille was the largest city taken. The king showed great bravery, remaining in the trenches most of the day. After this he conquered Franche Comté, a free county of Burgundy, through the great soldier Condé.

Holland became alarmed, and united with England and Sweden against the encroachments of France. Peace was finally concluded at Aix-la-Chapelle, May 2, 1668, whereby Louis received twelve fortified towns on the border of the Spanish Netherlands. He at once fortified strongly all the cities which he captured.

His next desire was to humble Holland. She was both republican and Protestant, and stood in his way in capturing Belgium. Louis tried by masterly diplomacy to set the weak Charles II. of England against Holland, and win the favor also of Sweden and Germany. At length, in 1672, at the head of 130,000 men, supported by a combined English and French fleet of one hundred and thirty vessels of war, Louis XIV. started for the conquest of Holland.

The little country had but 25,000 men, led by William, Prince of Orange, then but twenty-two years of age, and in feeble health, to oppose this great army. Louis crossed the Rhine June 12, where, the water being low, the horses needed to swim only about twenty feet, and on June 20 made a triumphal entry into the city of Utrecht. Several cities surrendered to the superior numbers. Holland was in despair. She sent four deputies to intercede with Louis for clemency.

His reply was that Holland should surrender all the territory on the left bank of the Rhine, pay twenty million francs, establish the Catholic religion over her Protestant country, and all the important cities should be garrisoned by French troops.

When the Hollanders learned the terms, with one accord they resolved to perish rather than be subject to France. "To subscribe to them would be suicide," said William; "even to discuss them is dangerous; but, if the majority of this assembly decide otherwise, there remains but one course for the friends of Protestantism and liberty, and that is, to retire to the colonies in the West Indies, and there found a new country, where their consciences and their persons will be beyond the reach of tyranny and despotism." Led by the intrepid William, the Hollanders pierced the dykes which had kept the ocean from overflowing, and let the sea destroy their homes, their flocks, their merchandise, their beautiful cities. Louis found his Moscow; and, like Napoleon, retreated, only to learn that Europe, alarmed at his ambition, had joined the Prince of Orange to defeat France. When the French had departed, the heroic Dutch closed their dykes, and by their windmills pumped the water out of their fertile fields; not, however, without tremendous losses.

The Emperor of Germany now took sides with Holland. Louis raised an immense army, and with his own hand made the orders for the march, showing that he understood the details of war. Louis was, as Napoleon said, "a great king. What king of France since Charlemagne can be compared to Louis XIV., under all his aspects?"

For six long years Europe was immersed in war. Condé was sent against the Prince of Orange; Turenne against Germany. The Palatinate, a country on both sides of the Rhine, with a territory of about sixteen hundred square miles, Turenne laid waste, destroying the cattle and harvests, that the German army might have nothing to subsist on when it crossed the country. When the peasants saw their harvests destroyed, they tore several of the French soldiers in pieces. In return, twenty-seven villages were burned by the French army. The Elector Palatine protested, but it had no effect upon Turenne.

This great general fell at the battle of Salzbach, June 27, 1675, at the age of sixty-four. He was watching his army, and saying to M. de St. Hilaire, who sat by him on horseback, "I don't at all want to be killed to-day." At that moment a cannon-ball carried away the left arm of St. Hilaire and the neck of his horse, and nearly cut Turenne's body in two parts.

"Do not weep for me," said St. Hilaire to his son; "it is the death of that great man. You may perhaps lose your father, but neither your country nor you will ever have a general like that again."

The soldiers threw a cloak over the body of Turenne, and "raised a cry," writes Madame de Sévigné, "that was heard two leagues off. . . . They roared to be led to battle. They wanted to avenge the death of their father; with him they had feared nothing, but they would show how to avenge him."

Europe was tired of war; and peace was made at Nimeguen, in 1678, between Holland and France, August 10; and Spain and France, September 17. "Holland," says Guizot, in his history of France, "had not lost an inch of her territory during this war, so long, so desperate, and notoriously undertaken to destroy her."

Louis had offered the now famous Prince of Orange one of his natural daughters; but William had wisely married, Nov. 15, 1677, Princess Mary of England, eldest daughter of the Duke of York, afterwards James II., with whom he was soon to reign on an English throne.

For the next ten years Louis XIV. seemed to have the world at his feet. When James II., the Catholic king of England, fled to Louis for protection, as the English had called the Protestant Prince of Orange to their aid, Louis met the fallen monarch with a hundred six-horse carriages, and all his household. A casket was placed on the bureau of James's bed-chamber at the palace of St. Germain, containing six thousand louis d'or as a gift; and six hundred thousand livres were allotted for the annual expenses of his establishment.

The formalities of the daily life of Louis XIV. seemed

to enhance his grandeur before the people. At eight o'clock in the morning the first *valet-de-chambre* entered the king's chamber, opened the shutters, replenished the fire, if cold, and awoke him at half-past eight. The valet retired, and several persons entered, among them the king's sons, and his physician and surgeon. Then the first lord of the bed-chamber presented a dish of holy water, and the king made the sign of the cross upon his brow and breast. A collection of wigs was shown him, and he made his choice. The first lord drew on his costly dressing-gown. Bontemps, a valet, put on his stockings and his embroidered slippers. Several favored persons then entered, while he was being shaved.

The great monarch was after this to be dressed, and another distinguished company were permitted to witness the robing. One gentleman put on the shoes, while another clasped their diamond buckles. Two pages in crimson velvet carried away the slippers he had just worn. The royal shirt was then put on; the outer garments handed one by one; a cravat of rich lace fastened about the neck, and two handkerchiefs of costly point handed to him on an enamelled saucer.

After his breakfast, served with much ceremony, he entered his cabinet, and gave his orders for the day. Then he proceeded to his chapel for mass, and dined at one o'clock, alone, no person being allowed to sit in his presence. After this he fed his dogs, rode in the open air, or hunted. At ten in the evening he had supper with the royal household, the meats and other food, which had been tasted to be sure it was not poisoned, being brought in, preceded by two guards and several officials, so as to prevent all contact with the royal dishes. Six noblemen at each end of the table waited upon the king, tasting each kind before he ate of it. About midnight he again fed his dogs, and retired with the usual ceremony.

Into this stately etiquette and elegance Madame de Maintenon came by her marriage in 1684. No wonder she wrote a friend, "Save those who fill the highest station, I know of none more unfortunate than those who envy them. If you could only form an idea of what it is!"

From the time of their union, the great monarch never ceased his deferential attention to Madame de Maintenon or his love for her. He read his letters and despatches in her apartment. He asked her advice, saying, "What does 'Reason' say to that?" or, "What does your 'Solidity' advise as to this?" She was sometimes present at the grand council of ministers, and her judgment was highly valued.

She urged Louis to have good men about him. She hated war. "I long for peace," she wrote in 1684. "I shall never give the king any counsels prejudicial to his glory; but if he would believe me, he would be less dazzled with this *éclat* of victory, and would think seriously of his salvation."

Among her many good works she established a school at St. Cyr for poor girls of noble birth. Other poor girls were clothed, fed, instructed, under the same roof till they were twenty years of age. The king became deeply interested, and two thousand five hundred men were set at work upon the buildings. Madame de Maintenon visited the place every day, now seeing that the food was properly cooked, and now teaching or speaking to the girls. To her brother she wrote, "Think of my delight at coming back along the avenue, followed by the one hundred and twenty-four girls who are there now!"

Racine wrote for the girls the drama of "Esther;" and Louis, with James II. and his queen, Mary of Modena, came to see it acted.

In 1685, a year after Louis married Madame de Maintenon, he committed the great and irremediable error of his reign, — the Revocation of the Edict of Nantes. By the Edict of Nantes, granted by Henry IV. of Navarre in 1598, freedom of religious belief was guaranteed. People could be Roman Catholics or Protestants, as they preferred.

After Henry IV. had been stabbed by a fanatic, François Ravaillac, May 14, 1610, the Huguenots, or Protestants, had a varying fortune of tolerance and intolerance. Under the great minister of the son of Henry, Louis XIII., Cardinal Richelieu, they were generally unmolested. He died in 1642; and under Cardinal Mazarin, the prime minister of Anne of Austria, and during the youth of Louis XIV., though there were quarrels between Catholic and Protestant, the latter were usually allowed their rights.

From the death of Mazarin in 1660, the same year in which Louis was married to Maria Theresa of Spain, the freedom accorded to Protestants continually decreased. In 1661 it was forbidden the latter to sing psalms in private houses so as to be heard outside. Two years later those Protestants who had become Catholics, and then returned to their own faith, were banished; and those who kept on their hats when the Host was carried by were sent as galley-slaves to the fleet.

Louvois, the war minister, persuaded Louis that nothing would so hasten the *conversion* of Protestants as troops, — dragoonades. At once the army was sent into various provinces; and the Protestants, alarmed for their lives, abjured their faith in great numbers. Madame de Maintenon wrote to Madame de Brinon, "Think, for your consolation, of a hundred thousand souls being converted in Guienne in one month by public declaration." She wrote to Abbé Gobelin, "The king is very well, thank God, and is rejoicing in all the couriers who come in bringing news of millions of conversions."

It was finally decided to revoke the Edict of Nantes, by which Louis fondly hoped that Protestantism would be entirely suppressed, and all would embrace the Catholic religion. He signed the fatal declaration Oct. 17, 1685.

Protestant churches were at once demolished; all ministers who would not be converted were to leave the kingdom in a fortnight, but not take with them any of their children under seven years of age. The results of such a measure were perhaps not fully apprehended by the king. While Louvois was urging the "extremest rigors of the law," Louis was kept somewhat in ignorance of the brutal measures used. Men and women were thrown into subterranean dungeons. They were tortured with the horrors of the inquisition, as one may read in "The Huguenots," by Charles Tylor. "From torture to abjuration, and from this to communion, there was often not twenty-four hours' distance," says

Saint Simon; "and their executioners were their guides and witnesses." Thousands starved in the recesses of the mountains, were burned, or were shot down like criminals.

When Madame de Maintenon, having heard some of these things, remonstrated against this severity towards those of the faith of her childhood, the king replied, "I fear the indulgence you would ask proceeds only from a lingering affection for your old religion."

Bossuet, the great Catholic preacher, as well as others high in authority, lauded Louis for his work. "You have strengthened the faith!" exclaimed Bossuet; "you have exterminated the heretics: this is the meritorious work of your reign, its peculiar characteristic. Through you, heresy is no more. God alone could have wrought this wonder." The Pope, Innocent XI., celebrated the Revocation by a *Te Deum*. Madam de Sévigné wrote, "This is the grandest and finest thing that ever was conceived and accomplished."

Michelet says Madame de Maintenon "allowed a written decision for the Revocation of the Edict of Nantes to be extorted from her," which is probably true; for while she rejoiced in the conversions (?), she doubtless foresaw something of the misfortune it might bring to France. Besides, she knew that conversion by force was not genuine. "The state of those who abjure without being truly Catholic," she wrote, "is infamous."

For years Madame de Maintenon was greatly blamed, as it was believed that she instigated or encouraged the Revocation. Her letters, edited by La Beaumelle, intended to prove this, have been found by comparison with the originals to have been much changed by him, or even made up from a sentence or a phrase. Later years have changed the verdict of historians.

Although the Protestants were forbidden to leave the country, they fled in all directions. Probably 250,000 escaped to England, Germany, Switzerland, Holland, Ireland, and elsewhere, — manufacturers, skilled laborers, merchants, and others. Berlin received watchmakers, carvers, and jewellers. Silk-weavers went to Spitalfields, a suburb of London. Nobles trained in arms sought other battle-fields for glory, and later helped defeat James II. of England, and put William III., the bitter enemy of Louis, on the throne. It is said that the fugitives carried out of France sixty million francs in five years.

So eager were they to get away from the hateful rule of the "Most Christian King," Louis, that they used every device possible. A woman had herself packed up in a bundle of iron rods, and carried six leagues beyond the frontier. Sometimes whole boat-loads starved or froze on the ocean in the bitter winter, and their bodies were washed ashore.

For five years after his marriage, till he was again at war, Louis enjoyed what he had never enjoyed before, a home of rest and congenial companionship. Saint Simon thus describes the king and Madame de Maintenon in her room: "The king's arm-chair against the wall, a table in front of him, and a folding-chair around it for the minister who was working. On the other side of the chimney-piece a niche of red damask, an arm-chair, where Madame de Maintenon sat with a small table in front of her. A little farther off was her bed, in an alcove. . . . Madame de Maintenon read, or worked tapestry, hearing all that passed; for the king and the minister conversed aloud. She seldom offered a word, more rarely one of any moment; but the king often asked her opinion, when she replied in measured terms."

When the king asked her opinion, "she would smile," says Saint Simon, "profess her incapacity, utter sometimes one sentiment, sometimes another . . . and in the end determine matters in such a way that three-fourths of all favors and promotions, and again three-fourths of the remaining fourth of all that was done by the ministers, were disposed of by her."

Some of the courtiers said that the reign ought no more to be spoken of as that of Louis the Great, but the "Reign of Françoise d'Aubigné."

She was very tired of life at court. She wrote to the Archbishop of Paris, "I have been enduring them [court pleasures] now for a week, and there are so many that I am overwhelmed with the dreariness of never hearing a single rational conversation. The chapter of pease still goes on. The intense desire to eat pease, the delight of having eaten pease, and the joyful expectation of eating yet more pease — these have been the three points of discussion for the last four days. There are even ladies who, after having supped, and well supped, with the king, find more pease to eat when they get home before they go to bed. You have some strange sheep, Monseigneur. Forgive this outburst of annoyance to my pastor."

When Louis went to war, and Madame de Maintenon remained with the girls at St. Cyr, the king said to the pupils, "I am leaving you the dearest thing I have." Madame de Maintenon wrote the king when absent, "Sire, a single day of your Majesty's absence is an age to me. I am satisfied as to your feelings, but I cannot rest in peace away from you. My whole happiness, all the pleasure of my life, lie in seeing your Majesty."

Protestant Europe had become indignant at the consequences of the Revocation of the Edict of Nantes. Wherever the exiles went, their sorrows elicited sympathy. In 1686, the year following the Revocation, the League of Augsburg was formed, uniting Germany, Sweden, Spain, and the electors of Bavaria, Saxony, and the Palatinate, against France. Louis soon marched against the Palatinate, one pretext being a claim to the territory, as the male line of electors had become extinct, and Charlotte, the second wife of Louis's brother Philip, was the next heir.

The cities of the Palatinate soon surrendered. It was a difficult matter to garrison them all while the generals went to conquer other nations. Then Louvois, minister of war, prevailed upon Louis to give the barbarous order to burn them, and leave not one stone upon another. Manheim, Heidelberg, Spires, Worms, and Bingen, with their cathedrals and castles, were utterly destroyed. The Count of Tessé wrote to Louvois, "Nothing at all remains of the superb castle of Heidelberg. There were yesterday at noon, besides the castle, four hundred and thirty-two houses burned; and the fire was still going on."

One hundred thousand people, homeless and without subsistence, were scattered abroad. Germany was exasperated against France; and Gravelotte and Sedan, with the crowning of Emperor William at Versailles, scarcely obliterated old remembrances.

Louvois besought the king to burn Treves also; but Louis, already influenced by Madame de Maintenon against his war minister, refused. Louvois was angry, and said he had already given the order. Louis, in his rage, it is said, was about to strike the minister with the tongs, when Madame de Maintenon separated them. Louvois died very soon after. Louis said calmly to his brother, who mourned the loss they had sustained, "If M. de Louvois had not died so suddenly, he would have been in the Bastile within two days."

England and Holland joined the coalition against France. Louis XIV. hoped to reinstate the Catholic James II. on the throne; but Protestant England declared in favor of William and Mary, jointly, Feb. 13, 1689; and they were crowned April 11. James was totally defeated at the battle of the Boyne in Ireland, July 1, 1690. After various victories and defeats, all parties were tired of war, and the Peace of Ryswick, a village near the Hague, was declared Sept. 30, 1697, between France, England, Spain, and Holland. War had brought its usual disasters. William III. said, "My poverty is incredible." Voltaire wrote of France, "People were dying of want to the sound of the 'Te Deum.'" Fénelon, the great bishop, wrote the king anonymously, "The whole of France is no longer anything but one vast hospital. The people, who so loved you, are beginning to lose affection, confidence, and even respect; the allies prefer carrying on war with loss, to concluding a peace which would not be observed." . . .

A treaty of peace had been made a year previous to

that of Ryswick, between Louis and the Duke of Savoy, whose wife was the daughter of Philip by his first wife, the beautiful Henrietta of England. By this compact the duke's eldest daughter, Marie Adelaide, eleven years old, was betrothed to the Duke of Burgundy, the son of the dauphin, and grandson of Louis XIV.

The king was delighted with the little girl, and wrote to Madame de Maintenon a description of her: "The eyes bright and very beautiful; black and admirable lashes; the skin smooth, red and white, just as one would have it; the most beautiful and abundant hair that one can see; a very red mouth, full lips. . . . I am quite satisfied. . . . I hope you will be so too."

Madame de Maintenon was equally delighted with her. She wrote to the Duchess of Savoy about the king's delight in her daughter, as she had come to Paris to be educated for her high station. "She is so polite that she cannot bear to say the least disagreeable thing. Yesterday I demurred to the caresses she was giving me, on the ground that I was too old; and she replied, 'Ah, not so very old!' . . . Having very soon noticed that I cannot remain standing, she made me sit down; and, putting herself coaxingly almost on my lap, she said, 'Mamma charged me to say a thousand kind things to you for her, and to beg you to be a friend to me. Pray teach me everything that I must do to please.'"

Madame de Maintenon superintended the education of little Marie Adelaide, taking her to St. Cyr about three times a week, for the whole day. The day the Princess was twelve, she was married to the Duke of Burgundy, fifteen and a half years old. The boy bridegroom wore a black mantle lined with rose satin, the outside embroidered with gold; the bride a robe of cloth of silver, bordered with precious stones, and a cross of diamonds. Her dress was so heavy she could hardly bear the weight of it.

Marie Adelaide became the idol of the court and of the king. "In private," says Saint Simon, "prattling, skipping, flying around them; now perched upon the sides of their arm-chairs, now playing upon their knees, she clasped them round the neck, embraced them, kissed them, caressed them, rumpled them, tickled them under the chin, tormented them; rummaged their tables, their papers, their letters; broke open the seals, and read the contents in spite of opposition. . . . The king really could not do without her."

"Our sweet princess is only too sweet," wrote Madame de Maintenon, "and I begin to think she is too good." Her husband, a noble young man, idolized her, and was, like herself, the pride and hope of the nation. It had been foretold her by an astrologer, that she would die at twenty-seven. She said to her husband one day, "See! the time is coming when I must die. You cannot remain without a wife on account of your rank and your devotion. Tell me, I entreat you, whom you will marry."

"I hope God will never punish me enough to let me see you die," was his answer; "and if this misfortune must befall me, I shall never remarry, for I should follow you to the grave in eight days."

Louis's son, the dauphin, died in April, 1711, of malignant small-pox. He was carried in his own carriage to St. Denis. "This is where all greatness ends," said Madame de Maintenon. The king was much overcome.

In February, 1712, the following year, a more crushing blow came to Louis XIV. The idolized Marie Adelaide died of scarlet-fever, February 12, after five days' illness, at the age of twenty-seven. Her husband was prostrated with grief, and died six days later of the same fever. Their eldest son, five years old, died the next month, March 8. A baby two years old remained, who became Louis XV. France, as well as Louis and Madame de Maintenon, was crushed by this triple sorrow.

The king had already been engaged in one more devastating war, called the War of the Spanish Succession. Charles II. of Spain had died without children. Louis XIV. had married his *elder* sister, Maria Theresa, and felt that his grandson was entitled to the throne. Charles II. had willed it to him. Leopold of Germany had married a younger sister of Charles II., Margaret Theresa, and felt that he also was entitled to the throne of Spain for his heirs. England and Holland did not wish France and Spain to be so closely united, or to possess so much power.

Louis sent his grandson of nineteen, Philip V., to Spain, where he was welcomed as king. Unfortunately, Louis recognized the son of James II. as James III., King of England. William III. was indignant that Louis should seem to decide upon a ruler for England, and made ready at once for battle. His sudden death, March 19, 1702, resulting from a fall from his horse, brought Anne of Denmark to the throne, who was governed by John Churchill, Duke of Marlborough, and

Sarah Jennings, his wife, the famous Duchess of Marlborough.

In vain Madame de Maintenon urged the king not to enter upon another war. The old love of power and conquest was strong, and twelve years of desperate warfare resulted. Eugene, Prince of Savoy, and Marlborough of England, were the great generals opposed to Louis. Eugene was the son of the noted Olympia Mancini, sister of Mary, both nieces of Cardinal Mazarin, and both of whom Louis had loved in his youth.

The greatest battles fought were at Blenheim, Aug. 13, 1704, a village in Bavaria on the Danube; Ramillies, May 23, 1706, twenty-eight miles south-east of Brussels, where Marlborough overcame the French marshal Villeroy; Oudenarde, July 11, 1708, situated in Belgium on the Scheldt, where Marlborough and Eugene conquered the Duke de Vendôme, the leader of the French; and Malplaquet, Sept. 11, 1709, on the Belgian frontier, where Marlborough and Eugene gained a great victory over the able marshal Villars. This was the bloodiest battle of the war, in which the allies lost twenty thousand men.

The battle of Blenheim was one of the decisive battles of history. The allies, says Martin, numbered about 33,000 foot and 29,000 horse, — 62,000 in all; while the Franco-Bavarians had about 35,000 foot and 18,000 horse, — 53,000 in all. Guizot makes the numbers about equal. Eugene was repulsed five times by the French under Marsin; but Tallart, the other French marshal, who opposed Marlborough, was surrounded, and made prisoner, while his son was killed by his side. The cavalry fled towards the Danube, and perished in the river, or were slaughtered before they reached it. Fourteen thousand or more soldiers lay dead or wounded upon the battle-field. "Twenty-seven battalions," says Martin, "of veteran infantry, and twelve squadrons of dragoons, or at least what remained of them, surrendered themselves prisoners of war; the regiment of Navarre burned its colors and broke its arms in rage! . . . The flying army did not stop till it reached the left bank of the Rhine. It abandoned all Germany to the allies, as the price of a single victory!"

Marlborough was the hero of the hour. Queen Anne gave him the estate of Woodstock, Oxfordshire, a perpetual pension of four thousand pounds a year, and half a million pounds for the erection of a beautiful palace.

France was in a deplorable condition. "Imagine the horror of seeing an army without bread!" wrote Villars. "There was none delivered to-day until the evening, and very late. Yesterday, to have bread to serve out to the brigades I had ordered to march, I made those fast that remained behind. On these occasions I pass along the ranks. I coax the soldier; I speak to him in such a way as to make him have patience; and I have had the consolation of hearing several of them say, 'The marshal is quite right; we must suffer sometimes.' . . . It is a miracle how we subsist."

The king spared no effort to raise money for his suffering soldiers. He sent his gold plate to the Mint to be melted. Madame de Maintenon ate only oaten bread. "I was one of the first," she wrote to the Duc de Noailles, "to send away my plate. . . . There was enough to bring thirteen or fourteen thousand francs. . . . Starvation will soon reach even ourselves. We have not a penny, and corn rises every day." She was constantly urging for peace, and the people were murmuring and clamoring for it. Finally the proud Louis humbled himself to seek peace; but the conditions of the conquerors were such that they could not be accepted. He was asked to send armies against his grandson, Philip V. of Spain; but this he refused. He wrote to Philip, suggesting that, as the feeble child, afterwards Louis XV., might die, and the crown thus revert to Philip, that it might be wise to renounce the monarchy of Spain. This the young grandson refused to do. He would give up France, but never Spain, where they adored their young king, and were willing to die for him.

Meantime, Leopold of Germany had died; Marlborough was in disgrace in England, and his opponents were in the cabinet. The Peace of Utrecht was effected April 11, 1713, and Europe rested for a time.

These years had been full of care and sorrow to Louis XIV. and his wife. Her apartment, as she told Madame de Glapion, at St. Cyr was "just like a church. It is a regular procession; everybody passes through, and the comings and goings are perpetual. When the king has heard mass he comes back again to my room. Then . . . a great many ladies, and they stay while I am at dinner. . . . It is necessary to entertain the company, and in some way to keep them all in union. If anybody does anything indiscreet, I feel it; I am worried by the way something that is said is taken.

"Some one of the ladies wishes to speak to me in private. . . . One has had a quarrel with her husband, another wants to beg something of the king; one has had some evil turn done her, another has suffered from some misunderstanding. . . . I see myself there in the midst of them all — this person, this old person, the sole object of their attention! I am the one whom they address, through whom everything passes. And God gives me the grace never to see my own position on its dazzling side; I only feel the pain of it. . . . I look upon myself as an instrument of which God makes use to do good.

"If the king has any troubles, I must share them; his sadness, his depressed spirits. Sometimes he is subject to fits of uncontrolled weeping."

" You know," said Madame de Maintenon, "that my maxim is to spend myself and spare others. Great people are not usually like this." At another time she said, " I am not a great person. I am only raised." . . . " As to the king's gentleness, you could never believe how far he carries it, and I am more free in telling him when he does wrong than I am with a thousand other people. Some days ago, I said to him frankly, ' You have not done well, sire, in that; you have been very wrong.' He took this admirably, even humbly, from me. The next day, when it was necessary to speak of what had been so ill done, I wanted to let it pass quietly by, saying, ' That is past, sire; we must not think of it again.' He replied, ' Do not make excuses for me, madame; I was very wrong.' "

All through the last war Madame de Maintenon was writing letters to the marshals, cheering and counselling, to the bishops, seeking their aid and prayers, and to those who were suffering, giving consolation and courage. At St. Cyr over forty volumes of her letters are preserved. "They possess," said a prominent author, "to the highest degree, a certain nameless quality of discretion, simplicity, efficacy."

When she could find a moment of leisure she went among the poor. To some she gave money, to some bread, and to others clothes. "When she speaks of God to these peasants," wrote her secretary, Mademoiselle d'Aumale, "you see a great gladness in her face, and a very strong wish to make them know Him."

Two years after the war of the Spanish Succession, the king was drawing near the end of life. He was leaving a child of five to sit upon his throne, his great-great-grandson. A Regent had to be appointed; and Madame de Maintenon urged the Duke du Maine, the son of Madame de Montespan, whom she had educated, and whom she tenderly loved. Another person had strong adherents, the dissolute nephew of the king, Philip, Duke of Orleans. He was the son of Louis' only brother Philip, and had married the daughter of Madame de Montespan, with great ceremony, at Versailles, in 1692.

Louis XIV. tried to compromise matters by appointing a council of regency, with the Duke of Orleans as president, and the Duke du Maine as a member with the charge of the young king.

In August, 1715, Louis was taken ill. He asked to have the little dauphin brought to his bedside. "My child," said Louis XIV., "you will soon be the king of a great kingdom. Never forget your obligation to God; remember that you owe to him all that you are. Try to preserve peace with your neighbors. I have loved war too well; do not imitate me in this, any more than in my too lavish expenditure. Take counsel in all things. Relieve the distress of your people as soon as you can, and do what I have had the misfortune to be unable to do myself." These words were afterwards inscribed at the head of the bed of Louis XV.

As the child was leaving him, Louis kissed him and said, "Darling, I give you my blessing with all my heart." He asked for the boy to be brought back once more for his kiss and blessing.

The king saw two grooms of the chamber weeping. "What are you crying for?" he asked; "did you think I was immortal?" To Madame de Maintenon, now eighty years old — he was seventy-seven — he said, "I have always heard that it was difficult to make up one's mind to die. I do not find it so hard."

To his nephew he commended Madame de Maintenon. "You know," he said, "what consideration and esteem I have entertained for her. She has never given me any but good counsel; I should have done well if I had always followed it. She has been useful to me in everything, but, above all, in regard to the salvation of my soul. Do everything that she asks you to do for herself, for her relations, and her friends. She will never encroach upon you."

Towards the last he begged Madame de Maintenon to forgive him whenever he had not made her happy; for he had, he said, always loved and esteemed her just the same. He shed tears as he spoke; and, in spite of all her efforts to prevent it, tears streamed down her cheeks. "What will become of you?" he asked. "You have nothing."

"Do not think of me," was the answer; "I am nothing; pray occupy yourself with God alone."

"There is no one that I regret to leave but you," he said, "and we shall soon see one another again."

On August 29, Thursday, as the king was unconscious, and it was supposed he would not live through the day, she repaired to St. Cyr, with the approval of her confessor and advice of Marshal Villeroy. The next day, Friday, he regained consciousness, and asked for her. She at once returned, when he spoke a few words, and then seemed to sleep. In the evening she returned to St. Cyr. The king lived a day longer, much in the same condition. The last words he was heard to utter were those of the psalm: "Have mercy upon me, O my God! Come unto my aid; make haste to help me!"

Marshal Villeroy sent Madame de Maintenon in his own coach to St. Cyr, and posted royal guards along the road, that she might pass in safety. "Some popular commotion may be feared," he said. The whole of Sunday, September 1, — the king died at quarter-past eight in the morning, — Madame de Maintenon spent in tears and prayers. She had hoped to die first. "I should like to die before the king," she had said to Madame de Glapion. "I would go to God; I would cast myself at the foot of his throne; I would offer him the desires of a soul that he would have purified; I would pray him to grant the king greater lights, more love for his people, more knowledge of the state of the provinces, more aversion for the perfidy of the courtiers, more horror of the ways in which his authority is abused; and God would hear my prayers."

No one dared at first to tell the aged woman, now partially deaf and infirm, that her kingly companion was dead. When she learned it, she sent away her men-servants, and sold her carriage and horses, as she said she could not "reconcile herself to feeding horses while so many young girls were in need."

A week later the Duke of Orleans, whose habits had always received her just censure, came to tell her that the king's pension of four thousand livres a month would be continued to her. He then said, "She had done all the good she could to everybody, and never wronged anyone."

Madame de Maintenon lived four years, devoting her time to the poor, and teaching the girls. She wrote to the Princess des Ursins, a letter now in the British Museum, "There is nothing to be done but to bow one's head to the hand that has struck us. I wish with my whole heart, madame, that your condition were as happy as mine. I have seen the king die like a saint and like a hero. I have left the world which I did not love, and I am in the pleasantest retreat that I could wish for."

Two years after the death of Louis, Madame de Maintenon received an illustrious visitor at St. Cyr. Peter the Great came to see her with his interpreter. She was ill in bed. When asked her malady, she replied, smiling, "Very great age." He had the curtains of the bed drawn aside that he might look at the woman whom the great Louis XIV. had loved and depended upon. She wrote to a friend, with something of the buoyancy of early days, "You will believe that he must have been pleased."

Devoted to her church, she yet loved to hear all the changes in the political world. She wrote to Villeroy two years before her death, "Between ourselves, I should be happier than I am if I had any society; however clever a nun may be, she has no knowledge of what has occupied us all our lives."

April 14, 1719, after a severe cold and cough, she seemed to rally. "I am better," she said to her friends, "but I am still going."

A violent thunder-storm came on towards evening, and visibly affected her. Near midnight she received the sacrament. When her confessor asked her to bless the daughters of St. Cyr, she said, "I am not worthy;" but when he urged, she lifted her hand, though unable to speak. She became unconscious, and passed away at dawn, April 15, 1719, at the age of eighty-four.

For two days she lay in death, "with an air so sweet and so devout, that one would have said she was praying to God." On April 17 she was buried in the nuns' choir, and a slab of marble marked the place of sepulture.

Seventy-five years later, in 1794, when the wars and expenditures of Louis XIV., and the follies of Louis XV., had helped to bring on the French Revolution, and the people needed cannon, the church of St. Denis was despoiled of its graves, the coffins melted for lead, and the bodies of Louis XIV., Maria Theresa, the lovely Marie Adelaide, Duchess of Burgundy, whose untimely death had saddened all France, and many others, were thrust into one common grave.

A little later, when the church of St. Cyr was being tranformed into hospital wards, the slab of black marble showed where the aged Madame de Maintenon rested. The vault was broken open, says Saint-Amand, and the body, with "dreadful yells," was thrown into a hole in the cemetery. The friend of the poor was thus punished for being the friend of a king.

Madame de Maintenon is without doubt, as the scholarly opponent of Papal infallibity, Dr. J. J. I. Döllinger calls her, "the most influential woman of French history." In the midst of a corrupt court she gave no occasion for scandal. She had sufficient self-control and tact to know how to control a high-spirited, proud, dominant king. She was a charming conversationalist upon all great topics, with no love for the trivial and simply amusing. And yet she was vivacious; and the king at first disliked her " because he thought her a' wit."

Her Christian character was never hidden, even before the highest. To one she wrote, " We are never at rest till we have given ourselves to God." Again, " I find nothing does so much good as prayer; it rests and strengthens both the heart and mind at the same time."

She made mistakes, even with her excellent judgment. Her hopes that the Catholic and Protestant religions could become one in France were futile. " I intended to do good," she said, " when I obtained the nomination of M. de Noailles and M. de Fénelon as Archbishops of Paris and Cambrai; but I was so grieved about them in the end that the king said to me, ' Well, madame, are we to see you die for this matter?'"

She was gentle in manner, and noted for her grace and modesty. Fénelon said of her, "Wisdom spoke by the voice of the Graces." Saint Simon, who did not like her, said she had "incomparable grace, with language gentle, exact, well-expressed, and naturally eloquent and brief."

Madame de Maintenon is one of the most striking examples in history of the type of woman able to keep the affection she has won. Louise de la Vallière was not only beautiful and gentle, but gave the king her intense and undivided love. She lived for him alone, taking no part in the affairs of state. Madame de Montespan, extremely beautiful and queenly, fond of gayety, and the centre of all eyes from her brilliancy, faded out of the heart of Louis XIV. Madame de Maintenon, neither very beautiful nor young, but able to be his intellectual companion, adviser, and unselfish friend when at the zenith of his power, was, at eighty years of age, the only one that filled his heart. As he said in dying, "There is no one that I regret to leave but you, and we shall soon see one another again."

CATHARINE II. OF RUSSIA.

CATHARINE II. OF RUSSIA.

IN the ancient town of Stettin, in Prussia, May 2, 1729, a little girl was born, Sophia Augusta Frederika, who was destined for a great career. Her father was an officer in the army, a brave and good man, Prince Christian-August of Anhalt-Zerbst; her mother, an ambitious and pleasure-loving woman, Princess Jeanne-Elizabeth of Holstein-Gottorp.

The child, Sophia, was brought up simply, as was necessary in a home of small means. Her governess was French, Mademoiselle Cardel, who taught her to admire Racine, Corneille, and Molière. She was a good-natured child, quick mentally, witty, intelligent, and with great decision of character, even in these early years.

When Sophia was ten years old, she met for the first time Peter Ulric, the lad, then eleven, whom she afterwards married. He was her first cousin on her mother's side, the son of Anna Petrovna, daughter of Peter the Great, and of Charles Friedrich, Duke of Holstein-Gottorp. The boy seems to have had a bad disposition, and Sophia was not attracted towards him.

Elizabeth, the daughter of Peter the Great, had come to the throne of Russia. She was a woman of much beauty and ability. She had been engaged to Prince

Karl-August of Holstein, the uncle of little Sophia, who had died before the marriage. She therefore felt a deep interest in his family, and asked for the portraits of his brothers and his sister, Jeanne-Elizabeth. In 1742 the empress sent to the latter a portrait of herself in a frame of magnificent diamonds.

A little more than a year after this gift was made, a message came to Jeanne-Elizabeth, urging her to visit the Imperial Court at Moscow, and to *bring her daughter*. There must have been visions now before both their minds of a broader life than the quiet one at ancient Stettin.

In January, 1744, Sophia and her mother started on their long journey. The girl of fifteen had but three dresses in her simple wardrobe; but she carried with her a father's love in a book of counsel written with his own hand, and a gift from him of a volume on religious matters.

As soon as the travellers were within the borders of Russia, they were treated with every attention. State chariots were at their command, scarlet sledges lined with sable, one of them drawn by sixteen horses, many servants, and all the luxuries that wealth could give.

The Tsaritsa was waiting anxiously for the arrival of her visitors at her splendid court. She is said to have possessed fifteen thousand silk dresses, and five thousand pairs of shoes! Her attendants were also dressed magnificently. Another person was also waiting with intense interest, — Peter Ulric, the cousin of Sophia, the nephew of Elizabeth, whom she had made heir to the throne.

He was then a youth of sixteen, very inferior in body

as well as in mind, poorly educated, badly trained by a brutal tutor, and unsuited for the great position to which he was to be called. It was evident that Sophia had been wanted in Russia for a marriage. Frederick the Great had desired this union, to cement the friendship of Russia and Prussia.

The pretty Sophia pleased the empress and her nephew. It was not asked whether the girl herself was pleased. Evidently her mother was rejoiced at the prospect of seeing her child ruling over a great empire.

With admirable sense, the girl at once decided to make the Russian nation her nation; to study the language, walking barefoot in her room at night to keep herself awake while she studied. She became ill in consequence of a chill, and nearly lost her life. She gave up the Lutheran religion, and adopted the faith of the Greek Church, assuming the name of Yekaterina Alekseievna. The empress then presented her with a collar of diamonds worth one hundred thousand roubles. The next day, June 29, 1744, she was betrothed; and on August 25 she was married in the church of Our Lady of Kazan, the ceremony lasting from ten o'clock in the morning till four in the afternoon.

For many days balls, operas, dinners, and illuminations were enjoyed. The wealth of Crœsus seemed showered upon the girlish German princess. Her apartments were hung with cloth of silver embroidered with silk, and red velvet embroidered with silver.

If there was any happiness in this royal marriage, it did not last long. Peter was immoral; he drank to excess; he even struck his wife when she did not please him. He kept in his bedroom a pack of hounds, whose barking and frantic cries when beaten made Catharine's life miserable. He called her a fool publicly before a dinner company of four hundred persons. Catharine tells in the "Memoirs" written by herself, and published by Appleton in 1859, that Peter passed his time in childish pursuits unworthy of his age. He amused himself with paper soldiers, and had a rat tried and executed because it had eaten a pasteboard sentinel placed before a pasteboard fortress.

Alfred Rambaud, in his history of Russia, quotes de Breteuil, the French ambassador: "Peter smokes and drinks beer for hours together, and only ceases from these amusements at five or six in the morning, when he is dead drunk."

Peter wished to divorce his wife and marry Elizabeth Vorontsof, the daughter of Count Roman Vorontsof. It is said that she drank with him, and did not hesitate to beat him when he deserved it. Peter gave an order to have his wife arrested and placed in a convent; but the order was not carried out.

Catharine, too, caused scandal at court by the attention she bestowed upon the young and handsome Sergius Saltykof, chamberlain to Peter, belonging to one of the most important families in Russia. Very attractive in face and manner, pitied and loved by the people on account of her unhappy life, Catharine was constantly surrounded by temptations.

She did not forget, however, to cultivate her mind while her husband was wasting his life. She read all the Russian books which she could find. She studied Montesquieu, and thought his "L'Esprit des Lois" ought to be "the breviary of every sovereign of common-sense." She read carefully his "Causes of the Greatness and Fall of the Roman Empire." She was very fond of Plutarch's "Lives," and other biographies of noted persons. She read nine volumes of German History by Father Barre, giving a week to each volume. The letters of Madame de Sévigné greatly pleased her. She pored over the "Annals of Tacitus," the Latin historian. She corresponded with Voltaire, whom Goethe called "the greatest literary man of all time." She wrote him, says James Parton in his "Life of Voltaire," "Since the year 1746," — she was then seventeen — "when I became mistress of my own time, I have been under the greatest obligation to you. Before that period I read nothing but romances; but by chance your works fell into my hands, and ever since I have not ceased to read them, and I have desired no books which were not as well written as yours, or as instructive. . . . I am reading at present your 'Essay upon General History,' and I should like to learn every page of it by heart."

After Catharine had been married ten years, her first child was born, Sept. 20, 1754, named Paul. He was taken away from his mother, and cared for during the next six years, for the most part, by Elizabeth, who seems to have thought of disinheriting the incapable Peter, and placing Paul on the throne.

The young mother, Catharine, was therefore left alone with her books and her courtiers. Ambassadors from other countries soon learned that Catharine, well-read and charming, knew more about the needs and wishes of Russia than Peter, or even the empress. Count Poniatowski, one of her admirers, a fine-looking and scholarly young Pole of twenty-two, whom she afterwards made King of Poland, thus describes Catharine, who was then twenty-five years old: —

"With her black hair, she had a dazzling whiteness of skin; the color of the eyelids black and very long; a Grecian nose, a mouth that seemed made for kisses, hands and arms perfect, a slim figure, rather tall than short, an extremely active bearing, and nevertheless full of nobility; the sound of her voice agreeable, and her laugh as gay as her humor, which caused her to pass with facility from the most sportive, the most childish amusements to the driest mathematical calculation."

Chevalier d'Eon wrote: "The grand duchess is romantic, ardent, passionate; her eyes are brilliant, their look fascinating, glassy, like those of a wild beast. Her brow is high; and, if I mistake not, there is a long and awful future written on that brow. She is kind and affable; but when she comes near me, I draw back with a movement which I cannot control. She frightens me."

In February, 1758, a daughter, Anna, was born to Catharine; but lived only fifteen months. Another child, Alexis, Count Bobrinski, was born later. Catharine became more than ever interested in affairs of State. "She is now," says R. Waliszewski in his "Romance of an Empress," "in full possession of all her gifts, natural and acquired, of one of the most marvellous intellectual and physical organizations that have ever been made for combat, for the conduct of affairs, and for the government of men and things."

Her correspondence with high officials on state matters, with perhaps some hints of her own reign in the future, was at this time discovered by Elizabeth, and Catharine was in disgrace. Equal to the occasion, she demanded an audience with the empress, and asked that she be allowed to leave Russia forever, a country where she had suffered so much from false accusations and at the hands of a drunken husband, who still depended upon her.

"The Grand Duke," says Catharine in her "Memoirs," "for a long time called me *Madame la Ressource;* and however vexed he might be with me, if ever he found himself in distress on any point, he came running to me at full speed to have my advice; and as soon as he had it, he would dash away again at full speed."

The empress could not send away the mother of little Paul, whom she idolized. She forgave Catharine, and restored her and her husband to favor.

Elizabeth was breaking down physically, from care and anxiety. She had, like her father, Peter the Great, done many good things for Russia. She had proved a powerful opponent to Frederick the Great in his wars for conquest. She had founded the University of Moscow, and helped forward both science and commerce.

"In January, 1759, she had," writes the Marquis de l'Hôpital, "sunk into a singular state of superstition. She remains whole hours before an image for which she has great devotion. She talks to it, consults it. She comes to the opera at eleven, sups at one, and goes to bed at five."

Three years later, Jan. 5, 1762, Elizabeth died, at the age of fifty-three, and Peter Ulric became Peter III. He did not endear himself to his people. "Even in the burial chamber of his aunt," says the Princess Dashkof, the sister of Elizabeth Vorontsof, Peter's favorite, "he was seen whispering and laughing with the ladies-in-waiting, turning the priests into ridicule, picking quarrels with the officers, or even with the sentinels, about the way their cravats were folded, the length of their curls, or the cut of their uniforms."

Peter at once made peace with his great friend, Frederick of Prussia, restored all that Elizabeth had taken from him in war, introduced Prussian dress and drill into his army, drank to the health "of the king, our master," meaning Frederick the Great, and knelt before his portrait with glass in hand, exclaiming, "My brother, we will conquer the universe together!" He dismissed his body-guards, whom Elizabeth had valued so highly, and put a Holstein regiment in their place. This, of course, exasperated the army. He began to confiscate the property of the church, and turn it over to the state, thus setting the priests against him.

Peter, however, did some creditable things. He put an end to a secret tribunal established by Elizabeth, whereby any one could be arrested and punished for criticisms upon the government. He recalled, it is said, by the advice of Catherine, many political offenders who had been banished to Siberia; Biron, General Münnich, and others. Duke Biron, then seventy-two, had been in prison for twenty years. He was the favorite of the Empress Anna Ivanovna, the daughter of Ivan V., the brother of Peter the Great. She lived in the greatest luxury at court, and was as eccentric as she was prodigal of money.

A singular punishment was inflicted by her on a prince who had displeased her. He was condemned to personate a hen, sit on a large nest of eggs in a basket of straw, in one of the principal rooms at court, and, on pain of death, cackle like the fowl.

The Russians disliked their empress, and said the corn did not grow because a woman ruled; but they disliked "Biren, the cursed German," still more. He was finally sent to Siberia by Anne Leopoldovna, the niece of Anne Ivanovna, while she was regent, and her little son, Ivan VI., was emperor.

When Elizabeth, the daughter of Peter the Great, came to the throne through a revolution, she sent Anne and her husband, Anton, Duke of Brunswick, to a prison in the north of Russia, where Anne died after four years. During this time two sons and two daughters were born to Anne Leopoldovna. The baby emperor, Ivan VI., was separated from his mother, and confined in the fortress of Schlüsselburg. His life was a pitiful one. He was not allowed to speak with his guards, it was said, in his dungeon, where a lamp was always burning, nor to read, and at twenty-one had become weak-minded, or had lost his reason. Peter III. brought him to St. Petersburg, and talked of making him his successor instead of his own son Paul.

Peter and his wife grew more and more unhappy. She had a new favorite in the person of a tall, handsome officer, Gregory Orlof, who had received three wounds at the battle of Zorndorf, Aug. 25, 1758. He was noted for his great strength and fearlessness. He had four brothers in the guards, and Catharine could rely on these and their power with the army.

Without doubt there was much discontent among the people. Many preferred that the well-educated, agreeable Catharine should rule. The Orlofs had won the army to her side. The talented young Princess Dashkof was her ardent supporter. Of course these took their lives in their hands; for defeat in a revolution meant imprisonment in Siberia, or death.

Peter had received some hints of a conspiracy, and had arrested one of the conspirators. Passek, an officer, supposing that his commander was in the secret, asked when they were to march against the emperor. The officer pretended to be one of their number, and so obtained knowledge of the plot. As soon as Captain Passek was arrested, Alexis Orlof, the brother of Gregory, started for Peterhof, the summer palace of the Tsars, twenty miles from St. Petersburg, to bring Catharine at once to the city.

It was on July 9, 1762, at five in the morning. Catharine was asleep; but she dressed hastily, sprang into the coach beside her maid, while Orlof mounted in front. The horses were tired out by the journey from Petersburg; so two horses and a peasant's cart, found on the way, were used to hurry the royal lady to the capital.

When they reached the barracks, three regiments of foot-guards took the oath of allegiance to Catharine. At Our Lady of Kazan she received her subjects, kneeling before her. From the Winter Palace she issued her proclamation; and the people cried, "Long live the empress!" She sent Admiral Talysine to Cronstadt, and secured its allegiance, and was soon at the head of twenty thousand men, marching against Oranienbaum, another summer home of the Tsar.

He, meantime, had started on the morning of that

fatal July 9 for Peterhof, where Catharine was to give a dinner in his honor before he started on his campaign against the Danes. He did not reach Peterhof till two o'clock, and then only to find it deserted.

He at once embarked for Cronstadt, to put himself at the head of the garrison. "There is no longer any emperor," said Admiral Talysine; and the astonished Peter hastened to Oranienbaum.

Catharine appeared on horseback at the head of her troops, wearing the uniform of the grenadiers, oakleaves around her sable cap, and her hair floating in the wind. The Princess Dashkof rode beside her, wearing a similar costume.

When the troops reached Peterhof, to which place Peter had been brought, he offered first to share the crown with Catharine; and then, as she disdained this offer, he abdicated. He begged that Elizabeth Vorontsof might go with him into exile; but this was denied. She was banished to Moscow.

Peter was sent to a place named Ropcha, "a secluded spot, but very pleasant," writes Catharine, fifteen miles from Peterhof. He asked for his dog and his violin; but these requests were not granted. Four days from this time it was given out that Peter had died of a "hemorrhoidal colic . . . flying to the brain!"

That he was strangled, after having been poisoned in his wine by Alexis Orlof and some accomplices, is extremely probable; that Catharine knew of it, and favored it, is equally probable.

Another stain rests upon the early years of her reign. Now that Peter was dead, some one might dislike her usurpation, and suggest Ivan VI. She therefore re-imprisoned him at Schlüsselburg, saying, "It is my opinion that he should not be allowed to escape, so as to place him beyond the power of doing harm. It would be best to tonsure him, and to transfer him to some monastery, neither too near nor too far off."

Two years after Catharine had become empress, Mirovitch, a lieutenant of the Guards, made an attempt to liberate Ivan VI. With his comrades, they battered down the door of the dungeon, when, to their horror, they found the mangled body of the prince, who had been killed by his guards. These had received strict orders to kill him if ever he attempted to escape. Ivan had made an heroic struggle for his life, and was badly cut by their swords. His body was wrapped in a sheepskin, and buried without ceremony.

"According to the information I received from those who had seen the body of Ivan," says Coxe, "he was six feet in height, handsome and athletic; he had small, fiery eyes, and a complexion uncommonly fair, which had been rendered pallid by confinement."

Mirovitch was tried and condemned to death, but from his manner evidently expected a reprieve up to the last moment. When he was beheaded, Sept. 26, 1764, the people who crowded to see the execution were so much overcome at the sight of his head, that they uttered shrieks, and the bridge over the Neva was partially broken by their weight. During the twenty years' reign of Elizabeth there had been no capital punishment, although many had been tortured with the knout.

Catharine II., at the time of her coming to power, was thirty-three years old. The French historian, Rulhière, thus describes her: "Her figure is noble and agreeable, her bearing proud, her person and her demeanor full of grace. Her air is that of a sovereign. All her features indicate character. . . . Her forehead is large and open, her nose almost aquiline; her mouth is fresh, and embellished by her teeth; her chin a little large, and inclined to fleshiness. Her hair is chestnut in color, and of the greatest beauty; her eyebrows brown, her eyes brown and very beautiful, . . . and her skin is of dazzling whiteness. . . . The amiability and good-nature which are also to be seen there, seem to a penetrating eye merely the effort of an extreme desire to make a pleasing impression." Catharine herself said that "her greatest gift was the gift of pleasing."

Loving Russia, Catharine had made herself ready for the task of ruling. Her desire was to make Russia great; and she succeeded beyond all expectation. It was not a fancy sketch that she sent to her correspondent, J. M. Grimm, in Paris, showing what she had accomplished between the year 1762 and 1781: "A hundred and forty-four towns built, thirty treaties made, seventy-eight victories won, eighty-eight notable edicts, decreeing laws, and a hundred and twenty-three edicts in behalf of the people;" and yet she said, "All that I can do for Russia is but a drop of water in the sea."

She had already studied the laws of other nations besides the complex ones of Russia. She at once, like Napoleon the Great, prepared, or caused to be prepared, a new code of laws for her people. For the framers of this code she wrote minute "instructions," enough to fill a book, with her own hand. She never dictated. She had "pillaged," as she said, from Montesquieu and Beccaria. When the work of her six hundred and fifty-two deputies was completed, she gave to each a gold medal, with her effigy, and the motto, "For the happiness of each and all, Dec. 14, 1766." She sent copies of her laws to the principal crowned heads of Europe. Frederick the Great wrote to her: "No woman has hitherto been a legislatrix. That glory was reserved for you, who so well deserve it."

Catharine was deeply interested in the serfs. One of the first acts of her reign was to give to the state the land and the one million serfs owned by the clergy. A commission made up of lay and ecclesiastical delegates settled an income on the clergy and the monks. She proposed, in 1766, to the Society of Political Economy which she had founded, a question as to the right of the laborer to the land which he cultivated. One hundred and twenty replies were sent, in Russian, Latin, French, and German. A prize of a thousand ducats was offered; but the publication of the paper favoring the emancipation of the serfs, which received the prize, was opposed by thirteen votes to three.

Catharine's plans met with the greatest opposition from the nobles, who had, in fact, placed her in power, and she could not make them enemies. She never ceased to think about the serfs, and corrected many abuses concerning them. It is declared that she projected a ukase making them free after the year 1785; but the great measure was not carried out till over seventy years later, in 1861, by Alexander II., when twenty-three million serfs obtained their liberty.

Catharine expedited trials by increasing the number of courts of justice and judges. She noted " with profoundest sorrow that corruption has progressed so rap-

CATHARINE II. OF RUSSIA. 69

idly that it is hardly possible to cite an administration or a tribunal that is not infected by it. If any one asks for a place, he must pay for it; if a man has to defend himself against calumny, it is with money; if you wish falsely to accuse your neighbor, you can, by gifts, insure the success of your wicked designs." All these abuses Catharine tried to abolish.

She was tolerant of all religions. She allowed the Jesuits to come into Russia; the Volga Tartars to rebuild their mosques. She welcomed colonists from all nations. The Moravians came in large numbers because they could have religious freedom. In the province of Saratof, says Rambaud, "she induced twelve thousand families to take up their abode, whose descendants, now very numerous, still inhabit the country."

Dr. S. M. Schmucker, in his life of Catharine, thus describes her Lombard or Loan Bank: "She became the great money-lender of the empire. She established a bank on this principle, possessing a capital of thirty-three millions of roubles; and empowered to issue bills possessing the currency of money, to the amount of a hundred millions more.

"Of the fund thus invested, twenty-two millions of roubles were to be lent to the nobility for twenty years, on mortgage on their estates at an interest of five per cent. . . . The remaining eleven millions of roubles of the principal of this Imperial Bank were devoted to the encouragement both of foreign and domestic commerce, and of the internal trade of the empire, by being loaned in smaller amounts to merchants and retail dealers. The bank also operated as an insurance company from losses by fire. All foreigners, as well as all

Russians, were allowed to deposit their funds in this bank, and to have the sovereign's word and credit pledged for their security."

In the second year of her reign, Catharine devised a new system of education for her empire. She sent to Oxford and Turin and Germany for the best teachers. She caused to be translated into the Russian language the works of Confucius, Plato, Homer, Horace, Vergil, and, indeed, the best from all the classics.

In 1762 a school of artillery and engineering was founded; later, a school of commerce, the academy of mines, and the academy of fine arts developed, which had been created under Elizabeth. Ten normal schools were established at St. Petersburg, where they soon had a thousand pupils.

The Russian Academy was founded in 1783, modelled after the French Academy, through the influence of a woman, Princess Dashkof, who was then president of the justly famous Academy of Sciences. "The task," says Rambaud, "of fixing the rules of the orthography, grammar, and prosody of the Russian language, and of encouraging the study of Russian history, was confided to her. She then undertook the publication of a dictionary, which appeared from 1789 to 1799, which included in its six volumes 43,257 words, and was re-edited from 1840 to 1850." The highest in the land, even Catharine herself, helped in the preparation of this dictionary. With such examples, it is not strange that to-day many of the Russian women are highly educated, and in the learned professions.

Catharine was the first sovereign of Russia to think of education for women. Loving the most abtruse philosophical works of her time, she could see no inferiority in the mind of woman, and no reason why she did not need the same education as man. She opened the institute of Smolna, a handsome edifice, for five hundred young women.

In 1763 she erected the Foundling Asylum at Moscow, to which thirteen thousand children are sent annually. Betzky, an eminent philanthropist, gave all his means, two million francs, to the institution, and twenty years of service. Procope Demidof erected the immense buildings at his own expense.

The great Foundling Asylum at St. Petersburg, covering twenty-eight acres, was also built during the reign of Catharine. It is one of the most interesting objects in the city to the traveller. In 1882 I went through every department, and found much to admire in this humane institution.

As I entered the marble hall, an official in a red cloak reaching to his feet, and his hat trimmed with yellow braid, made me welcome. While I waited, a poor girl came with her baby. The only question asked was, "Has the child been baptized?" A cord was clasped about its neck by a metal seal, with a number on it, and a similar one given to the mother, that she might come to visit it, or claim it at any time within ten years.

I was first shown into a room where the babies are washed in little copper tubs, flannel lined. Some cried, and some went to sleep in the warm water. Instead of a cloth for washing, a piece of hemp is used, on account of its softness. They are then laid on down pillows, on a table in the centre of the room, a flannel blanket wrapped around them up to their necks, their little arms being held down by their sides, their feet folded in, and the whole bundle tied about with a cord. A white cap is put on the head, and the only part visible is a wee face. They are then placed in iron cots about a foot and a half wide and two long, and each covered with a green blanket.

In the next room scores upon scores of babies were being cared for by the attendants, who wear red or green caps, white waists, and dark skirts. One mother had come from the country to see her baby, and was holding it to her cheek with a pitiful look, a bundle lying behind her in the chair. Our guide said she had walked many miles. Each nurse cares for two children, and receives as compensation her board, and about eighteen cents a day. A poor woman who comes and nurses her own baby daily, and thus saves the board of a wet-nurse, receives about thirty-seven cents a day. Married people may, if they are poor, bring their child for one year. If, at the end of that time, they cannot take it home, it belongs to the state.

Half of the infants usually die during their first year. The rest are educated, the girls usually as teachers, and the boys as mechanics, or as sailors and soldiers. The property devoted to this work of saving helpless children in Russia is estimated at five hundred million dollars.

The learned Diderot once wrote: "When time and the steadfastness of this great sovereign shall have brought these establishments to the point of perfection of which they are all susceptible . . . people will go to Russia for the sake of seeing them, as people formerly went to Egypt, Lacedæmon, and Crete; but with a curiosity which will, I venture to think, be better founded and better rewarded."

Catharine admired the philosopher, Diderot, and invited him to her palace, though she thought some of his plans visionary. She said to him, "You work on paper, which is tractable to everything; while I, a poor empress, must work on human nature, which is irritable and easily offended."

Catharine made St. Petersburg beautiful. She built elegant palaces, and costly bridges over the Neva. She caused to be erected a monument to Peter the Great, that will forever associate the name of Catharine the Great with his. It represents Peter on horseback, reining in the spirited animal, which stands on his hind legs on the brink of a rock. The granite pedestal weighs fifteen hundred tons, — it is fourteen feet high, twenty broad, and forty-three long, — and required five hundred men five weeks to move it with horses from a Finnish village four miles from St. Petersburg. It was hauled over cannon-balls on an iron tramway. The bronze statue and horse, weighing sixteen tons, were designed and cast by Falconet, a Frenchman. The head of the emperor was modelled by a woman, Marie Callot, who afterwards became the wife of Falconet. The artist spent nearly twelve years upon his work. The cost was 424,600 roubles. While all these improvements were carried forward, Catharine was engaged in wars which increased her territory and added to her fame.

Poland was distracted by internal dissensions over religion and reforms in government. The aid of Catharine was sought; and by a treaty made between Poland and Russia in 1768, the constitution could never be modified without the consent of the latter.

74   CATHARINE II. OF RUSSIA.

Insurrections broke out among the liberty-loving Poles, and were put down by Catharine. Turkey, claiming that her territory had been violated, took up arms against Russia, and was signally defeated by Rumiantsof, in July, 1770, with 17,000 Russians against 150,000 Mussulmans at Kagoul. The Russians took 140 pieces of cannon, and 7,000 wagons laden with provisions. Alexis Orlof, the brother of Gregory Orlof, the favorite, was sent to the Mediterranean with twenty-five sail-of-the-line. He annihilated the Turkish fleet at Tchesme, aided by the fire-ships of the English. There were public rejoicings at St. Petersburg in consequence, and Catharine laid the foundations of a new palace to commemorate the event.

When any of Catharine's generals expressed fear of failure from lack of provisions or numbers, with her usual fearlessness and hope she wrote them: "The Romans did not concern themselves with the number of their enemies; they only asked, 'Where are they?'"

She says in her private journals, upon her coming to the throne: "I found the army stationed in Prussia, without pay for the past eight months; in the treasury seventeen millions of roubles of unpaid bonds; . . . a loan of two millions attempted in Holland by the Empress Elizabeth, but without success; no credit, and no confidence abroad; at home, the peasants in revolt everywhere, and, in certain districts, the proprietors themselves ready to imitate their example." The Turkish war cost forty-seven and one-half million roubles; but Catharine was able to meet her payments.

In 1772 it was decided to divide the republic of Poland between Russia, Prussia, and Austria. It is generally claimed that Frederick the Great has the dishonor of this suggestion to recompense Catharine, his ally, for her losses in war. It was the old story of might making right, the weak succumbing to the strong.

Russia, by the division of Poland, obtained White Russia, with 1,600,000 inhabitants; Austria had Western Gallicia and Red Russia, with 2,500,000 people; Prussia took Western Prussia, with 900,000 people.

Catharine had conquered the Turks, but they were to be avenged. Her soldiers had brought back the dreaded plague to Moscow. During July and August, 1771, the deaths amounted to a thousand a day. Forty thousand persons perished in the suburbs of Moscow and Kief. The dead lay unburied in the houses and upon the streets. Churches were turned into hospitals. The people were frantic.

Catharine sent Gregory Orlof with a hundred thousand roubles to appoint a health commission, to check the disease in all ways possible, and to allay the frenzy of the people. The severity of winter stopped the disease in January, 1772.

Catharine had other obstacles to contend with. There were never wanting claimants to the throne, even though the position was a very unstable one. Among the pretenders was Emelian Pugatchef, a Cossack who had deserted from the army. He was said to resemble Peter III.

He attacked several towns, and compelled them to surrender; then with ten thousand Kalmucks, besides a multitude of Poles, who had been banished to Siberia, he marched towards Moscow. The hundred thousand serfs there began to think of rising. For almost a year his numbers increased; he hanged the nobles, and punished as rebels all who resisted him.

Finally Catharine sent Alexander Bibikof against him, with thirty-five thousand men. Pugatchef fought for five hours, was defeated, fled to the mountains, again rallied his forces, and was finally taken prisoner, and brought to Moscow in a cage in September, 1774. He was beheaded, and five of his accomplices were hanged, and twenty more were knouted, and sent to Siberia.

It was not strange that Catharine grew more watchful of her throne. The tragic story of Princess Tarakanof has been often told. Some claim that she was the daughter of Elizabeth by Count Razumofsky, her chancellor, whom she secretly married. Others, that the real daughter became the nun Dosythea, and that she is buried at Moscow in the Novospaski Monastery.

Prince Radzivil, a Pole, angered at Catharine II. for her policy towards his nation, determined to place this granddaughter of Peter the Great on the throne. Princess Tarakanof was conveyed to Rome, and Radzivil waited for the proper hour to carry out his plans.

Catharine learned of his purpose, and seized his estates, leaving him poor, though she offered to restore them if he would deliver the princess to her. This he refused to do.

Alexis Orlof was then sent to Italy. He found the princess at Rome; told her that he believed she was the lawful sovereign; pretended to fall in love with her; procured a false marriage through some make-believe Greek priests; took her with great ceremony on board a Russian fleet, and carried her to Russia.

As soon as she was on the ship, he caused her to be

put in chains. She fell at his feet; but the murderer of Peter III. did not even deign to look at her. When she reached St. Petersburg she was put in prison, and never seen afterwards. It was said by some that, six years later, the waters of the Neva rose to an unusual height, and drowned her in her cell.

In the Academy of Arts at St. Petersburg may be seen a painting by Flavitzky, representing the young princess struck with terror at the water rising about her, making death certain. Other authorities say that the sword did its bloody work with her.

The claimants to the throne being disposed of, Catharine turned her attention to increasing her possessions. The Crimea had been declared independent by a treaty in 1774, but it had been in a state of anarchy ever since. Catharine interfered, and the Sultan finally ceded Crimea to Russia in 1783.

Catharine had always had the "Greek project" in mind; viz., the expelling of the Turks from Constantinople, and the establishment of a large Greek empire, to be governed by her grandson, Grand Duke Constantine. He had early learned the Greek language, and had been provided with a Greek nurse, thus to help prepare him for his destiny.

Early in 1787 Catharine made a triumphal journey to the Crimea and other newly conquered provinces. Potemkin, the favorite who had taken the place of Gregory Orlof, arranged the journey for her. Count Orlof, to whom she gave one hundred and fifty thousand roubles a year, ten thousand peasants, a mansion, and court equipages, was in disfavor at court, though Catharine never ceased to be fond of him.

He had married a young and beautiful wife, who died at Lausanne in 1782. This and other disappointments so preyed upon Orlof's mind, that he died in June, 1783, before Catharine had completed the beautiful marble palace for him at St. Petersburg. The prince had helped her to gain the throne; he had bought for her the magnificent Orlof diamond, which weighs one hundred and eighty-five carats, and is valued at more than two million roubles. It once formed the eye of an idol in a temple in India, from which it was stolen by a soldier, and sold to a dealer.

Potemkin, who had become prime minister and field-marshal, was a handsome and accomplished Pole, a soldier and an able statesman. Having conquered the Crimea for her, the ancient name of which was Taurida, he was surnamed Tauridan; and Catharine had built for him the magnificent Taurida palace at St. Pétersburg. In two years she bestowed upon him thirty-seven thousand peasants, and about nine million roubles in palaces, pensions, and jewels; in all, about fifty million roubles.

During this triumphal journey, early in 1787, to the provinces of which Catharine had made Potemkin governor, she travelled in a gilded coach, followed by fourteen coaches and one hundred and twenty-four sleighs. There were about six hundred horses at each relay. Palaces were erected along the route, to last but a single night. Forests were ignited to illumine the darkness. Herds of sheep along the roadside were transported to other places in the night, while the empress slept, to grace the landscape on the day following.

The empress, says Prince de Ligne, carried a green bag filled with four-ducat gold-pieces, which she scattered among the people along the route, as often as ten times a day. She left in presents in every good-sized town as much as one hundred thousand roubles.

At Kief three hundred young women strewed flowers before the carriage of the empress. She remained at that city three months, and in March sailed down the Dnieper to Cherson, with eighty vessels and three thousand men. On one of the gates of the city, facing east, were the words, "This is the road that leads to Byzantium." Potemkin had erected a throne for her at Cherson, costing 14,000 roubles.

After a short voyage she stopped at Kamief, to welcome Poniatowski, the King of Poland, her former favorite. They dined together. Near Cherson she met Joseph II. of Austria, who went with her as far as Moscow.

Catharine remarked, looking out upon her possessions, "Rather than sign the secession of thirteen provinces, as my brother George has done [George III. in giving up the American colonies], I would have shot myself." Doubtless the ambitious queen said the truth, for she loved power.

Turkey could not help seeing that Catharine was seeking to gain Constantinople. The two nations were soon at war again.

Potemkin was not hopeful at first, and wrote to the empress about evacuating the Crimea, as his fleet at Sevastopol had suffered from a tempest. All the strength of the fearless woman rose against it. "I implore you to take courage and reflect," she wrote Potemkin; "with courage all can be repaired, even a disaster. . . . It would be better to attack Otchakof or

Bender, thus substituting the offensive for the defensive attitude. . . . Courage! courage! I write all this to you as my best friend, my pupil and scholar, who at times shows more resolution than I; but at this moment I have more courage than you, because you are ill and I am well."

The siege of Otchakof was begun, with one hundred thousand Russians. The besiegers suffered from cold and hunger, but both Russians and Turks fought heroically. Nearly the whole Turkish garrison were put to the sword. Twenty-five thousand captives were taken, and more than twenty thousand Turks were slain. The Russians lost twelve thousand.

Catharine appreciated this great victory, and sent to Potemkin one hundred thousand roubles, and a medal struck in his honor. To her great generals, Souvorof and Repnin, she gave swords set with diamonds, and plumes with brilliants. When Catharine had first met Souvorof, and all were asking favors, she asked, "And what do you wish, Souvorof?"

"Three roubles to pay for a lodging," was the answer.

On Sept. 22, 1789, Suvorof and the Austrian general, the Prince of Coburg, with twenty thousand soldiers, defeated one hundred thousand Turks. The next year Ismaïl, on the northern side of the Danube, defended by forty thousand men, was taken after three assaults by the fearless Suvorof. Ten thousand Russians were killed, and thirty thousand Turks. Repnin, with forty thousand men, defeated the Grand Vizier with one hundred thousand men at Matchin. Turkey sued for peace, which was made at Jassy in January, 1792.

CATHARINE II. OF RUSSIA. 81

Three months before the treaty was concluded, Potemkin died, Oct. 15, 1791. He was travelling; and unable to bear the motion of his carriage, he was laid on a piece of carpet, under a tree by the roadside, and died in the arms of his niece, Countess Branicki.

He was buried with great ceremony at Cherson, the city which he had built, the empress sending one hundred thousand roubles for his tomb. When her son Paul, who disliked Potemkin, came to the throne, he had the body disinterred, and placed in an obscure corner. It was afterwards discovered, and buried in a church.

Ever since the first partition in 1772, Poland had made rapid strides in education and other needed reforms. It seemed necessary to reform the constitution once guaranteed by Russia, and a liberal one was adopted May 3, 1791.

Catharine, having wars on her hands with Turkey and Sweden, dared not protest. Soon, however, some disaffected Poles besought her to interfere. She authorized them to form the Confederation of Targovitsa, and at once sent one hundred thousand Russian soldiers into Poland. The Poles asked the aid of Frederick William II. of Prussia, the nephew of Frederick the Great, who had died in 1786. He wished to be excused, but very soon joined Catharine for the sake of the spoils.

The Poles fought heroically under Prince Joseph Poniatowski at Ziélincé, and under Thaddeus Kosciuszko at Dubienka, July 17, 1792, where with four thousand men he kept fifteen thousand Russians at bay for six hours. The Poles were defeated, Russia taking three million people in the second division of Poland, and Prussia a million and a half.

Again the Poles rose to arms, and called Kosciuszko to lead them. He had fought bravely in our Revolutionary War, was one of the adjutants of Washington, and received the public thanks of Congress for his services. He was a finely educated man, somewhat saddened in early life because a Polish nobleman would not allow his daughter to marry an officer so poor as Kosciusko. The Polish peasants were armed with scythes. At Warsaw and elsewhere the Poles drove out the Russian garrisons.

Austria now joined Prussia and Russia, eager to secure more territory. The Poles were unequal to a contest with a hundred and fifty thousand men. On the eve of the assault before Praga, opposite Warsaw, the Russians put on white shirts, as though going to a wedding. Souvorof gave orders to spare the vanquished, but the command was not heeded. The dead numbered twelve thousand, while scarcely one thousand were taken prisoners. Suvorof wrote to the empress: "The streets are covered with corpses; blood flows in torrents."

Catharine made Suvorof field-marshal for his bravery and success. She never forgot the supporters of her throne. She said, "I make it a point to praise aloud, and to complain quietly." When men failed in battle she encouraged them. " Have not the greatest captains had their unlucky days?" she said. "The late King of Prussia was only great after a great reverse." After the battle of Kilburn she sent quantities of ribbon for the heroes, arranging them with her own hands.

Kosciuszko was taken prisoner at Maciejowice, Oct. 10, 1794, and imprisoned in St. Petersburg. After the death of Catharine he was liberated by her son Paul.

He died in Switzerland, Oct. 16, 1817. His body was removed by Emperor Alexander I. to the Cathedral Church of Cracow, and buried by the side of Poniatowski and Sobieski. The Poles have raised a large mound of earth, one hundred and fifty feet high, to his memory, the earth having been brought from all the great Polish battle-fields. Poland was divided for the third time between Russia, Prussia, and Austria, and the kingdom annihilated.

If Catharine had loved liberty in her early years, the excesses of the French Revolution, and the struggles under her own reign, had made her believe fully in absolutism. She prophesied that a Cæsar would come to control France after the Revolution; and he came in the person of Napoleon.

Nothing was too great or too good for her adopted country. While she increased the size of Russia, she did not forget its mental development. She loved books. She purchased Diderot's library for fifteen thousand francs, but insisted that he should retain it till his death, with a pension of a thousand francs a year.

As the pension was forgotten the year following, she directed that it be paid for several years in advance, and accompanied her letter with twenty-five thousand francs. After Voltaire's death she bought his library of about seven thousand volumes, though many protested against its leaving France. It is now in the Imperial Library of St. Petersburg.

Catharine loved to write as well as read. She rose at five or six o'clock in the morning, even in the bleak Russian winters, often kindling her own fire, to put her thoughts on paper, either to noted correspondents, or into books. To Grimm she wrote that her two plays, "Le Trompeur" and "Le Trompé," had "each brought in at Moscow ten thousand roubles to the management."

She wrote fiction, philosophical tales, sometimes poetry, and historical works suitable for her dearly loved grandchildren, Alexander and Constantine, the sons of Paul. She also began to translate the Iliad.

She caused her country to be explored in the interest of science. Eight hundred men, with a hundred officers, provided with all necessary instruments, studied the geography, natural history, and prospects for civilization, of her thousands of uninhabited acres. They explored the coasts of Japan and China, and the straits which bear the name of their discoverer, Bering.

Catharine built the Hermitage as a museum and a place in which she could have conversations with her gifted friends, and gathered into it some of the treasures of the world. She hung up ten rules at the entrance, the first being, "Leave your rank outside, as well as your hat, and especially your sword." The sixth was, "Argue without anger and without excitement." The tenth, "Tell no tales out of school; whatever goes in at one ear must go out at the other before leaving the room." If the last rule was broken, the person was not again admitted. In 1768 she bought the Dresden gallery of Count Brühl for a hundred and eighty thousand roubles.

She had copies made at Rome of the frescoes of Raphael in the Vatican. She filled several rooms with valuable prints, ten thousand drawings, and ten thousand engraved gems. She commissioned the great artists of Europe to procure their best for her. Sir Joshua

Reynolds painted for her "The Infant Hercules Strangling the Serpents," a fit emblem of Catharine. She allowed him to select his subject and name his price. She paid him fifteen hundred guineas, and sent him a gold snuff-box, with her portrait set in diamonds.

Catharine could not refrain from building. "The mania of building," she said, "is an infernal thing; it runs away with money; and the more one builds, the more one wants to build."

She embellished Tsarskoé-Sélo, the favorite summer home of royalty, fifteen miles from St. Petersburg. All is beautiful; but the amber room is especially so, the walls being panelled with amber which was given to Catharine the Great by Frederick the Great. The arms of Frederick are moulded with the imperial cipher, the Russian E. for Ekaterina. The bedchamber of Catharine has walls of porcelain with pilasters of purple glass. The walls of most of the rooms are covered with gold. In these grounds, eighteen miles in circumference, Catharine erected several monuments to her favorites.

The best beloved of all, a youth of twenty-two, was Lanskoï, a refined and cultivated officer, a Pole, elegant in manner, beautiful in person, and lovable in disposition. He died at Tsarskoé-Sélo, July 2, 1784, in her arms. She wrote, "I had hoped that he would be the support of my old age," — she was then fifty-five years old, — "he was attentive, he learned much, he had acquired all my tastes. He was a young man whom I was bringing up, who was grateful, kind, and good, who shared my sorrows when I had them, and rejoiced in my joys. . . . I cannot sleep or eat; reading wearies me, and writing is too much for me."

At his death, Lanskoï returned to his adored sovereign the seven million rubles which she had given him; but she refused to receive them, and gave the money to his sisters. She erected a beautiful mausoleum for him in the gardens of her palace, and could never visit it without tears. When Lady Bruce, an intimate friend, said to Catharine, " I notice that your majesty's favorites are very young," she replied, " I desire them to be so; if they were older, people would say they governed me."

With all Catharine's ambition and intellect, she had a warm heart. Her servants were devoted to her. " Will you kindly look for my snuff-box ? " was her usual way of speaking. She wrote Grimm, concerning an old German nurse who had just died : " Whenever she saw me, she would seize me by the head, and kiss me again and again till she half-stifled me. And she always smelt of tobacco, which her respected husband used largely."

" There is one among her cooks who cooks abominably," says Waliszewski. " For years she had never noticed it. When it has been pointed out to her, she has refused to dismiss the man, saying that he has been in her service too long. She merely inquires when his turn comes, and then says, on sitting down to table, ' Ladies and gentlemen, we must exercise our patience; we have a week's fast before us.' "

The empress, like Frederick the Great, was especially fond of dogs. A whole family of English greyhounds usually slept by her bed. Dr. Dimsdale brought from England a couple of these dogs to her in 1770, when he came to vaccinate her.

She had a pet cat, whose paws on the paper some

times hindered her writing. Her white squirrel was fed with nuts from her own hands. She also had a pet monkey. Madame Vigée Le Brun, who went to St. Petersburg hoping to paint the portrait of the empress, wrote: "I used to see her every morning open the shutters and throw out crumbs to hundreds of crows, who came every day at the same hour to seek their pittance."

Catharine II. had learned some of the things which help to make greatness. She had remarkable self-control, though she was naturally of a quick temper. If she gave way to her temper, she walked to and fro in her private room, drinking glass after glass of water, till she had conquered herself. She so far overcame this defect, that getting angry seemed impossible to her. She used to say, "I have imperturbability."

She had great courage. She wrote, "Courage! Forward! That is the motto with which I have passed through good years and bad years alike." When there was a riot in the streets, she mounted on horseback, and rode about the city at midnight, with a few trusted officers, to see if her orders had been obeyed.

In her war with Sweden, she thought seriously of going to the scene of action. "Had it been needful," she said, "I should have left my bones in the last battalion. I have never known fear." Like Napoleon, she had great will-power. She wrote Grimm, "I am constrained to will terribly what I will." She willed to make Russia a leading power among the nations of the world, and she succeeded.

She was natural in manner, and simple in her daily life. She urged ladies to be natural, and said experience would do the rest. She offered a cup of coffee to her secretary when he was cold. She talked with her subjects, but did not wish to be seen often in public. She cared little about her eating, never taking supper, and rarely using wine or any intoxicant.

She was usually an excellent judge of the characters and abilities of others, and she likewise knew herself. "With talents of a superior order, — and both Frederick and Napoleon were probably her inferiors in this respect," — says Waliszewski, "Catharine had more flexibility, was more fruitful in resources, had a more delicate sense of touch." Her executive ability was amazing. She placed men where she thought they ought to be, and then trusted them. She wrote to Grimm: "Men of worth are never lacking; for it is affairs which make men, and men which make affairs. I have never tried to look for them, and I have always found close at hand the men who have served me."

She did not waste time, and therein gave a valuable lesson to the world. She rose early, and retired usually before ten, lived methodically, never seemed in a hurry, was extremely punctual, was read to when she had a few spare moments, took very little time in her dressing, and often talked with others on important matters during this time. On state occasions she usually wore red velvet; at home, quite generally, white or gray silk, or violet.

There was apparently little love between her and her son Paul, probably because he seemed a dangerous rival for the throne of his father, Peter III., and felt that he should have ruled in her stead. When he did come to the throne at forty-two, he reigned only four years, when he was strangled, on the night of March 23, 1801, because he would not abdicate.

He introduced the Prussian costume; forbade the importation of European books and music; indeed, he made his policy exactly opposite to that of his mother. It is quite probable that Catharine, foreseeing much of this, intended to make Paul's son, her idolized grandson, Alexander I., her heir; but death came too suddenly.

She arose in good health, as usual, on the morning of Nov. 16, 1796, and took her strong coffee. Going to her room for a moment, her servants were surprised that she did not return. A half-hour later they found her stretched on her floor. She was speechless until her death, from apoplexy, at ten o'clock the following evening. She was sixty-seven, and had reigned for thirty-four years, for the most part with great power, wisdom, and success.

As in the reign of Peter the Great, some shadows darken "the light from the North," as Catharine was called. The partition of Poland cannot be forgotten, or the deaths of the innocent Ivan VI., and that of the misled Princess Tarakanof. There was little sorrow at the death of Peter III., but the world cannot sanction murder.

The obsequies were imposing, as befitted so remarkable a woman and so renowned a sovereign. By order of Paul, the tomb of Peter III. was opened, and his coffin laid in state beside that of Catharine. A love-knot reached from the side of one coffin to the other, with the words, " Divided in life — united in death."

As though to make the scene still more tragic, Alexis Orlof and Prince Bariatinski, supposed to have been the chief murderers of Peter III., stood during the three hours' ceremony on either side of the coffin, and viewed the work of their hands. Only a few bones and one sleeve of his uniform remained in the coffin of Peter III. Orlof was unmoved; but Bariatinski, it is said, would have fainted but for stimulants.

Catharine lies buried in the fortress and cathedral of St. Peter and St. Paul at St. Petersburg, an immense yellow building of stucco, surmounted by a tall spire with an angel and cross. Within, upon the walls, are flags and other trophies of battle. It is a weird place to visit. Priests in red velvet embroidered with gold were conducting service as we entered, and swinging their censers of incense. Thousands have looked with interest upon Catharine's marble coffin. Her son Paul lies here.

On the coffin of the idloized Nicholas, who died at Nice in 1865, and who was to have married Dagmar, is a wreath of red and white porcelain roses, tied with a blue ribbon. The nation is not through sorrowing, even yet, for the liberator of the serfs, Alexander II., over whose coffin hang several silver wreaths. Many kneel and kiss his coffin as they pass.

And now, in 1894, on Nov. 19, with great ceremony, and evidently sincere mourning, Alexander III. has been buried in this tomb of his ancestors. Royalty gathered from all over Europe. Emperor William II. of Germany sent a wreath of green and gold laurel, twined with real blossoms and fruit, bound with white ribbons, with the monograms and crowns of the emperor and empress in gold. It was so large that a car of the greatest size was necessary for its transportation.

The wreath sent by Francis Joseph occupied thirty florists for several days. It is estimated that about two million roubles were spent in decorating the route to the fortress and cathedral of St. Peter and St. Paul.

On Nov. 26, a week after the death of Alexander III., his son, Nicholas II., married the beautiful Princess Alix, daughter of the deeply lamented Alice, and granddaughter of Queen Victoria. They have begun the task of governing one hundred million people, in that country, more than twice as large as our own, over which Catharine reigned so ably.

In 1873 her statue, a monument forty-nine feet high, was unveiled with great ceremony before the Imperial Public Library, which her genius helped to build. The nine figures around the pedestal represent such able helpers as the Princess Dashkof, Potemkin, Suvorof, and others.

Lord Brougham of England truly said of Catharine II.: "Her capacity was of an exalted order. Her judgment was clear and sure; her apprehension extraordinarily quick; her sagacity penetrating. . . . There have been few abler monarchs in any part of the world."

MADAME LE BRUN.

THOSE who have visited the Louvre in Paris will recall in the French gallery, among the paintings by David, Greuze, Gérard, and Joseph Vernet, a beautiful portrait of Madame Le Brun, with her little daughter, Jeanne-Julie-Louise, in her arms, painted by herself.

Her life is as interesting as her face is charming. Élise-Louise Vigée was born in Paris, April 16, 1755, the daughter of a portrait painter, Louis Vigée.

As a child, she loved to play with his brushes and his pencils, and at seven, much to the joy of her father, drew a man's head with a beard. The proud parent said, "Thou wilt be a painter, my child, if ever there was one."

Like most artists, he seems to have been without means, though knowing and associating with prominent persons, like Diderot, d'Alembert, and others. If the home lacked luxury, it did not lack affection, especially from the father, who, like many another, not realizing all the success he had hoped for in his own life, looked forward to great things from his daughter.

The mother, Jeanne, was very beautiful, so that on the street she attracted much attention. She seems not to have been averse to such attention; for she often walked, with her equally beautiful young daughter, in

MADAME LE BRUN.

the Tuileries, or the gardens of the Palais Royal. She was very religious, never omitting a service. Her daughter never read a novel until after her marriage, her first being "Clarissa Harlowe." Her books were all religious ones.

The child, Élise, was in a convent from the age of six to eleven, at which time, not being strong in health, she was allowed to come home to her parents. Two happy years followed; and then the father died, May 9, 1768, leaving a wife and two children to care for themselves as best they could.

Élise was well-nigh heart-broken. She had already been taught in drawing and painting by the historical painter, Gabriel Doyen, and in color by Davesne, who painted the picture of Marie Antoinette as dauphine of France.

Nothing seemed to comfort the young girl, except her art work. Gabriel Briard, member of the Royal Academy, aided her in drawing; and Claude-Joseph Vernet, who was then, on the invitation of Louis XV., painting his famous sea-ports of France, encouraged and helped the girl of fourteen.

"My child," said he, "do not follow any particular school. Only consult the works of the great Italian and Flemish masters; but, above all, do as much as you can from nature. Nature is the best master. If you study it diligently, you will never get into mannerisms."

Day after day the girl copied the works of Rembrandt, Van Dyck, and Rubens, and some of the lovely female heads by Greuze, besides making portraits. But she could not support herself, her mother, and her brother, two years younger, whose schooling, books, and clothes she was obliged to provide.

A rich jeweller offered himself to the beautiful mother, and was accepted, probably on account of the needs of her children. The marriage proved a most unsatisfactory one. The miserly husband compelled Élise to give him all she earned from her work, and would not provide for them the necessities of life. This was enough to discourage the young artist, but she toiled on. She must by this time have learned that labor is essential to success, and that only the strongest will-power can overcome disappointments and poverty.

The new father profited by the marriage. He wore Louis Vigée's clothes without alteration, and had a wife and a daughter to earn money for him. Vernet begged Élise to save her money, and allow her step-father only a pension; but she feared that her mother would suffer, and so gave all she earned.

From the age of fourteen to twenty, Élise, by constant labor, was fast winning renown. Prominent persons sat for their portraits, and each told some other of the charming young worker and her excellent work.

Madame Geoffrin, to whose *salon* came the most distinguished men and women, both French and foreign, heard of Élise Vigée, and called upon her. This woman had won a place for herself in Paris without "distinguished birth, talents, or fortune." She was at that time probably about seventy; though Madame Le Brun says in her Memoirs that she "should have thought her at least a hundred, for not only did she stoop a great deal, but her costume aged her immensely. She wore an iron-gray dress, with a large flapped cape, covered with a black hood, tied under her chin."

Count Gregory Orlof, the favorite of Catharine II. of

Russia, who had helped her to gain her throne, was travelling in France with the greatest display. He was said to wear, on grand occasions, a coat whose every button was an immense diamond. He called upon Élise to see her portraits. She remembered that he was a colossal man, and wore a remarkable diamond ring upon his finger. About this time she painted the portrait of Count Shuvalof, grand-chamberlain, and one of the two favorites of Empress Elizabeth of Russia, a man of charming manners, who did much for the advancement of the Russian Empire. The noble Duchess de Chartres, wife of Philippe Égalité, sent for Élise to come to the Palais Royal and paint her portrait. After that, several court ladies sat to her.

Élise had many social invitations, but could rarely accept them, save in the evening, as "the daylight was too precious," she says, "for me to give its hours to society." She relates an amusing incident in connection with an invitation to dine with the Princess de Rohan-Rochefort.

Élise dressed herself for dinner in a new white satin; and then, thinking she would look at a picture which she had been working upon, she sat down in a chair opposite her easel. Her palette, covered with various paints, happened to be in the chair. Of course the dress was spoiled, and the dinner had to be given up.

At the house of this princess, Élise met some of the most noted persons in Paris. Often she took her guitar, and played and sang for them, when the evening was devoted to music. Cardinal de Rohan was often one of the guests. He was ambassador from Louis XV. to Vienna, then Bishop of Strasburg, and later Cardinal, but was ruined in the diamond necklace affair, for which he was confined for a time in the Bastile.

The Duc de Choiseul, another guest, was minister of foreign affairs under Louis XV., through the friendship of Madame de Pompadour, who governed the king. When Madame du Barri became the favorite, he was dismissed, and banished to his estate. He opposed the division of Poland; and when it took place Louis said, "This would not have been if Choiseul had been minister."

When Élise was twenty, she received from d'Alembert, secretary of the French Academy, " free entry to all their public Assemblies," by reason of her gift to the Academy of two portraits made from the engravings of the time, of Cardinal Fleury, tutor and finally minister to Louis XV., and La Bruyère, the noted author. D'Alembert, " a little man, very hard and cold, but exquisitely polite," she says, came to thank her in person. Catharine II. had offered him twenty-five thousand livres a year to become the tutor of her son Paul, with all facilities for completing his encyclopædia, but he declined.

While the young artist was winning fame for herself, and money for her step-father, he had become averse to the attention she and her mother received in public, and removed them to a quiet and obscure place in the country. "And what a place!" she writes. "Imagine a very tiny garden, no trees and no shade, except in a little arbor where my father had planted beans and runners which never grew; and we had not the whole even of this charming garden. It was divided into four parts by little sticks, and the three others were let to shop-boys who used to spend their Sundays in firing at the birds." The girl fretted at the confinement and separation from friends, but kept steadily at her work.

When they returned to Paris, they lodged in the same house as a picture-dealer and painter, Jean-Baptiste-Pierre Le Brun. He had a fine collection from the various schools of painting, and cordially gave the beautiful artist the privilege of copying. At the end of six months he offered himself in marriage. Élise did not wish to accept him; but the mother thought he was very rich, and repeatedly urged her not to lose so fine an opportunity.

Élise earned a good support for herself; but she so longed to escape living with her step-father, that she finally consented. All the way to church on that unfortunate day, Jan. 11, 1776, she kept saying to herself, "Shall I say 'yes?' shall I say 'no'?"

"Alas!" she writes, "I said 'yes,' and I exchanged my old troubles for other troubles. It was not that M. Le Brun was considered a bad-hearted man; he was good-tempered with all — in a word, he was very amiable; but his headstrong passion for low women, added to a love of gambling, brought about the loss of his fortune and mine, which he entirely disposed of in such a complete manner, that when I left France in 1789 I did not possess twenty francs, though I had earned over a million. He had dissipated it completely."

As he was already engaged to the daughter of a Dutch picture-dealer, he insisted that his marriage with Élise be kept secret till his business matters were settled with the dealer.

As soon as it began to be surmised that a marriage

might result from the acquaintance of Élise with Le Brun, her friends came to her and told her "she would better throw herself into the river" than marry him. They informed her of his character and his debts. The foolish mother of Élise could hardly restrain her tears, but it was too late. The artist had only exchanged one bad master for another. Le Brun made her give him every dollar she earned by painting, and compelled her to take pupils besides. The girl of twenty-one had become a servant.

His "old masters" were kept in richly furnished rooms in the front of his house; his wife in an anteroom and bedroom. She writes, "I never left my painting till it was quite dark, and the number of portraits I finished at that time was simply prodigious." Two years after her marriage her daughter, Jeanne, was born. The child brought sunshine into the young mother's heart; though so devoted was she to her painting, that she had never become depressed.

Her work and her talents were constantly increasing her fame. In 1779 she made her first portrait of Marie Antoinette. The queen was at this time twenty-four years old, six months younger than Élise Le Brun. She was tall, and held her head very erect, while her manner was most sweet and gracious. "It is very difficult," says the artist, "to give any idea to those who have not seen the queen, how very elegant and beautiful she was. . . . Her eyes were not large, and were almost blue in color; her expression was clear and very soft, her nose was thin and pretty, and her mouth was not large. . . . The most remarkable thing about her face was the brilliancy of her complexion. I never saw anything like it.

... Her skin was so transparent that it allowed of no shadow. ... Paints failed to depict the freshness, the delicate tints, of that charming face, which I never beheld in any other woman."

The portrait of Marie Antoinette, in a satin robe and holding a rose, was for her brother, the Emperor Joseph II. of Austria. She ordered two copies, one for Catharine II. of Russia, and the other for herself to be placed at Versailles or Fontainebleau.

Madame Le Brun painted several others of the queen, one in blue velvet, and one in a simple dress of white muslin, which gave especial satisfaction. It was taken to the theatre, and the audience all arose and greeted the artist with vehement applause. Still another represented Marie Antoinette ascending into heaven, with Louis XVI. and two of their children, who had died.

Madame Le Brun became very fond of the queen; sang duets with her at nearly every sitting, and never tired of praising her loveliness or thoughtfulness of others. She painted for the *salon* in 1788 the queen and all her children, the dauphin, Madame Royale, and the Duc de Normandie. It was so much liked that Louis XVI. said to the artist, "I do not understand much about painting, but you make me love it." The picture was hung at Versailles; but the dauphin dying the following year, in 1789, the queen could not see it without weeping, and it was removed, though she made known to the artist the reason for its removal.

Madame Le Brun then painted the brother of the king, afterwards Louis XVIII., the wife of the Comte d'Artois, afterwards Charles X., the aunts of Louis XVI., Adelaide and Victoria, and his sister, the lovely

Madame Elizabeth, who met her death heroically on the scaffold, May 10, 1799.

Madame Le Brun also painted the unfortunate Princess de Lamballe. "She had small features," says Madame Le Brun, "a brilliant complexion, splendid blond hair, and an elegant figure." She was married at nineteen to the Prince de Lamballe, who died the year following. After the death of the queen of Louis XV., Marie Leszczinska, and of Madame de Pompadour, a marriage was proposed between the beautiful Princess de Lamballe and the dissolute monarch; but the minister, Choiseul, defeated it. She became the superintendent of the royal household, under Marie Antoinette, to whom she was devoted, and met her death during the horrors of the French Revolution.

When she was brought out of La Force, one of the city prisons, on Sept. 3, 1792, and called before Hébert, a Jacobin, who sat at the gate, under pretence of trial, he said to her, " Swear devotion to liberty and to the nation, and hatred to the king and queen, and you shall live." "I will take the first oath," she replied, "but the second never; it is not in my heart. The king and queen I have ever loved and honored."

She was rudely pushed into the gateway. A brutal fellow struck her with his sabre. As soon as she fell, a butcher boy cut off her head. Her clothes were torn from her body. Her heart was torn out and, with her bleeding head, stuck on a pike, and paraded through the streets, followed by a shouting rabble, to the prison where Louis XVI. and Marie Antoinette were confined, awaiting their doom.

During these busy years, Madame Le Brun had one

pleasant vacation in 1782. Her husband was going to Brussels on business, and she accompanied him. Here she met the Prince de Ligne, — descended on his mother's side from Mary, Queen of Scots, — the Austrian general and French writer, who was with Catharine II. in that sumptuous journey to the Crimea in 1787.

Madame de Staël said of him, " He is the only foreigner who, in French manners, has become a model instead of being an imitator." Madame Le Brun thought, "for elegance of mind and manners, the prince has never had an equal." He took her to his home, and showed her his masterpieces by Rubens, Van Dyck, and others. He was as brave in war as he was fascinating in peace. His father and grandfather were both field-marshals of Austria, and he also held a like position. His literary works numbered thirty-six volumes.

Amsterdam and Antwerp interested the artist, who had known only France. Greatly admiring the famous painting of one of Rubens's wives in a straw hat, she made a portrait of herself in a straw hat with a garland of field flowers. Müller engraved it. Joseph Vernet liked it so much that he proposed Madame Le Brun as a member of the Royal Academy of Painting. M. Pierre, chief painter to the king, opposed the admission of a woman, but was finally over-ruled by his associates. Her presentation picture, in 1783, was "Peace returning and bringing Plenty with her."

She was now twenty-five, and more popular than ever. Famous men and women gathered at her *soirées;* and when in her modest apartments, on the Rue de Cléry, there were not seats enough for the guests, some of the marshals of France even sat upon the floor. The Marshal de Noailles, very large and very old, found it almost impossible to get up again. Prince Henry of Prussia brought his violin, and the most famous singers of Paris were glad to add their talent to these delightful evenings. The poet, Le Brun, sometimes called the French Pindar, read his poems to the assembled guests.

Once Madame Le Brun gave a Greek Supper, which occasioned much comment. Her brother having read to her some pages of the "Travels of Anacharsis," she resolved to try the food of the ancients, and imitate their costumes. All the ladies wore Greek styles, arrayed from Madame Le Brun's studio; the poet Le Brun wore a large purple mantle, and the little daughter of the hostess and another child bore antique vases and served the guests. It was rumored that this supper cost twenty thousand francs; when the story reached Vienna it had grown to sixty thousand, and at St. Petersburg eighty thousand. She tells us in her Memoirs that it cost exactly fifteen francs!

In the *salon* of 1785 she exhibited a picture of M. de Calonne, the comptroller-general, for which she received four thousand francs; for another portrait eight thousand francs; for the picture of the handsome youth, Prince Lubomirski, in 1788, twelve thousand francs. All this money went to the husband, who said, with truth probably, that he needed it all for his debts. His wife begged for two louis, but they were refused her.

Her dress was usually of the simplest kind, white muslin or linen, with a muslin kerchief around her head, as may be seen in her portraits in Florence, St. Petersburg, and at Paris. In the Louvre she is painted as a Greek. Her talent, her charming manner, and her kind heart had won her position, despite her plain wardrobe and simple home.

In 1786 Madame Le Brun went to Louveciennes to paint a portrait of Madame du Barri, who was then forty years of age. "Her face," says Madame Le Brun, "was still charming, with regular and pleasing features; her hair was fair and curly like a child's; her complexion was the only part which was becoming withered."

Madame du Barri wore in summer, as in winter, dresses of white muslin or percale, and walked in her park daily, without regard to the weather. Madame Le Brun painted three portraits of her, one in a dressing-gown, with a straw hat, and another in white satin, holding a crown in her hand. The last was suggestive, for her ascendancy over Louis XV. had been complete.

A young milliner in Paris, leading a disreputable life, then the companion of a profligate nobleman, she had became the favorite of the king when she was twenty-three. She spent the nation's money prodigally, not so much for herself as for her relatives, and she gave large sums to artists and literary men. On the death of Louis XV., his grandson and successor, Louis XVI., banished Madame du Barri to an abbey near Meaux; but she was allowed after two years to return to her estate at Louveciennes, where by acts of charity she endeavored to make amends for her past life.

In 1790 diamonds and jewels to the amount of four hundred thousand francs were stolen from her. She traced them to England, and went there to obtain them. She greatly aided the loyalists there, and on her return to France befriended the adherents of Louis XVI. and

Marie Antoinette. This was enough to mark her for the guillotine. She fainted at her trial, and was carried insensible to prison. On her way to the scaffold, Dec. 7, 1793, her cries for mercy to the crowd were so heart-breaking that the executioner hastened his bloody work.

The wars of Louis XIV. and his extravagant building of Versailles fountains and similar luxuries, and the prodigality of Louis XV., had brought about the debt and the poverty which culminated in the French Revolution. In 1789 the populace were ready to strike down the rich, to rail at any who rode in carriages; and looked for the impossible time when there should be no inequalities of fortune. There was no question as to their grievances. The poor were suffering, and then, as now, too often the rich were indifferent, or lacked generosity.

Madame Le Brun, known as the friend of the royalists, had already been subjected to much that was terrifying. Sulphur was thrown into her cellar through the gratings. The Jacobins shook their fists at her as they passed her windows, and tore up the pavement of the street where she lived.

She had grown ill from anxiety and overwork, and resolved to leave France and go to Rome. Fortunately her husband was absent, so that one hundred louis, which she had received for a portrait in September, were not appropriated by him, and could be used for the journey.

Just before her departure some of the National Guard came, most of them intoxicated, and said, in a threatening manner, " You shall not leave." Two soon returned and spoke kindly, advising her to leave at once, not in a carriage, but by the public coach or diligence.

On Oct. 5, 1789, she and her daughter started for Rome. That very day the king and queen, with their family, were forced to leave Versailles and go to Paris, in the midst of a turbulent crowd, armed with pikes, bearing the heads of the body-guards whom they had killed.

Madame Le Brun had left not an hour too soon. Her disguise in the poor dress of a working-woman had probably saved her from the scaffold. She tarried for a few days at the principal cities along the route. At Bologna she was made a member of the Academy. At Florence she was asked for her portrait, to be hung in the gallery of modern painters. This she sent later from Rome.

She arrived in Rome without funds, and borrowed a little from an artist. She was soon at work on the portraits of noted persons. Miss Pitt, a daughter of Lord Comelford, was represented as Hebe on clouds, holding a goblet in her hand, from which an eagle was drinking. The eagle was from life, and, accustomed to being chained in the open air, was furious as a prisoner in the artist's room. A portrait of a Polish lady, Countess Potocki, was done next, and then Lord Bristol, and others. For three years Madame Le Brun worked untiringly, sending now and then one hundred louis to her husband, who wrote her pitiful letters concerning his poverty.

There was everything in Rome to interest and stimulate the artist — the Coliseum, St. Peters, the Pantheon, and the wonderful ruins of former splendor. Many noted French people had found an asylum there during the Reign of Terror, and these added to her happiness.

Pope Pius VI., a very handsome man, wished to have her paint his portrait; but she says in her Memoirs, that "It was necessary that I should be veiled whilst painting his Holiness, and the fear that under the circumstances I should not be able to do justice to my subject, compelled me to decline this honor."

In Rome Madame Le Brun met the celebrated Angelica Kaufmann. "I found her," says the artist, "very interesting, apart from her great talent, by her wit and intellectual powers. Her conversation is very gentle; she is very well informed."

Her life, like Madame Le Brun's, had been a sad one. In England, when she was about twenty-six, and had won great fame, she was deceived into marriage with a *valet*, who pretended to be a noted count. His desire was to be supported with the money earned by his wife. When it was found that he was already married to another, his marriage with Angelica was declared null and void.

When she was forty, to please her aged father, she married the painter, Antonio Zucchi, who died fourteen years later. At her own death in Rome, 1807, at the age of sixty-six, the funeral was a most impressive one. Canova took charge of the ceremonies. The pall of the bier was carried by four young girls dressed in white, the four tassels being held by the four first gentlemen of the Academy. Two of her famous pictures were carried immediately after her coffin. Then followed many of the distinguished persons of Rome, each bearing a lighted taper. Besides plate, valuable ancient paintings, furniture, and the work of her studio, she left two hundred thousand dollars earned by herself.

During Madame Le Brun's residence in Italy, she visited Naples. The beautiful scenery, the Island of Capri in the distance, Vesuvius in eruption, the exquisite Bay of Naples, all gave joy to her refined nature. She stood on the Island of Capri, where, on its highest peak, Tiberius had built his palace, one column only remaining. From this point the Roman emperor threw into the sea whoever displeased him.

She made the ascent of Vesuvius, when great streams of lava were running at her feet. "The stream of fire which suffocated me," she says, " was nine miles in circumference. Tongues of fire darted from the crater, sending out great stones from the mouth, and the earth shook beneath our feet. . . . My poor little girl said to me, crying, 'Mamma, must 1 be frightened?'"

She painted, as her first picture in Naples, the Countess Scawronski, the wife of the Russian ambassador, an indolent beauty, the niece of Potemkin, the favorite of Catharine II. He had showered riches upon her of which she made no use. She never wore the enormous diamonds he sent her, nor the dresses. "Her happiness," said Madame Le Brun, "was to lie stretched on a sofa, wrapped in a large black pelisse."

Sir William Hamilton, the English ambassador, desired a portrait of the beautiful Lady Hamilton, afterwards the beloved of Lord Nelson. Madame Le Brun painted her as a bacchante, reposing on the seashore, holding a painted cup in her hand. Her quantity of beautiful chestnut hair quite enveloped her figure. The artist painted the picture for twenty-four hundred francs, and afterwards Sir William sold it in London for eight thousand francs. Madame Le Brun also painted her as a sybil. One day the artist drew with chalk, at Sir William's casino on the seashore, two heads of cherubs, on the panels of the door. The ambassador, who was a shrewd business man, cut them out, and sold them to Lord Warwick in England.

Talleyrand, the French ambassador to Naples, showed the artist much courtesy. He came one morning with a request that she should paint the two eldest daughters of the Queen of Naples, who was the sister of Marie Antoinette. The Queen of Naples paid munificently for the portraits, and gave the artist a beautiful box of old lacquered work with her initials set in diamonds, worth ten thousand francs.

Carolina Maria, the Queen of Naples, resembled her beautiful sister of France, though not as pretty. "Her face was worn," writes Madame Le Brun, "but one could see she had been handsome; her hands and arms were perfection as to color and form. . . . She bore the whole weight of the government. The King Ferdinand would not reign." They were both deposed by Napoleon, who placed Murat and his sister Caroline upon the throne. Carolina Maria retired to Vienna, where she died at Schönbrunn, Sept. 8, 1814.

Through all these months of work, and success both social and artistic, Madame Le Brun's chief happiness was in her little daughter, about whose education she took the utmost pains. The child was sweet in disposition, gentle and lovable.

The artist had been made a member of the leading Academies of Italy, and this was most gratifying; but she longed to paint many of the scenes which inspired her. Alas! there was little or no time for anything but portraits; for money must be earned for herself and child, for her mother who lived in Paris, and considerable for her impecunious husband, who, unlike his wife, had been born with a natural disinclination for work.

Madame Le Brun left Rome, April 14, 1792, hoping to return to France. At Parma she was made a member of the Academy, to which she gave a head that she had painted of her daughter. At Turin the wife of Louis XVIII. received her most kindly. Here she stayed for some time, having learned the desperate condition of affairs in Paris. At Vienna she remained for two years and a half.

Here, as at Venice, her "Sybil," was exhibited, and won for her many patrons. She brought letters of introduction to Prince de Kaunitz, who had been minister under Maria Theresa, and other notables. The prince was a strange character. He would never hear a word about death. When the empress was dead, it was announced to him in the words, "The empress signs no more."

The artist met Prince Metternich and his son, afterwards prime minister; also the Russian ambassador, Count Razumofski, and the Prince de Ligne, both of whom encouraged her to visit St. Petersburg. She therefore left Vienna with her daughter and governess, April 19, 1795. She spent a week at Dresden, where the elector asked her to exhibit her "Sybil." All the court went to see the painting.

She reached St. Petersburg July 25, 1795, and found it much more beautiful than she had expected, with its wide streets, elegant churches, and fine mansions. She was surprised to see the nights scarcely an hour long, twilight not coming till after midnight. Before she had been in the city a day, Prince Esterhazy called, and promised to present her at court.

She had met him at Vienna, where on New Year's Day his horse was caparisoned with a cloth thickly sewn with diamonds. He was of an ancient and very rich Hungarian family, a distinguished diplomat, and patron of art. It is said that Napoleon offered him the crown of Hungary, which he declined. His family were the largest landholders in Austria. Madame Le Brun was soon presented to Catharine II., at her summer palace at Tsarskoé Sélo. She had been afraid to meet the great sovereign; but Catharine's cordial manner reassured her, as she said in a sweet voice, "I am charmed to see you here, Madame; your reputation has preceded you. I greatly love the arts, and above all painting. I am not a connoisseur, only an amateur."

The empress had removed one of her gloves, that her hand might be kissed, as was the custom; but the artist quite forgot it. "This celebrated woman made such an impression on me," said Madame Le Brun, "that it was impossible to think of anything else but looking at her." The artist had come in a plain muslin dress, not having had time to prepare any other; but the empress did not appear to notice it. She thought only of the talent of her visitor.

The proverbial Russian hospitality was extended to the newcomer. She spent a week with the Princess Dolgoruki, who had been beloved by Potemkin, the commander-in-chief of the army. At a great dinner given by him in honor of the empress, but really for the princess, at dessert spoonfuls of diamonds were served to the guests from crystal cups. Having heard that the princess needed shoes for a ball, he sent a courier to Paris, who travelled day and night till he returned with the shoes.

After the portrait of the Princess Dolgoruki had been painted, she sent Madame Le Brun, in appreciation of it, a very handsome carriage, and clasped a hair bracelet on her arm, with these words set in diamonds, " *Ornez celle qui orne son siècle.*"

During her first month in Russia, Madame Le Brun earned forty-five thousand francs by her brush. This she deposited with a banker who failed, and the artist lost it all. After a time fifteen thousand francs were stolen from her. If her art had not been "as dear to her as her life," as she used to say, these trials would have been almost unbearable.

Work was pressing upon her. She painted the two granddaughters of Catharine II., children of Paul I., Alexandrine and Hélène, thirteen and fourteen years old. Alexandrine had been promised in marriage to the young Gustavus IV., of Sweden, who came to St. Petersburg, Aug. 14, 1796, to claim his bride. He was seventeen and she fourteen. He greatly admired the lovely picture which Madame Le Brun had painted of Alexandrine.

The king was to make his appearance at court at seven in the evening, and Catharine and her guests were ready to receive him. At six he was asked to sign papers, promising that Alexandrine should have a Greek chapel and priests in Sweden. He refused to sign, saying that in public she must conform to the religion of his country. He would not place himself against the laws of the land. The king left the next morning for Sweden, and the disappointment and vexation of Catharine were said to have hastened her death. Gustavus married the same year the Princess Frederika of Baden.

Madame Le Brun's next picture was of the Princess Elizabeth, the young wife of Alexander I., son of Paul. It was a full length picture in court dress, the princess arranging flowers in a basket. When Madame Le Brun first saw her, she was watering a pot of carnations. Her lovely face was one "of angelic sweetness." She was dressed in white with a sash tied loosely about her waist. "She is Psyche!" exclaimed Madame Le Brun. She was very gracious to the artist, saying, "We have long been wanting to see you here, Madame, so much so, that I even dreamt you had arrived."

A portrait of the bride of Constantine, the brother of Alexander, was also made. She was a princess of Saxe-Coburg, about sixteen, "not less lovely and bewitching than Elizabeth," though "not possesing such a heavenly face." Neither princess seemed to find a Russian throne very desirable. Constantine and his wife were divorced.

When the picture of Elizabeth was finished, Madame Le Brun went to the royal palace to present it to Catharine II. The empress complimented her, and said, "They insist on your doing my portrait. I am very old; but since they desire it so much, I will give you the first sitting this day week." Before the day came for the sitting, the Autocrat of Russia was dead.

The artist, like everybody else, missed the great empress, and feared that there would be a revolution under the unpopular Paul, her son. He compelled women as well as men to get out of their carriages into the snow, whenever he appeared, either on horseback or in his sleigh. Once when he passed the carriage of Madame Le Brun, and saw her hastening to alight, he stepped from his sleigh, remarking, "That his command was not for foreigners, and certainly not for Madame Le Brun."

Paul's first wife, Augusta, princess of Hesse Darmstadt, died after three years of marriage; the second was a princess of Würtemberg, received into the Greek church as Maria Feodorovna.

Paul wished a portrait of the Empress Maria, which was made in court dress, with a crown of diamonds. Madame Le Brun thought her a handsome woman, tall and commanding, and as universally beloved as Paul was disliked; often while the artist painted, the emperor and his sons, Alexander and Constantine, were present. Sometimes Nicholas and Michael came. "I never saw a finer child than the Grand Duke Nicholas, afterwards emperor," said the artist. He was called in after years, the handsomest man in Europe.

While in Russia Madame Le Brun had the honor of being made, before a distinguished company, a member of the St. Petersburg Academy. She painted for the Academy a portrait of herself, with her palette in her hand.

A severe trial came to the artist while in Russia. Her daughter, at this time seventeen, extremely pretty and well educated, and much admired by all, wished to marry a man "without talent, fortune, or family." At first Madame Le Brun could not give her consent; but as her daughter grew ill in consequence, they were married. The impecunious M. Nigris, secretary to a count, asked Madame Le Brun for a few ducats to give to the church on the day of his wedding! She gave her daughter a handsome marriage portion, the result of her labors in St. Petersburg, and sad at heart, left for Moscow, Oct. 15, 1800.

Five years later her daughter and her husband came to Paris. He was commissioned to obtain singers for St. Petersburg, and was obliged to return alone, as his wife had long ceased to care for him.

At Moscow, Prince Demidof, the wealthiest man in Russia, placed a palace at the disposal of Madame Le Brun. In five months she painted several of the most distinguished persons in the city, — Prince Bezborodko, the privy councillor of Catharine II., who had thirteen thousand men on his estates; Marshall Soltikof, governor of the city, and others.

Sad and ill, the artist returned to St. Petersburg, to find that the Emperor Paul had been strangled in his bedroom. His body, embalmed, lay exposed on a state bed for six weeks. Each day the Empress Maria knelt and prayed before this funeral couch, taking with her her little sons, Nicholas and Michael. The former asked innocently, "Why papa was always asleep."

Alexander I., who had come to the throne amidst the acclamations of the people, asked Madame Le Brun to paint two portraits of himself — one of the head and shoulders, and another on horseback. She was too ill; and though she drew both the emperor and empress in pastels, she soon felt obliged to leave Russia. The emperor kindly urged her to remain, saying, "I will give you the empress's horse, and when you have had a few rides, you will be quite well again."

She reached Berlin toward the close of July, 1801, and three days later was asked by the beautiful Louise of Prussia to come to Potsdam and paint her portrait. The artist soon loved her, as did everybody else. " My pen is powerless," she wrote, " to describe the impression made on me by this princess. The charm of her lovely face, with its fine and regular features, her beautiful figure, neck, and arms, and the dazzling whiteness of her complexion — everything about her surpassed my expectations. She was clad in deep mourning, with a head-dress of wheat-ears in black jet, which added still more to the brilliancy of her skin."

She was always doing little kindnesses. When she heard incidentally that the coffee was poor at the hotel where the artist stayed, she sent some excellent coffee the following day. When the artist admired some antique bracelets which the queen wore, she took them off at once, and placed them on the arms of Madame Le Brun.

After painting some other portraits, and being made a member of the Berlin Academy, Madame Le Brun hastened to her home in Paris, after an absence of twelve years. Her husband had made the house attractive for her coming. The staircase was filled with flowers; and the hangings of her bedroom were of green cashmere, edged with gold-colored embroidery. A crown of gold stars was at the head of her bed. The artist appreciated the thought, though she remarked that he made her " pay very dearly for all this luxury."

Her friends welcomed her heartily. Madame Bonaparte called, and asked her to breakfast with the First Consul. She was surprised at the " little, slight man."

Lucien Bonaparte came to the studio, and praised her "Sybil." The famous painter Gérard, whose paintings of the mother of Napoleon and Madame Récamier were so greatly admired, came to her house as a guest.

At the home of the latter beauty, Madame Le Brun was welcomed with that grace which Madame Récamier possessed in so eminent a degree. " Only one woman in Paris rivalled her in beauty," said the artist, " and that was Madame Tallien. . . . I sought in vain for a defect in the whole appearance of this charming person. . . . She had an enchanting smile, and was admirably proportioned."

Madame Tallien, the daughter of a count in Spain, and early in life the wife of M. de Fontenay of the parliament of Bordeaux, became interested in the revolutionary movement, and was arrested by the government. Tallien, a leader in the French Revolution, being sent on a mission to Bordeaux, met the beautiful prisoner, who had been divorced from her husband, and married her. On her arrival in Paris, as she was a moderate Republican, she prevailed upon Tallien to overthrow the hated Robespierre. Her home became the centre of the most brilliant society in Paris. She saved many persons from death during the Revolution, on account of the influence she exercised over her husband. She was always ready to help even her enemies, and was called " Our Lady of Good Help."

Madame Le Brun was still depressed and worn, and on April 15, 1802, started for London. She found much to interest her in that great city. To Westminster Abbey, she went again and again. She stood by the monument of poor Chatterton, and said, " I could not help thinking that the money employed on raising his tomb would have sufficed to have procured him a comfortable existence."

She met all the great artists. Sir Joshua Reynolds she thought " as modest as he was clever." His coloring reminded her of Titian. When Reynolds saw her picture of Calonne, and was told, though inaccurately, that she had received £3,200 for it, he replied, "If they gave me £4,000 for it, I could not have done it as well."

Madame Le Brun was of course cordially welcomed. She was invited to the house of the noted wit and beauty, Georgiana, Duchess of Devonshire, "the most admired woman in London at this period;" a leader in politics, who had helped Fox into Parliament. "She was about forty-five years of age," says Madame Le Brun. "Her features were very regular. . . . She was of medium height, and not too stout for her age; her easy manners were extremely gracious."

Mrs. Siddons, the famous actress, came to her studio, and the Comte d'Artois, afterwards Charles X. Fox came several times. The Prince of Wales, afterwards George IV., came to her receptions and concerts. He said to the artist, "I take a passing look at all the *soirées*, but here I remain."

He was at this time about forty years of age, tall and well-proportioned, and elegant in appearance. Madame Le Brun painted his portrait nearly full length, and in uniform. As soon as it was finished he gave it to the beautiful Mrs. Fitzherbert. She was of an old Catholic family, a widow to whom he was privately married when she was twenty-nine and he twenty-three. His excesses compelled her to leave him; and she died at Brighton, seven years after his death.

Though Madame Le Brun remained three years in London, she was obliged frequently to go into the country to avoid the fogs and smoke. She visited Dr. Herschel, the astronomer, and his sister, and was shown through his telescope the planet which bears his name. She spent some days at Knole, near Seven Oaks, owned by the Duchess of Dorset, and enjoyed the castle and park, some of whose elms are said to be a thousand years old. The mansion dates back to the reign of King John. It was owned by the Archbishop of Canterbury, and Cranmer relinquished it to Henry VIII.

The mansion of Knole covers five acres; a great pile of buildings surrounding three square courts. It has long been famed for its fine collection of Italian, Venetian, Flemish, and Dutch pictures. One room contains portraits of the most eminent English poets, some by Sir Joshua Reynolds and Gainsborough. The hall has a fireplace and irons, supposed to have belonged to Henry VIII., as they bear the Tudor crown and the letters H. R. The great gallery contains copies from the cartoons of Raphael.

The Duchess of Dorset, who was very rich, had married the English ambassador to St. Petersburg, whom Madame Le Brun had met there. Before sitting down to dinner, the Duchess remarked to the artist, "You will find it very dull, for we never speak at table." At dessert the son of twelve ventured to speak a few words to the Duchess, and was sent away "without the smallest mark of tenderness."

Madame Le Brun went to the house of the Duc

d' Orléans, afterwards Louis Philippe, King of the French; and the Duc de Montpensier, his brother, found pleasure in taking his distinguished countrywoman out sketching with him. She spent some days at Warwick Castle, one of the most beautiful places in England. Through the invitation of Lord Warwick she went to the Isle of Wight, and thought it and the Island of Ischia were the only places where she would like to spend her life.

On her return from London she purchased a country home at Louveciennes. By order of Napoleon she painted a portrait of his sister, Madame Murat, and her little girl. After Napoleon's dethronement, when the allied armies entered Paris, they did not spare the villagers. On the night of March 21, 1814, the Prussians entered the house of Madame Le Brun, pillaged her wardrobe, took whatever gold and silver they could find, and cut out with a sabre a piece of the counterpane of the bed where she lay. After four hours of dreadful fright she managed to escape. Again in 1815, when the allies came to Louveciennes, the English took some valuable things from her, destroyed her court and garden, and she was obliged to flee for safety.

When Louis XVIII. returned to the throne, Madame Le Brun was overjoyed. He appeared in an open carriage, with the Duchess d'Angoulême by his side, whose lovely face and sad, sweet smile recalled that of her mother, Marie Antoinette. She had married the eldest son of the Comte d'Artois, afterwards Charles X., the brother of Louis XVIII. She was beloved by everybody for her virtues. Louis shook hands cordially with Madame Le Brun, and recalled the pleasant days when they knew each other at the court of his brother, Louis XVI. Louis XVIII. was infirm at this time; but the Comte d'Artois said, "He always suffers in his legs, but his head is excellent; we will walk for him, and he will think for us." He, like his brother, Charles X., was very good to artists.

Madame Le Brun divided her time between Louveciennes and Paris, spending eight months of each year in the former place. Here the noted in society, literature, and art came to see her; M. Desprès, Councillor of State in Holland, and member of the French University; M. Aimé Martin, author and friend of Bernardin de St. Pierre, who after his death married his widow, and adopted his daughter Virginie; the Comte de Forbin, artist and man of letters, director-general of the Louvre Museum.

In 1819 the Duc de Berri, second son of the Comte d'Artois, wished to buy Madame Le Brun's "Sybil." Much as she hated to part with it, she could not refuse him. The duke was assassinated the following year, Feb. 13, 1820, as he was helping his wife into her carriage at the opera. Lovel, a saddler, a violent Bonapartist, hoping to exterminate the Bourbon dynasty, stabbed the duke in the side. He died early the next morning. His last words were to ask pardon for his murderer. Seven months later, his little son Henri, Duc de Bordeaux, afterwards Count de Chambord, was born.

Some years after this, Madame Le Brun painted two portraits of the Duchess de Berri, Marie Thérèse of Savoy, one in red velvet and another in blue velvet.

Once, when she was sitting for the artist in the Tuileries, her little son Henri, six years old, came and showed her his copy-book, on which his teacher had written, "Very good." His mother thereupon gave him two louis. He was delighted and exclaimed, "There is something for my poor! but first for my old woman!" She was a person whom he met frequently in his play.

Madame Le Brun was now growing old. In 1813 her husband had died, and six years later, Dec. 18, 1819, her daughter. Gay in her tastes, she did not choose to live with her mother; but the sorrow at her death was, nevertheless, crushing. A year afterwards her only brother died; and she would have been left quite alone, save for two nieces, to whom she was devotedly attached.

During her last journeys in France, at Bordeaux, where she was lamenting over so many ruins, one of the towns-folk said: "I see that Madame la Countess had some châteaux near here." "No," answered the famous painter, "my châteaux are all in Spain!"

She died in Paris, in the Rue St. Lazare, May 29, 1842, at the age of eighty-seven; and her body was interred at Louveciennes. To the last, the charming woman, dignified yet lovable, received the most distinguished people at her home. She had acquired a competency which she left to her nieces. She had painted six hundred and sixty-two portraits and about two hundred landscapes, besides other pictures. Göthe admired the expression and fine execution of her portraits, and always praised them, as did Sir Joshua Reynolds, who said there were no portraits finer, not even those of Van Dyck. She suffered from unfair criticism, and from jealous persons who said her pictures were painted for her, or that she received high prices on account of favoritism; but nothing deterred her from her art. Her energy and her labor were extraordinary. Through a life of struggle and disappointment she won renown by her genius, her charming manners, and her generous, cheerful nature.

DOLLY MADISON.

DOLLY MADISON.

DOLLY MADISON, the gracious and beautiful social leader of her time, was born May 20, 1772, on a North Carolina plantation. Her grandfather, John Payne, was an English gentleman of wealth and education, married to Anna Fleming, the great granddaughter of the Earl of Wigton in Scotland. He settled on the James River in Virginia, but gave to his son, John Payne, a large plantation in North Carolina, where he married "a great belle," Mary Coles, whose father was a native of Enniscorthy, Ireland.

This young lady was desired in marriage by Thomas Jefferson, whom her friends favored; but his suit was not successful, as she preferred young Payne. When her child Dolly was born, she was named Dorothy, after a relative, Mrs. Patrick Henry.

The little girl inherited the beauty of her grandmother and her mother; and so careful was the latter to preserve it that her grand-niece says, in her "Memoirs," when the little girl went to school she was "equipped with a white linen mask to keep every ray of sunshine from the complexion, a sun-bonnet sewed on her head every morning by her careful mother, and long gloves covering the hands and arms."

Both father and mother were strict Quakers; and

while they were thankful for the gift of beauty for Dolly, they belived in no external adorning to enhance it. The pet of the grandmother, the child received from her some old-fashioned jewelry, which, not daring to wear, she sewed in a bag and tied it around her neck under her gown. During a long walk in the woods one day, the string must have become untied; for the precious treasures were all lost, and though tearful days were spent in searching for them, they were never found.

When Dorothy, or Dolly as she was called, was fourteen, in 1786, her parents moved to Philadelphia. Mr. Payne had become assured in his own heart that slavery was sinful. He sold his plantation and freed his slaves, several of whom refused to leave his service, and went with him to Philadelphia. His eldest son, John, who had been travelling in Europe, went into business with his father; but their Revolutionary money depreciated, they were unused to trade, and failed, bringing the family into reduced circumstances. "Mother Amy," one of the slaves, saved five hundred dollars by her wages, and left it at her death to Mrs. Payne. Mr. Payne was prostrated by the misfortune.

Dolly was at this time a tall, slight girl of nineteen, with black hair, blue eyes, an uncommonly fair complexion, and great sweetness of expression. A rich young lawyer, Mr. John Todd, with good looks and warm heart, also of the Society of Friends, offered himself to her in marriage, but she replied that she "never meant to marry."

The young man had shown Mr. Payne much kindness in his financial troubles. It was evident that if Dolly were given to him in marriage, the young man would feel compensated for all his pecuniary losses. The father therefore called the dutiful girl to his bedside, and explained to her his wishes. Taught to obey, she became the wife of Mr. Todd, and seems to have been rewarded in seeing her father happy for the remaining few months of his life.

Mr. Todd proved a devoted husband. About three years after his marriage the yellow fever broke out in Philadelphia in the summer of 1793. Mrs. Todd, and her two little children, one a baby of three weeks, were carried in a litter to Gray's Ferry to escape the disease, her young husband telling her that he would soon join her, "and never leave her again." He closed his office, stayed to minister to his father and mother, both dying of the dreadful plague, and then hastened to Gray's Ferry.

When he met his wife's mother, Mrs. Payne, at the door, he said, "I feel the fever in my veins, but I must see her once more." Dolly heard his voice, rushed down stairs and was clasped in his arms, begging to go back to Philadelphia with him. In a few hours he was dead, his baby also, and his lovely wife of twenty-two was believed to be dying.

She, however, finally recovered and returned to Philadelphia with her mother and remaining child, whom she named John Payne, after her father. Being very rich and very attractive, after a time she was sought by one and another admirer. A lady who was a bridesmaid at her wedding, says, "Gentlemen would station themselves to see her pass;" and finally the lady said to her, "Really, Dolly, thou must hide thy face, there are so many staring at thee."

Among those who saw the blue-eyed beauty on the street, and were urgent for an introduction, was a member of Congress, James Madison, forty-three years of age, twenty years older than Dolly. Madison, born March 16, 1751, was the son of a Virginia planter in comfortable circumstances. Though frail in health, he entered Princeton College at eighteen, and became a most devoted and distinguished scholar. It is said that he took but three hours of the twenty-four for sleep, that he might crowd two years into one in college. He was fond of Hebrew; and William C. Rives says in his life of Madison, "He explored the whole history and evidences of Christianity on every side, through clouds of witnesses and champions for and against, from the fathers and schoolmen down to the infidel philosophers of the eighteenth century." He probably inclined to the ministry, but finally took up law, meantime teaching his brothers and sisters at home.

He was elected at twenty-five a delegate to the Virginia Convention in 1776, and was made a member of a committee to frame a Bill of Rights and prepare a Constitution for that Province. From this time he became a prominent statesman.

His scholarship, especially his knowledge of English constitutional law, made him an able adviser, and his calm temperament and admirable self-control, a judicious leader. In 1780, while yet under thirty, he was chosen a delegate to the Continental Congress. Those were dark times for the Republic. Madison wrote to a friend: "The public treasury empty; . . . Congress complaining of the extortion of the people; the people of the improvidence of Congress, and the army of both. . . . Congress recommending plans to the several States for execution, and the States separately rejudging the expediency of such plans."

The United States as yet was a confederation of independent commonwealths, and Congress had little power. When it tried by taxes to raise seventy millions to pay the debts incurred by the war of the Revolution, the States would not sanction its suggestions.

The people talked about Eastern and Western and Southern confederacies. They were afraid of a paternal central government, and did not realize that we should be easily conquered if disunited. England began to ask if Congress or the separate States sent representatives to her.

Washington, Franklin, Hamilton, Madison, and a few others, gave themselves no rest, until, by years of argument and exhortation, in the great constitutional convention in Philadephia, in the summer of 1787, the Articles of Confederation were replaced by the Constitution of the United States.

"Mr. Madison," says Mr. Sidney Howard Gay, in his life of that statesman, "is called 'the Father of the Constitution.' A paper written by him was laid before his colleagues of Virginia, before the meeting of the Constitutional Convention at Philadelphia, and was made the basis of the 'Virginia Plan,' out of which the Constitution was evolved."

When, after months of heated debate, the Constitution was sent to the different States for adoption, and Virginia was a pivotal State, Mr. Madison was untiring in his efforts. "He was always on his feet," says Mr. Gay; "always ready to meet argument with argument;

always prompt to appeal from passion to reason; quick to brush aside mere declamation, and to bring the minds of his hearers back to a calm consideration of how much was at stake, and of the weight of the responsibility resting on that convention."

The position which Madison held before his countrymen is shown in the words of a distinguished French traveller, Brissot de Warville, in his "New Travels in the United States of America."

"The name of Madison," he says, "celebrated in America, is well known in Europe by the merited eulogism made of him by . . . Mr. Jefferson. Though still young, he has rendered the greatest services to Virginia, to the American Confederation, and to liberty and humanity in general. He contributed much, with Mr. White, in reforming the civil and criminal codes of his country. . . . This Republican appears to be about thirty-eight years of age. He had, when I saw him, an air of fatigue; perhaps it was the effect of the immense labors to which he has devoted himself for some time past. His look announces a censor, his conversation discovers the man of learning, and his reserve was that of a man conscious of his talents and of his duties."

The first Congress held under this new government was appointed at New York for March 4, 1789, and from that time our Presidents have been inaugurated on the same day of the month. Mr. Madison became the leader of the House of Representatives, introducing as his first measure a duty to protect our "infant industries." This tariff debate lasted six weeks, and nearly everything was taxed, "except slaves from Africa," says Mr. Gay; for already the quarrel about slavery had begun, as well as the long list of "compromises."

During the eight years of Washington's Presidency, Madison was a power in Congress. He differed radically from Alexander Hamilton in matters of finance, banking, the public debt, etc.; but he was always the scholar, and the man of dignity and self-control.

During all these busy and eventful years Mr. Madison had remained a bachelor. He had once been in love, and had become engaged, in 1783, while in the Continental Congress, to a daughter of General William Floyd, of Long Island, one of the signers of the Declaration of Independence. Madison was thirty-two, and Catherine Floyd sixteen.

General Floyd seemed delighted at so wise a choice, when lo! the girl changed her mind, and married a young clergyman "who hung around her at the harpsichord." History does not state whether the rectory proved as agreeable as the White House; but the father was grievously disappointed.

The blow was a cruel one to Madison. His devoted friend Thomas Jefferson wrote him, "I sincerely lament the misadventure which has happened, from whatever cause it may have happened. Should it be final, however, the world presents the same and many other resources of happiness, and you possess many within yourself. Firmness of mind and unintermitting occupation will not long leave you in pain." The rector's wife died three or four years before ex-President Madison.

It was about ten years after Miss Floyd broke her engagement, that Madison met, while walking, the beautiful widow of twenty-two, Mrs. Dolly Todd, and asked a friend for an introduction. Dolly was evidently pleased at the request, and wrote to Mrs. Lee: "Dear friend, thou must come to me. Aaron Burr says that the 'great little Madison' has asked to be brought to see me this evening."

When he came Mrs. Todd received him in a mulberry colored satin, with a silk tulle handkerchief about her neck, and a dainty cap on her head, from which a curl of black hair now and then escaped. Mr. Madison found the young lady even more attractive than Congressional debates and constitutional law, and it was soon rumored that they were engaged. Mr. Madison, had, as in the former instance, chosen a lady just half his age.

When President and Mrs. Washington heard of the engagement, the latter said, "Dolly, if it is so, do not be ashamed to confess it; rather be proud. He will make thee a good husband, and all the better for being so much older. We both approve of it: the esteem and friendship existing between Mr. Madison and my husband is very great, and we would wish thee to be happy."

In September, 1794, Mrs. Todd and Mr. Madison, with their friends, drove from Philadelphia to Harewood, the home of the bride's sister in Virginia. Two years previous to this, Lucy Payne, fifteen years old, had married George Washington's nephew, George Steptoe Washington; and at this handsome estate of Harewood, after a week's journey thither, the lovable Dolly and scholarly James Madison were married. The girls at the wedding cut off bits of Mechlin lace from the groom's ruffled shirt, as a memento of the occasion, and threw rice as they departed for Montpelier, the home of Mr. Madison's father in Orange County, Virginia.

At the close of the year Mr. and Mrs. Madison returned to Philadelphia. The latter laid aside her Quaker garb at her husband's desire, and began to mingle in society. At the drawing-rooms of Mrs. Washton she was cordially welcomed, her sweet manner, tact, and thorough kindness of heart, soon making her many friends.

When General Washington retired from the Presidency, Madison too gave up official life, and went back to the ancestral home in Virginia, building for himself a house at Montpelier. His wife was wealthy, so that all comforts could be supplied; and her little sister Anna, with her idolized child, John Payne, made the home of the quiet scholar a delight. He wrote to Thomas Jefferson about his sheep and lambs; he gave himself to his beloved natural history, but, as had been his habit through life, spent most of his days in reading and copious writing about matters of state.

When Washington died, Dec. 14, 1799, Mr. and Mrs. Madison, with Thomas Jefferson, visited the lonely widow at Mount Vernon, and were sincere mourners for the self-centred, great-hearted, broad-minded patriot.

Public life could not long spare so able a man as Madison, or so amiable a woman as his wife. When Thomas Jefferson became president in 1800, James Madison was made Secretary of State. Mrs. Jefferson was dead, the two daughters of the president were married and living in Virginia, and Mrs. Madison, with her sister Anna, often presided at the White House.

This sister was married three years later, in 1804, to the Hon. Richard Cutts, a member of Congress from Maine, then a part of Massachusetts. He was a capable and well-educated young man, having studied at Harvard University and in Europe, and was chosen to represent his district when he was twenty-eight.

Mrs. Madison was eminently fitted for the position which Jefferson asked her to take at the White House. She had not a trace of self-conceit. She wished to please, and she succeeded. She remembered every face, every name, and the slightest incident in connection with the history of each visitor: this at once gave a suitable topic for conversation, and made a bond of friendship. Her dress, her manner, her language, never gave occasion for criticism. Her power of adaptation was marvellous. To her father she had been the loving daughter; to John Todd, the true wife; to James Madison, the helpful promoter of every enterprise; to the nation, the courteous, interested servant of the people, and therefore the leader of the people.

When Captain Meriwether Lewis and Captain William Clarke were sent by Jefferson to explore the Missouri River, and the country this side of the Rocky Mountains, then an unknown wilderness, Mrs. Madison spared no pains to see that everything was provided for the perilous journey. The travellers were gone nearly three years, and brought back much valuable information.

When Alexander von Humboldt, the great scholar and explorer, came to Washington, Mrs. Madison, with her accustomed tact, made his visit a happy one. She wrote to her sister Anna: "He is the most polite, modest, well-informed, and interesting traveller we have ever met, and is much pleased with America. . . . He had with him a train of philosophers, who, though clever and entertaining, did not compare with the Baron."

Gilbert Stuart, the celebrated painter, came to Washington early in 1803, and received a perfect ovation. Mr. and Mrs. Madison had their portraits painted. Mrs. Madison considered her husband's "an admirable likeness." "He is almost worked to death," wrote a lady concerning Stuart, "and every one is afraid that they will be the last to be finished." The painter said, "The ladies come and say, '*Dear* Mr. Stuart, I am afraid you will be very much tired; you really must rest when my picture is done.'"

Stuart's life had been a most interesting one. Born Dec. 22, 1755, in Narragansett, R.I., of humble parentage, the son of a snuff-grinder, his drawing had been made on fences and wagon boards. When his parents moved to Newport, he obtained some colors and a palette, and painted two Spanish dogs. At thirteen he painted two portraits, Mr. and Mrs. John Bannister of Newport. When he was fifteen he met Cosmo Alexander, an artist, who took a fancy to the bright lad, taught him all he was able to teach, and carried him to England when he returned. Alexander soon died, commending Stuart to the care of a friend. He also died, and the boy was thrown upon his own resources.

For two years life was a bitter struggle to obtain food and lodging. At the end of this time he returned home in a coal-vessel. He had seen some fine pictures, and he had gained every bit of knowledge possible in his poverty. He was soon asked to paint the portraits of some wealthy Jews in Rhode Island, which gave him a little money. Feeling the need of studying the human figure, with a friend to share the expense, a blacksmith was hired as a model at fifty cents an evening.

He was all the time eager to become a pupil of Benjamin West, a distinguished American painter in England. He hired a cheap passage to London, and waited for a little time, hoping in some way to get a letter of introduction to the great man. Want at last compelled him to go at once and seek an interview.

West received the young man of twenty-two years kindly, asked to see some of his work, and finally took him into his own house. Eight years later Stuart opened a studio; and West and Sir Joshua Reynolds sat to him for their pictures to bring him into notice, and thus open the door to fame. His prices were second only to those of Reynolds and Gainsborough.

In 1792 he returned to America, famous, and everywhere sought after. A request soon followed him, asking that he return to paint a portrait of the Duke of Kent, the father of Queen Victoria, and a ship of war — quite in contrast to the coal-barge of a few years before — was placed at his disposal. He had determined, however, to paint the great man with whom his fame as an artist will be ever associated, George Washington; and he declined the honor from England. His first portrait of Washington was made in Philadelphia, in a house on the corner of Fifth and Chestnut Streets. He was a welcome guest on every festal occasion, and more work came to him than he could possibly attempt.

When he came to Washington, in 1803, the demands upon him were rather increased than lessened. He remained for two years, and then settled in Boston. He painted to the last, even when ill. He died June 27, 1828, at the age of seventy-two, and is buried in the cemetery on Boston Common; but the number of the tomb being unknown, no one can tell the place of burial.

The Madison home continued to be a happy one. After the sister Anna was married, Mrs. Madison took home her brother's child, Anna Payne, who lived with her ever afterward.

When they had been married eleven years, Mrs. Madison injured her knee, and was obliged to go to Philadelphia for treatment. This was almost the first separation since their marriage, and both felt it keenly. She wrote her husband: " A few hours only have passed since you left me, my beloved, and I find nothing can relieve the oppression of my mind but speaking to you, in this, the only way. . . . Betsy Pemberton and Amy are sitting by me, and seem to respect the grief they know I feel at even so short a separation from one who is all to me."

The next day she wrote: " The watchman announced a cloudy morning at one o'clock; and from that moment I found myself unable to sleep, from anxiety for thee, my dearest husband. Detention, cold, and accident seem to menace thee. . . . The doctor, during his short visits, talks of you. He regards you more than any man he knows, and nothing could please him so much as a prospect of passing his life near you; sentiments so congenial to my own, and in such cases, like dewdrops on flowers, exhilarate as they fall."

Two days later she wrote: " I have at this moment perused with delight thy letter, my darling husband, with its enclosures. To find you love me, have my child safe, and that my mother is well, seems to comprise all my happiness." In a few weeks Mrs. Madison rejoined her husband and son, Payne, in Washington.

A letter written sometime later from Mr. Madison, at Washington shows the same warm affection on his part: "My dearest, . . . what number of days I may be detained here it is impossible to say. The period, you may be sure, will be shortened as much as possible. Everything around and within reminds me that you are absent, and makes me anxious to quit this solitude. . . . God bless you, and be assured of my constant affection."

When Jefferson had served eight years as president, James Madison was elected to fill his place, in 1809. At the inauguration ball, Mrs. Madison wore buff-colored velvet, rich pearls on neck and arms, and a Paris turban with a bird of Paradise plume. When the manager brought her the first number in the dance, she said smiling, "I never dance; what shall I do with it?"

"Give it to the lady next to you."

"No, that would look like partiality."

"Then I will," said the manager, and gave it to her sister.

Mrs. Madison proved herself an able helper in these times of political ferment, and later of war. Animosities between public men seemed to be forgotten in her presence. She was tolerant of all opinions, political or religious. She conversed well, listened well, was always cheerful, and unselfish.

President Madison said, when worn with the cares of state, a visit to his wife's sitting-room, where he was sure of a bright story or a hearty laugh, was as refreshing as a long walk in the open air. Her sympathy went alike to rich and poor, the servant in her own household, the orphan and the invalid.

She was sincere in her expressions of attachment.

When Henry Clay voiced the common sentiment, and said, "Everybody loves Mrs. Madison," she replied with truth, "Mrs. Madison loves everybody." Washington Irving describes her as "a fine, portly, buxom dame, who has a smile and a pleasant word for everybody."

A writer of that time says; "We had the pleasure of seeing her on the occasion of a splendid *fête* which was given by his excellency, Mr. Dashkof, the minister of Russia, in honor of the natal day of his sovereign. We remarked the ease with which she glided into the stream of conversation and accommodated herself to its endless variety."

There was no stiffness or shyness in her presence. Like the noble woman who filled this same position years afterward, Lucy Webb Hayes, Mrs. Madison seemed never unkind in word, or look, or act. She gave generously of her wealth, and the poor of the District had reason to love her. She entertained cordially without extravagance. Though not a learned woman, as this was not the fashion of the day, she was an excellent counsellor for her husband, who prized her common sense and good judgment.

When arguments between persons became heated, she left the room for a few moments, and the parties usually saw their mistake, and were peaceful on her return. "I would rather fight with my hands than with my tongue," she used to say.

Though Mr. Madison had no children, the home was always full of young people. Lucy Payne, at whose house Mrs. Madison was married, became a widow about the time Mr. Madison was made president, and came to live with them in Washington. Some time after she married Judge Todd of Kentucky, who had five children. "How wise Lucy is to choose him in preference to the gay ones who courted her," said Mrs. Madison.

For three years the life at the White House was peaceful and happy, but the nation was soon to be plunged into a bloody conflict with England, and the President and his wife were to suffer with the rest, in the War of 1812.

The French Revolution had produced strong factions in our own country. France had aided us in our Revolutionary War, and our sympathy was with her in her desire for a Republic, till her excesses cooled the ardor of all lovers of freedom. Louis XVI. had been beheaded, saying, with his latest breath, "I forgive my enemies; may God forgive them, and not lay my innocent blood to the charge of the nation! God bless my people!"

The Revolutionists had plunged into war with England, and "Citizen Genet" had been sent as minister to the United States, to secure our aid in the struggle. Washington, wiser than many who surrounded him, had little faith in the French leaders, and knew that our own country was unable to bear the strain of another long war. He issued a proclamation of neutrality, April 17, 1793; and though the French sympathizers were furious, his wisdom was shown in the end.

Our commerce became seriously crippled by the prohibitions of trade made by both France and England. In 1793, June 18, England issued an "Order in Council," declaring that all vessels laden wholly or in part with breadstuffs, bound to any port in France, or places occupied by French armies, should be carried into England, or sold only in some port friendly to England. This destroyed our extensive commerce with the French West Indies.

War with England seemed probable; but Washington was determined to avert it, and nominated John Jay, Chief Justice of the United States, as envoy extraordinary to Great Britain, to make a treaty if possible. This treaty was effected, which for a time prevented war with England, but produced great enmity on the part of France.

Jan. 10, 1798, the Directory of France proclaimed that all vessels having merchandise on board, the production of England or her colonies, whoever the owner, were liable to seizure as good prizes. Within a few months French cruisers seized as many as a thousand American vessels, under the pretext that these were aiding England.

John Adams, then President, anxious to avoid a war, sent three envoys to France: they were rudely treated, and ordered to leave the country. America made ready for war with France, which was actually begun on the ocean; but another embassy, sent by John Adams, was cordially received by the First Consul, Napoleon, and a treaty happily was concluded.

Later, in the struggles between France and England, May 16, 1806, the latter, by "Order in Council," declared the whole coast of Europe from the Elbe in Germany to Brest in France, a distance of about eight hundred miles, to be in a state of blockade. Napoleon retaliated by the Berlin decree of Nov. 21, 1806, declaring the whole coast of Great Britain to be under blockade, and claiming the right to seize all vessels trading with England or her colonies.

England replied by another "Order in Council," Nov. 17, 1807, and Napoleon by his Milan decree, Dec. 17, 1807. The result of all this was that American commerce was practically ruined. England had taken over nine hundred of our vessels since 1803, and our losses by France and England were estimated at seventy million dollars.

America had become especially incensed at England through the carrying out of her declared "right of search" for British seamen on American vessels. England needed every Englishman to help carry on her wars, and when these had left her country to find higher wages, or security from danger, in America, she boarded vessels, and in hundreds of cases impressed into her service men who were really Americans, and had never been on British soil.

Sometimes the officers resisted and bloodshed followed. The "impressed" men were often unmercifully whipped with the cat-o'-nine-tails, or hanged for desertion as a warning to their comrades.

Lossing tells, among other cases, of James Tompkins, and three others, Americans, who were imprisoned on board the British ship Acton, in April, 1812. "When they refused to do duty they were whipped five dozen lashes each. Two days afterward they received four dozen lashes each. They still refused to do duty, and, after the lapse of another two days, they received two dozen lashes each. They still refused; and, after being whipped again, they were put in irons, where they were kept three months."

Lord Castlereagh admitted in Parliament that there were in the British Navy three thousand five hundred impressed men who claimed to be Americans. There were six thousand such cases on the records of our State Department.

Things like these inflamed the nation, and war against England was declared by Congress, June 18, 1812. Mr. Madison, like a large party in America, was opposed to war, hoping that it might be avoided by treaties, and knowing how poorly we were prepared to meet England on the sea.

"Against the thousand vessels and one hundred and forty-four thousand sailors of the British navy," says Rossiter Johnson in his "War of 1812" "the Americans had twenty war-ships and a few gunboats, the whole carrying about three hundred guns." The United States, however, had a fine merchant marine, and England was using many of her ships in warfare with other nations.

Like every other conflict, the War of 1812 had its ghastly features. The English made the Indians their allies, and the battles at the West were frequently those of the tomahawk and the scalping-knife. The United States determined to invade Canada from Detroit, Michigan, and on the Niagara frontier from the State of New York. It was believed, though only by a portion of the people, that Canada would be glad to unite with the States and be free from British rule.

General William Hull, governor of Michigan, was sent to command the forces at Detroit. He had done good service in the War of the Revolution, but here he seems to have failed utterly. At Fort Dearborn, a place now within the city of Chicago, where there were fifty soldiers and their families, a massacre occurred. They had been ordered by General Hull to go to Detroit, two hundred miles through the wilderness; and before going they destroyed their alcohol, firearms, and gunpowder, that these might not be used by the Indians. As the red men had been promised the property in the fort, they were indignant; fell upon the little band, murdered and scalped them all, men, women, and children, and sent these trophies to the British Colonel Proctor, who had offered a premium for American scalps.

General Hull, fearing that he could not hold out against superior forces, and that his provisions would soon be exhausted, surrendered Detroit, and thus the North-west, to the enemy. He was tried by court-martial and sentenced to be shot, but was pardoned by President Madison, who had much of the coolness of Washington, and who did not forget Hull's honesty, even if he had erred in judgment. At Niagara River the attempt to invade Canada proved a failure also.

On the ocean, for the most part, there were victories instead of disasters. On the 19th of August, 1812, the Constitution, a frigate of forty-four guns, nicknamed "Old Ironsides" because her frame of live-oak was so strong, commanded by Captain Isaac Hull, met the English frigate Guerriere of thirty-eight guns, south of the Gulf of St. Lawrence, at the point due east from Cape Cod. About five in the afternoon the battle was begun by the Guerriere. Captain Dacres gallantly allowed ten impressed American sailors to go below, that they might not fight against their country. At six o'clock the ships came along side each other and the battle was terrific, for a half hour or more, when the Guerriere became a wreck. The Americans had attempted to board her, and to lash the ships together, but were shot down.

The Constitution lay near her prize all night; and in the morning Captain Hull removed the wounded to his own vessel, as the Guerriere was filling with water. When Captain Dacres handed his sword to Captain Hull, the latter replied, "No, no, Captain; I'll not take a sword from one who knows so well how to use it." The Constitution lost seven killed and seven wounded; the Guerriere twenty-three dead or mortally wounded, and fifty-six other wounded men. The English wreck was set on fire; and when, in fifteen minutes, the magazine was reached by the flames, she was blown to pieces.

When Captain Hull reached Boston, the whole city was gay with banners, and his officers were given a banquet to which six hundred were invited. New York and Philadelphia sent swords and plate, and Congress gold medals and $50,000 to be divided as prize money among the officers and crew.

The London *Times* said, "Never before in the history of the world did an English frigate strike to an American," and it shared in "the gloom which that event cast over high and honorable minds."

Captain Hull, who was at this time thirty-eight years of age, was a native of Connecticut. In later years he had charge of the navy-yards at Boston and Washington. He died in Philadelphia in 1845, and is buried in Laurel Hill Cemetery under a beautiful marble monument, copied from one in Rome.

Commodore Decatur, in the frigate United States, on Sunday, Oct. 25, captured the British frigate Macedonian. The former lost five killed and seven wounded; the latter thirty-six killed and sixty-eight wounded. Commodore Decatur brought his prize to New York on New Year's Day, and was, like Hull, received with banquets and gold medals. Congress, the Legislatures of Massachusetts, New York, Maryland, Pennsylvania, and Virginia, voted him thanks. The corporation of New York also gave the crew a banquet.

News was brought to Washington of this victory while a grand ball to the officers of the navy was in progress at the White House. The captured colors of the Guerriere and other ships were draped on the walls of the hall. When the colors of the Macedonian were brought, the distinguished Captains Hull and Stewart, says Willis J. Abbot, in his "Blue Jackets of 1812," "marched the length of the hall, amid the plaudits of the gay company, and laid the colors before Mrs. Madison, — the Dolly Madison who is still remembered as the most popular of the 'ladies of the White House.'"
In six months nearly three hundred British vessels, with three thousand prisoners, were brought into the ports of the United States.

While there were some defeats on land, in the second year of the war, there were several victories at sea. Lieutenant James Lawrence, while cruising off the coast of Guiana, Feb. 24, 1813, in the Hornet, of twenty guns, met the English brig Peacock, also of twenty guns, and gained a victory. The latter struck her colors in fifteen minutes, giving also the signal of distress. She soon filled with water and went down, taking with her nine of her own crew and three of the Hornet's.

Lawrence was made captain, and given the command

of the Chesapeake, lying in Boston Harbor. A battle with the English frigate Shannon, under Captain Philip Bowes Vere, was fought June 1, 1813, about thirty miles from Boston Light, between Cape Cod and Cape Ann. The ships were seen from Salem. The men, stripped to the waist, at the beat of the drums came pouring from all parts of the ship to their posts. The two ships lay side by side. The first broadside of the Shannon so swept the deck of the Chesapeake, that not more than fifty were left standing of the one hundred and fifty men. The men cheered as they fired the guns and fell. Most of the officers were shot, among them Captain Lawrence. As he was carried below, he said, "Tell the men to fire faster, and not give up the ship. Fight her till she sinks!"

His men were soon overpowered. The ships were lashed together by a veteran in the British navy, whose right arm was cut off by the cutlass of an American in the attempt. The Shannon took her prize to Halifax, where Lawrence was buried with imposing naval honors. Two months later, his body, with that of his brave officer, Lieutenant Ludlow, was brought to New York, and buried under a massive sandstone monument in Trinity churchyard. Lawrence was only thirty-one years old.

Two months later there was a great naval battle on Lake Erie, north of Ohio. Several vessels had been built at Presque Isle, now Erie, Pa.; and Captain Oliver Hazard Perry, a young man of twenty-eight, — he was born in South Kingston, R.I., Aug. 23, 1785, — was asked to come on from Newport and take charge of the fleet. There were two brigs, the Lawrence and Niagara, carrying twenty guns each, and several smaller vessels. The Lawrence was Perry's flagship. He anchored in Put-in-Bay Harbor, on the north side of Put-in-Bay Island, one of the largest in a group of twenty islands in the western part of Lake Erie.

Perry met the British fleet of six vessels, on Sept. 10, 1813, a clear, beautiful autumn day. A large blue flag, with the dying words of Lawrence, "Don't give up the ship," in big white muslin letters across it, was run up the mast-head as the signal for battle. The cooks passed along the deck giving the men food, as it was near noon; and sand was strewn upon the floor, that the feet should not slip when they were wet with blood. Perry's little brother of thirteen stood by his side ready for action.

For two hours after twelve o'clock the battle raged, the Lawrence receiving the most destructive fire. Soon the officers were all or nearly all dead. Out of one hundred men on board, twenty-two were killed and sixty-one wounded. Perry seemed preserved as if by miracle. He said afterwards, "The prayers of my wife have prevailed in saving me."

He determined to transfer his flag to the Niagara. The only uninjured boat of the Lawrence was lowered; Perry sprang into it, followed by his little brother, and four oarsmen rowed them in fifteen minutes to the Niagara. He had been standing in the boat with the blue banner half folded around him, but finally sat down at the earnest entreaty of the men, as the shot and shell were splintering the oars and the boat, and his life was in imminent danger.

Perry at once gave the order for close action. In

another hour, at three o'clock, every British vessel had surrendered, and Perry was writing to General William Henry Harrison on the back of an old letter, resting on his navy cap, "We have met the enemy and they are ours; two ships, two brigs, one schooner, and one sloop."

"Never before," says Lossing, "had a whole British fleet or squadron been captured."

At twilight, after the reading of the burial service, the bodies of all the slain, except the officers, wrapped in rude shrouds, with a cannon-ball at the feet of each, were dropped into the lake. The officers were buried on the margin of South Bass Island.

Perry died of yellow fever, on his birthday, Aug. 23, 1819, at the age of thirty-four, and was buried at Port Spain, Trinidad. Seven years later his body was removed to Newport, and buried with distinguished honors. Congress made liberal provision for his family, and his mother, who was dependent upon him. A beautiful statue, twenty-five feet high, was erected to his memory in Cleveland, Ohio, Sept. 10, 1860.

In 1814 the Americans for the third time attempted to invade Canada; and the severe battles of Chippewa and Lundy's Lane, or Niagara, were fought and won. England planned to send an army from Canada southward, while another was to march northward from New Orleans. In both these plans they were thwarted.

Admiral Sir George Cockburn sailed up the Potomac, and attacked the city of Washington. The British general, Ross, and a guard of two hundred men, came at eight o'clock in the evening. Commodore Barney had not been able to withstand the vessels of Admiral Cockburn or the four thousand soldiers of General Ross.

Washington was in a panic. Mr. Monroe, Secretary of State, and afterwards President, ordered his papers to be removed in wagons to Leesburg, about thirty-five miles from the city. The people fled in all directions, sleeping all night in the fields.

At three o'clock in the afternoon of Wednesday, Aug. 24, 1814, Mrs. Madison was waiting for some definite word from her husband, who had gone to the fight at Bladensburg, six miles from Washington. She wrote her sister Anna: "We have had a battle, or skirmish, near Bladensburg; and here I am still, within sound of the cannon! Mr. Madison comes not. May God protect us! Two messengers, covered with dust, come to bid me fly; but here I mean to wait for him. . . . One kind friend, Mr. Carroll, has come to hasten my departure, and in a very bad humor with me, because I insist on waiting until the large picture of General Washington is secured, and it requires to be unscrewed from the wall. This process was found to be too tedious for these perilous moments; I have ordered the frame to be broken, and the canvas taken out. [The frame was broken with an axe.] It is done! and the precious picture placed in the hands of two gentlemen of New York for safe keeping."

"Save that picture," said Mrs. Madison to Mr. Jacob Barker, a banker, and to Mr. R. G. L. De Peyster, "save that picture, if possible; if not possible, destroy it; under no circumstances allow it to fall into the hands of the British." It was sent in a hack to a woman named Baker, living beyond Georgetown, and eventually restored to Mrs. Madison, and hangs at the White House.

Mrs. Madison managed to carry away the Declaration of Independence, with the autographs of the signers, thus saving the precious mementoes of our early history. "I lived a lifetime in those last moments," said Mrs. Madison afterwards, "waiting for Mr. Madison's return, and in an agony of fear lest he might have been taken prisoner!"

The British set fire to the public buildings; the President's house, the furniture and library of which had cost Mr. Madison twelve thousand dollars, the new Capitol, the library of Congress, the Treasury buildings, the Arsenal, and barracks for almost three thousand troops, besides many private buildings. Admiral Cockburn was said to have led his men into the House of Representatives, and, standing in the Speaker's chair, shouted, "Shall this harbor of Yankee democracy be burned? All for it will say, Ay!"

Mrs. Madison, as well as thousands of others, did not sleep that night, but from their hiding-places watched the flames. Long before daylight, Mrs. Madison left her retreat in the house of an acquaintance two miles beyond Georgetown, and travelled to a little tavern in the middle of an apple orchard, sixteen miles from Washington, where she met her husband.

During the journey there was a dreadful thunderstorm, which drenched the travellers. Trees were struck by lightning, houses were blown down, and several persons were buried in the ruins. Toward midnight a courier arrived, telling that the British had ascertained the President's hiding-place, and would soon be there. At the earnest entreaties of his wife, Mr. Madison sought refuge in a little hovel in the woods. At dawn

Mrs. Madison disguised herself, and started away in a small wagon. The English had boasted that they would capture the beautiful woman, and "show her in England." Later in the day both Mr. and Mrs. Madison, learning that the British had evacuated the city, returned to their ruined home. The burning of Washington roused the utmost indignation throughout America. Even many in England declared that it was "a return to the times of barbarism."

The British attempted to take Baltimore, but were repulsed, and General Ross was killed. A fleet of sixteen vessels, for twenty-four hours poured shot and shell into Fort Henry. The people of Baltimore were filled with anxiety.

It was during this bombardment that Francis Scott Key composed the "Star Spangled Banner," which has immortalized him. Going to the British fleet, under flag of truce, to ask for the surrender of his friend, Dr. Beanes, they were detained until after the bombardment. They waited anxiously to see if the flag was still waving on the morning of Sept. 14, 1814, and to their great delight saw it through their glasses. Key wrote the words on the back of an old letter, between midnight and dawn, as he paced the deck of his ship.

Both English and Americans were glad to make peace, after three years of fierce conflict; and a treaty was signed at Ghent, Dec. 24, 1814. The war cost the United States 30,000 lives, and $100,000,000. It was a fearful price to pay for grievances, real though they were.

Nobody was more rejoiced that the war was over than President and Mrs. Madison, whose hearts had never been really in favor of it, and who had been blamed for all the misfortunes. Mr. Madison, amiable and upright, had been drawn by his party into the war; Washington, perhaps, would have controlled the party, and found a way of escape.

When the President and his wife returned to Washington, they occupied a large house on the northeast corner of Pennsylvania Avenue and Nineteenth Streets. Here Mrs. Madison entertained many distinguished guests, — Talleyrand, Chateaubriand, Joseph and Jerome Bonaparte, and others. Here she graciously presided, as Sir Charles Bagot, Minister from Great Britain said, "looking every inch a queen."

Everybody wished to see the charming Mrs. Madison. Two elderly ladies from the West, passing through the city, asked a gentleman on the street how they might meet her. He showed them the way to the President's house, and being a friend of the family, asked for Mrs. Madison, who was at breakfast. She came into the room and met them cordially. So pleased were they that one of them said, "P'r'aps you wouldn't mind if I just kissed you, to tell my girls about." And the beautiful woman embraced them both, to their great delight.

"She had," says a friend, writing about her, "a sweet, natural dignity of manner, which attracted while it commanded respect; a proper degree of reserve without stiffness in company with strangers; and a stamp of frankness and sincerity, which, with her intimate friends, became gayety and playfulness of manner. There was, too, a cordial, genial, sunny atmosphere surrounding her, which won all hearts, and was one of the secrets of her prosperity.

"She was said to be, during Mr. Madison's administration, the most popular person in the United States; and she certainly had a remarkable memory for names and faces. No person introduced to Mrs. Madison at one of the crowded levees of the White House required a second presentation on meeting her again, but had the gratification of being recognized and addressed by name."

When Mr. Madison's Secretary of State, James Monroe, became President, March 4, 1817, Mr. and Mrs. Madison retired to their summer home, Montpelier, in Virginia. He was now sixty-six and she but forty-five, in the prime of life. A writer in the *Portfolio*, February, 1818, says of Mrs. Madison: "Like a summer's sun she rose in our political horizon gloriously, and she sunk benignly."

At Montpelier, for twenty years, Mr. Madison devoted himself largely to writing. "I have rarely during the period of my public life," he said in 1827, "found my time less at my disposal than since I took my leave of it." He wrote upon every prominent topic of the time. He wished slavery abolished, though he owned over one hundred slaves.

His slave and body-servant, Paul Jennings, who thought his master "one of the best men that ever lived," wrote, "I never saw him in a passion, and never knew him to strike a slave; neither would he allow an overseer to do it." He was so considerate of their feelings that when he was obliged to rebuke his slaves he would "never mortify them by doing it before others."

He was an earnest advocate of temperance, and for many years was a total abstainer. He worked earnestly for education — he was rector of the University of Virginia — believing that the well-being, and even the perpetuity, of the nation depended upon that. He advocated equal educational privileges for men and women. He thought the capacity of woman for the highest education had "been sufficiently illustrated by her works of genius, of erudition, and of science."

He loved agriculture, and was deeply interested in his crops of wheat and his animals. The property consisted of twenty-five hundred acres. The house, which belonged to his father, had been greatly enlarged, and his aged mother lived in the original part of the old homestead. She received at two o'clock each day the distinguished friends and tourists who came to visit her son and his wife. Surrounded by the Blue Ridge Mountains, the house made a picture not unlike that of a beautiful English estate.

On the wide porch of the house, supported by pillars, Mr. Madison, in his black coat, knee-breeches with buckles, and powdered hair worn in a queue behind, walked his allotted number of miles for exercise in stormy weather. Near by was his study, a little building in the form of a temple, surmounted by a statue of Liberty. Trees abounded, — silver poplars, tulip-trees, and weeping willows. The garden was laid out in the form of a large horse-shoe, and kept in order by a French gardener named Beazée, who had come to Virginia at the time of the French Revolution.

Roses and white jessamine clambered over the porticoes, as is usual in Southern homes. Tiger lilies abounded, the seed being sent from France by General Lafayette, who went to Montpelier in his last visit to our country in 1825. The much-disliked thistle, says Mrs. Madison's grand-niece, was first propagated here, the seed coming from France, and marked " very rare."

Mr. Madison's sitting-room, where he spent much time at his desk, was furnished with chairs and an iron bed with high posts and crimson damask canopy, brought by Mr. Monroe from the palace of the Tuileries, after the French Revolution. In the various rooms were many pictures and statues. In the dining-room, Napoleon in his ermine robes, Louis the Fourteenth, Thomas Jefferson by Kosciusko, with many gifts of friends, and on the mahogany sideboard the silver of their families. The "clock-room," with its old-fashioned clock, had about fifty statues and busts, — Washington, Jefferson, Adams, and others. The drawing-room, with Persian rugs, had its walls quite covered with mirrors and pictures, six by Gilbert Stuart, and the Declaration of Independence framed. The library up-stairs was filled with books, while pamphlets were piled on every chair and table.

The home life was arranged with order and comfort. Every Sunday Mr. and Mrs. Madison rode five miles to the Episcopal Church for worship, taking as many of their guests as chose to accompany them. She wielded, says a writer of the time, "as skilfully the domestic, as she had done worthily and popularly the public, sceptre."

The one sorrow of Mrs. Madison's life was the conduct of her son, Payne Todd. He passed several years travelling in Europe, spending his fortune and much of his mother's. Mr. Madison treated him like a son, and paid many of his debts. His mother wrote him affectionately: "I am impatient to hear from you, my dearest Payne, and had I known where to direct, I should have written you before this."

Some months later she wrote: "Every one inquires after you; but, my dear son, it seems to be the wonder of them all that you should stay away from us for so long a time; and now I am ashamed to tell, when asked, how long my only child has been absent from the home of his mother. . . . I have said in my late letters, as well as this, all that I thought sufficient to influence you. I must now put my trust in God alone. . . . We should rejoice in any occurrence that would bring you speedily to our arms, who love you with inexpressible tenderness and constancy.   YOUR OWN MOTHER."

For several years before Mr. Madison's death, at the age of eighty-five, his wife was his devoted nurse. Five years before his death she wrote to one of her nieces: "I have so long been confined by the side of my dear sick husband, never seeing or hearing outside of his room, that I make a dull correspondent. . . . His poor hands are so swollen as to be almost useless, and so I lend him mine. The music-box is playing beside me, and seems well adapted to solitude, as I look out at our mountains, white with snow, and the winter's wind sounding loud and cold."

She was also caring for Mr. Madison's aged mother, who died at ninety-eight. "Dolly is my mother, now," said the mother-in-law, "and cares most tenderly for all my wants. . . . I owe everything to her." Later Mrs. Madison wrote to a friend concerning the ex-president, now completely crippled by rheumatism: "I never leave my husband more than a few moments at a time, and have not left the enclosure around my house for eight months." After his death, June 28, 1836, Mrs. Madison's health gave way for a time, on account of the severe strain upon her nerves. She wrote, with her own hand, replies to the various letters of condolence, from General Jackson, then President of the United States, and other distinguished persons both at home and abroad. Jefferson said Madison had "a pure and spotless virtue, which no calumny has ever attempted to sully."

All Mr. Madison's unpublished manuscript was left with his wife to be published. President Jackson sent a special message to Congress, proposing the purchase of the manuscript, comprising a record of the Debates of Congress during 1782-1787. The nation bought it for thirty thousand dollars. Later, in 1846, Congress bought the remaining letters and private correspondence of Mr. Madison for fifteen thousand dollars.

A year after Mr. Madison died, his wife, unable to bear the loneliness of the country home, returned to Washington, keeping some of her nieces and nephews with her. She received all the homage of former times. At New Year's, Fourth of July, and other holidays, her house on the corner of Lafayette Square and H Street was as thronged with visitors as the White House.

She had several narrow escapes from death. In 1844 she was on board the steamer Princeton, when the great cannon, " the Peacemaker," exploded, killing and wounding many. Her house was set on fire; and she was saved by her serving-man, Ralph, who broke open her door, where she was found quietly sleeping in the dense smoke, and bore her down the burning staircase and out into the garden.

Through her spendthrift son, and perhaps her own inability to manage her finances, she was obliged to sell her beloved Montpelier, with the slaves, to Mr. Moncure of Richmond. Her souvenirs were removed to the home of her son, where he had erected several small buildings around a tower-like structure, containing the ball-room and dining-room. His mother was to reside in one of the cottages. She did not live to see the plan carried out, because money was lacking.

"My poor boy," she used to say, "forgive his eccentricities, for his heart is all right." She wrote him, "You know the little I have in my power is at your command, though but 'a drop in the bucket'. . . . Dolly and Mary wrote me yesterday that you were very popular in Washington; and I should like to be with you to witness it — the respect and love shown my son would be the highest gratification the world could bestow upon me."

As life neared its close, and its burdens fatigued her, she would say, remembering the strong and calm President, "Oh for my counsellor!" To her niece, who worried over some small matters, she said, "My dear, do not trouble about it; there is nothing in *this* world worth really caring for."

She wanted the Bible read to her often, especially the Gospel of St. John. Toward the last she slept almost constantly, occasionally reviving and putting out her hands to embrace her loved ones, murmuring from time to time, "My poor boy!"

She died July 12, 1849, having survived President

Madison thirteen years. Her funeral was held in St. John's Church, Washington; and later she was buried in the cemetery at Montpelier, by the grave of her husband. Her son Payne died two years later of typhoid fever, it is said, "full of grief for a wasted life."

Lossing truly says, "Mrs. Madison adorned every station in life in which she was placed." She once wrote her niece, Mary Cutts, the daughter of her favorite sister, Anna, "We must press on that intricate path leading to perfection and happiness, by doing all that is good and noble, before we can be taken under the silver wing of our rewarding angel."

Dolly Madison will ever be remembered as a woman whose loveliness of disposition, whose cheerful, helpful nature, and whose remarkable tact, were only equalled by her beauty and her grace. She won the heart of the nation.

CATHERINE BOOTH.

CATHERINE BOOTH.

IN London, in 1882, I heard, for the first time, Mrs. Booth, well called the Mother of the Salvation Army. The great hall was packed to listen to the words of a tall, fine-looking woman, very plainly dressed in black, quiet in manner, eloquent in language, and wholly devoted to her work.

Her theme was the conversion of children. No Christian parents could have left that meeting without feeling that they were responsible for the salvation of their children. Her remarkable strength of character, her shining example, her constant watchfulness and prayer, had brought her whole family into a consecrated life.

Catherine Booth was born in Ashbourne, Derbyshire, England, Jan. 17, 1829, the only daughter in a family of five. Three brothers died in infancy. John, the only surviving brother, went to America when he was sixteen.

Catherine's father, John Mumford, had been a very eloquent lay preacher in the Methodist church, but during the childhood of his daughter grew cold in heart, and gave up even his profession of religion. He was a coach-builder, and earned a good living; but material comfort did not satisfy his devoted wife, who had loved him, more than all else, for his piety. Perhaps this disappointment bound her more closely to her daughter, whom she early taught to love the Scriptures. Before the girl was twelve, she had read the Bible through eight times!

"The longer I live," wrote Mrs. Booth years afterward, "the more I appreciate my mother's character. She was one of the Puritan type. I have often heard my husband remark that she was a woman of the sternest principle he had ever met, and yet the very embodiment of tenderness. To her, right was right, no matter what it might entail. . . .

"She had an intense realization of spiritual things. Heaven seemed quite near, instead of being, as with so many, a far-off unreality. It was a positive joy to her that her three eldest children were there. I never heard her thank the Lord for anything so fervently as for this, although they were fine, promising boys."

Catherine was a frail, nervous child, never strong and equal to out-door plays, but passionately fond of dolls, which she would feed and put to bed and pray with!

When twelve years of age she became the secretary of a juvenile temperance society, arranged meetings, wrote articles for the papers over an assumed name, and was a brilliant talker for one so young.

She was always on the side of the weak or the unfortunate. One day, trundling her hoop along the street, she saw an officer dragging a prisoner to jail, while a crowd were jeering behind him. The little girl, feeling at least that the man was friendless, hastened to his side, and walked along the street with him.

She was extremely fond of animals, as are all sensitive and lovable natures, and was keenly alive to their sufferings. She owned a beautiful retriever, Waterford, which was her inseparable companion. If he heard her praying or weeping, as he lay on the rug outside her door, he would whine and scratch to come in.

Going one day to her father's place of business, she closed the door after her, leaving Waterford outside. Striking her foot against something, she cried out with the pain, when the dog, thinking some one was hurting her, sprang through a large glass window to save his playmate. The father, very angry, caused the dog to be shot immediately. It was too evident that the lay preacher had given up his religion with such a temper.

For days, the child, half-dead with grief, could not speak to her father, and for months suffered unspeakably. When the man's anger was cooled, he regretted his action, but that could not bring back the pet which had lost his life for her sake.

Whenever she found a horse in the field, worn with work or thin from lack of food, she would buy a bushel of corn, and with some friend go at evening and give it to the grateful animal. Wherever she saw a horse or a donkey beaten, she would, by kindness or decision, compel its driver to cease.

She raised money among her little friends to send the gospel to the heathen. She was especially interested in the colored people, and renounced sugar, and practised other measures of self-denial, that the down-trodden and the ignorant might be helped a little through her savings.

When she was twelve she was sent to a good school, where she remained two years, but was obliged to leave it on account of disease of the spine, which compelled her to spend most of her time in a recumbent position.

She was already very fond of history and biography, the life of any one who had benefited others being eagerly read. During her illness she studied many theological works — Wesley, Finney, Mosheim, Neander, Bunyan, and other authors. Butler's "Analogy" she read with enthusiasm, and Newton on "Prophecy."

When Catherine was fifteen, the family moved from Boston, England, to London. A year later, the girl, though so religiously brought up, felt that she was not a Christian. She says, "I used to pace my room till two o'clock in the morning, and when, utterly exhausted, I lay down at length to sleep, I would place my Bible and hymn-book under my pillow, praying that I might wake up with the assurance of salvation. One morning, as I opened my hymn-book, my eyes fell upon the words: —

"'My God, I am Thine!
What a comfort Divine, —
What a blessing to know that my Jesus is mine!'

. . . . .

"I no longer hoped that I was saved. I was certain of it. The assurances of my salvation seemed to flood and fill my soul. . . . For the next six months I was so happy that I felt as if I was walking on air."

Catherine soon joined the Wesleyan church of which her mother was a member, and a Bible-class, conducted by the wife of a minister. The teacher used to insist on the timid Catherine praying, and "would often keep the class on their knees five minutes, waiting for me to begin," says Mrs. Booth. "When I told her one day that the excitement and exertion had made me ill, she replied, 'Never mind! you will be of use by and by, if you overcome this timidity, and employ your gifts. But if you don't, you won't.'" Who could then have imagined that Catherine would one day hold thousands spellbound by her eloquence and her spiritual power?

In 1847, when she was eighteen, she seemed likely to die of consumption, and was sent to the seashore at Brighton. Here her love of nature made her happy. She was "heartily sick of looking at the brick and mortar" of a great city. Fresh air and youth finally brought back her health, and she was again in London, teaching her Sunday-school class of fifteen girls from twelve to nineteen years of age, visiting the sick, and doing other good work.

In June, 1851, a young man came to preach at the chapel in Binfield Road, Clapham, where Catherine and her mother worshipped. He was twenty-two, three months younger than Catherine; a tall, slight, delicate looking young man, thoroughly in earnest, and evidently possessing a warm heart.

His father, once a man of means, had lost his fortune, and died early, leaving his family to struggle for themselves. William Booth, the only son, was apprenticed to a firm, where he soon showed much energy and ability for business. At fifteen he was converted, and, with a band of young men, began to hold cottage and open-air meetings.

At seventeen he was made a local preacher in the Methodist Church, but advised not to prepare himself for regular ministerial work, as his health was so precarious, it was thought that he could not bear the strain for twelve months. When he was twenty, he left Nottingham and settled in London. It was a great grief to his devoted mother, whose saintly character the son always regarded as scarcely short of angelic.

The wish to enter the ministry grew stronger. He thought of offering himself as chaplain to a convict-ship, and thus work his way to Australia. He wrote to a friend, " You know I would prefer by far the homework. But the difficulties are so great. My ability is not equal to the task. *Preachers are not wanted*, my superintendent told me so." Moody and Spurgeon had a somewhat similar experience.

Young Booth carried on his business, and preached as he had opportunity. Both Catherine and her mother were pleased with the young man, and thought they had not heard so good a sermon before in the chapel.

Shortly after, all three were invited to the house of a mutual friend. Catherine was drawn into conversation on the temperance question by some one present. The old arguments were used — " You cannot make people sober by Act of Parliament."

" I am not so sure of that," replied the intelligent girl of twenty-two; "by shutting up the liquor dens you can certainly minimize the evil, since you remove the temptation from those who are too weak to resist it. What is there to prevent the government from doing this? It has been done in some places with the best possible results. In the villages and districts where its use has been prohibited, drunkenness is comparatively unknown, thus proving that people *can* be made sober by Act of Parliament."

" But what would become of the revenue ? "

"What would become of a man," was her response, "if he were to suck his own blood and eat his own flesh? How can a kingdom flourish that lives upon the destruction of its subjects, and that draws its revenues from their very graves?"

Mr. Booth was pleased with the bright girl, and the acquaintance grew into a sincere and unchangeable affection. He was invited to become the settled pastor at the chapel, a friend paying the salary of fifty pounds a year, or about two hundred and fifty dollars. He gave up a business in which he was doing well, and accepted for life his hard labor for souls, with poverty. A year after their first meeting, Catherine Mumford promised to share this labor and poverty with the young preacher, and she kept her promise nobly till the end.

The following year, 1852, Mr. Booth was asked to take charge of the Spalding circuit, a country district some thirty miles in extent. He accepted, and Catherine's letters came often to cheer and aid him. "I was pleased," she wrote, "to hear that you were going to read Mr. Fletcher's life. I hope you'll always keep some stirring biography on hand. It is most profitable. . . .

"Do not be anxious about the future. Spalding *will not be your final destination*, if you *make the best of your ability*."

A physician had urged Mr. Booth to take port wine for his health. Catherine wrote: "I need not say how willing, nay, how anxious, I am that you should have anything and everything which would tend to promote your *health* and happiness. But so thoroughly am I convinced that port wine would do neither, that I should hear of you taking it with unfeigned grief. . . . I abominate that hackneyed but monstrously inconsistent tale — a teetotaler in principle, but obliged to take a little for 'my stomach's sake!' . . . I have far more hope for your health *because* you abstain from stimulating drinks, than I should if you took them. Flee the detestable thing as you would a serpent. Be a teetotaler in principle and practice."

In 1854 Mr. Booth, at the age of twenty-five, was called to London as an assistant pastor. For two years past Catherine Mumford had been preparing herself by study and work for the broad field she was one day to occupy. She disliked novels, but she read other books eagerly. "Being so much alone in my youth," she said in after life, "and so thrown on my own thoughts, and those of the mighty dead as expressed in books, has been helpful to me. Had I been given to gossip, and had there been people for me to gossip with, I should certainly never have accomplished what I did. I believe gossip is one of the greatest enemies to both mental and spiritual improvement."

On Mr. Booth's return to London he had already been so successful in evangelistic work, that he was not permitted to remain long in the great city. Bristol asked for his services, and he spent a week there. At Oldham, Bradford, Manchester, Guernsey, and other places, he won many to a changed life. About two thousand persons in different cities sought conversion during the four previous months.

On June 16, 1855, Catherine was married to the man of her choice, at the Stockwell New Chapel, none being present but her father, Mr. Booth's sister, and the minister, Dr. Thomas. Mr. Booth and his wife proceeded immediately to Ryde, in the Isle of Wight, where, after staying a week, they took the steamer for Guernsey. Here the revival meetings were begun again, "the doors being open," the bride wrote her mother, "at half-past five, to admit the seat-holders *before the crush.*"

At York and Hull Mr. Booth's pointed and earnest preaching produced the same results. Mrs. Booth was happy in the companionship of a congenial Christian man. She wrote years later, "Unhappy marriages are usually the consequences of too great a disparity of mind, age, temperament, training, or antecedents."

To one of her sons she wrote, "You will want a companion and a counsellor — a 'help-meet.' The original word means a *help corresponding* to *his dignity.* . . . A wrong step on this point, and you are undone! . . . When God's time and person are come, he will bring you together." She told her son to pray for such a companion; and, with an unselfishness somewhat rare in mothers for their sons, she added that she was praying for it also.

Mrs. Booth wrote her mother: "My precious husband is kinder and more tender than ever. . . . We are to have apartments at Sheffield. . . . Though I get literally oppressed with kindness, I must say I would prefer a home, where we could sit down together at our own little table, myself the mistress and my husband the only guest. But the work of God so abundantly prospers that I dare not repine, or else I feel this constant packing and locating among strangers to be a great burden, especially while so weak and poorly." . . .

Again she wrote, "I never was so happy before. My cup, so far as this world goes, seems full. . . . My precious William grows every day more to my mind and heart. . . . William preached with marvellous power. For an hour and ten minutes everybody was absorbed and riveted. . . .

"They finished up last night gloriously. Though it was a very wet night the chapel was packed in every part, and scores went away unable to get in." Six hundred and sixty-three professed conversion during the month at Sheffield.

Catherine's first child, William Bramwell, named after a noted preacher, was born in 1856. She wrote her beloved mother: "I feel as though I had never loved you half as well as I ought to have done. Forgive all my shortcomings, and be assured I now appreciate all your self-sacrifice on my behalf. . . . My precious babe is a beauty, and very good."

It seems impossible for any man to succeed without arousing jealousy. Mr. Booth was only twenty-seven, and it was thought that his influence was becoming too great for so young and untried a man. It was decided by Conference that he should give up evangelistic work for a time, and take a pastorate.

Mr. Booth was appointed to Brighouse, a low, smoky town, where a second son, Ballington, was born July 28, 1857. Here, with much timidity, Mrs. Booth began her work in public. At the request of her husband, she became class-leader in a company of twenty-nine members. "I felt very tremulous at first," she wrote, "but gained confidence and freedom as I went on. I feel a good deal exhausted, but otherwise no worse."

Mr. Booth had often urged her to give a series of lectures on temperance, feeling that she had the ability if she could only overcome her timidity. At first she spoke to the children. "I got on," she wrote her father, " far better than I expected. . . . I shall give a lecture to the females of Brighouse first, and then to a mixed audience. But I must not be too sanguine. Perhaps I may lose my confidence next time. I am so anxious to succeed for the cause's sake."

After the ordination of Mr. Booth in 1858, he was removed to Gateshead, a town of fifty thousand people. The chapel numbered about ninety members, and the Sunday evening congregations about one hundred and twenty, though the building would seat twelve hundred and fifty. Before many weeks Bethesda Chapel was filled to overflowing with two thousand people. It was called by outsiders the " Converting Shop."

The revival services were begun by one all-day meeting of fasting and prayer. Bills were distributed from house to house, Mrs. Booth taking one district which contained about one hundred and fifty houses. Every Sunday night a band of workers marched along the street from five to six o'clock, singing as they went, and stopping at suitable places for a brief meeting. The saloons sometimes sent out bands to out-sing the Christians, but the latter often sang a hymn to the popular tune which the saloonists started. Many hundreds were added to the churches through this revival.

This year, 1858, Catherine, their first daughter and third child, was born. Mrs. Booth wrote to her mother: " Her hair is exactly the color of mine. She has a nice nose and mouth, a fine forehead, and a plump, round face. She is the picture of health and happiness, and thrives daily." Concerning her husband, she wrote: "William never was kinder or more loving and attentive than now. He often tells me I grow more beautiful in his sight and more precious to his heart day by day."

With health very frail, she still found time for earnest Christian effort. One Sunday on her way to church, she reasoned with herself that she should ask others to come, instead of going for mere enjoyment. She spoke to a group of women sitting on a door-step, and was not repulsed. Seeing a woman with a jug in her hand, and thinking she might be intoxicated, she asked with tact, " Are the people out who live on this floor ? "

" Yes," was the reply, " they are gone to chapel."

" Oh, I am glad to hear that; how is it that you are not gone to a place of worship ? "

The poor woman looked at her torn clothes, and then said that she must stay at home to keep a drunken husband from going to the saloons. Mrs. Booth went to see the man, a clever workman who could earn three or four pounds a week, talked and prayed with him, and the following day he took the pledge. After this she visited among the drunkards at night, so as to find them at home, and secured a good number who met with her once a week for reading the Bible, and prayer.

Of course the destitution of these people was great. One woman lay with her twin babies on a heap of rags. By her side was her only sustenance, a crust of bread and a bit of lard. "I fancied a bit o' bootter, and my mon, he'd do owt for me he could, bless 'im; he couldna' git me iny bootter, so he fitcht me this bit o' lard. Have *you* iver tried lard i'ste'd o' bootter ? It's *rare good!*"

Mrs. Booth washed the babies in a broken pie-dish, and wished she had used lard for butter all her life, thus to have been able to give the poor woman more comforts.

In 1859 a neighboring minister wrought more good than he could have imagined, by a pamphlet, trying to prove from the Bible that women should not preach. It was directed more especially against the American evangelists, Dr. and Mrs. Palmer, the latter a lovable woman who had done great good.

Mrs. Booth had done little public work herself, but felt that the church had long been crippled from the silence of its women. She had always believed in the equality of woman, and said, " Never till woman is estimated and educated as man's equal — the literal 'she-man' of the Hebrew — will the foundation of human influence become pure, or the bias of mind noble and lofty." At once she wrote an excellent pamphlet in answer to that of the minister. Those who care to investigate the subject more fully will find Miss Willard's "Woman in the Pulpit" a most interesting and helpful book.

Of course such passages as "I suffer not a woman to teach," cannot be taken literally, for more than half the Sunday-school teachers are women. Happily such grand organizations as the Christian Endeavor Society are fulfilling the law, "There is neither male nor female; for ye are all one in Christ Jesus."

More important than Mrs. Booth's pamphlet, was the fact that she had laid out a path for other women, in which, to be consistent, she herself had to walk. After much inward struggle on account of her natural shrinking, she promised her Lord that she would speak for him, if she died in the attempt.

In the spring of 1860, one Sunday at church, when more than a thousand were present, the Holy Spirit seemed to urge her to speak. She said to herself, "I cannot do it." Satan seemed to whisper, "You will look like a fool, and will have nothing to say." "Ah!" said the delicate woman, "I have never yet been willing to be a fool for Christ; now I will be one."

She rose up from her seat, and walked down the aisle. Her astonished husband stepped down from his desk and said, "What is the matter, my dear?" "I want to say a word," was the reply. "My dear wife wishes to speak," said Mr. Booth, and sat down.

"I stood," says Mrs. Booth, — "God only knows how — and if any mortal ever did hang on the arm of Omnipotence, I did. I felt as if I were clinging to some human arm, but it was a divine one which held me up. I just stood and told the people how it had come about. I confessed, as I think everybody should who has been in the wrong." Hundreds wept as the earnest woman spoke, and dated their conversion from that hour.

Mrs. Booth said, "I never imagined the life of publicity and trial that it would lead me to, for I was never allowed to have another quiet Sabbath when I was well enough to stand and speak. All I did was to take the first step. I could not see in advance."

Mr. Booth at once urged his wife to speak in the evening. Although much exhausted by the effort in the morning, knowing that she could do good, she consented. The chapel was packed, the people crowding to the doors, and sitting on the window-sills. For twenty years this magnetic power never lessened. High and low, rich and poor, in elegant halls and in forlorn waste places, gathered to hear a consecrated woman preach the gospel. Her voice and her example led thousands of other women to speak for Christ. The minister's opposition pamphlet proved a blessing to almost unnumbered homes and hearts.

Invitations now poured in upon Mrs. Booth, to hold revival meetings, or to supply in her husband's absence. Gentlemen came who had never entered a Dissenters' place of worship, attending only the Established Church.

About this time her husband broke down from overwork; and she was urged to preach for him, and take charge of the interests of the circuit. She wrote to her parents, "I never was in such a state in my life. I could neither eat nor sleep." When she saw the congregation she " felt almost like melting away."

She wrote her husband, " With time and pains and more of the Spirit, I believe I shall be useful yet. . . . My own health appears a trifle compared with yours, and I feel that infinitely easier could I meet death myself than its approach to you."

Her greatest difficulty was to find time for preparation for preaching, with her four little children, Emma having been born early this year, 1860. But by saving the time which so many give to shopping or society, she found it possible. The children were never neglected, as their wonderful record in Christian work during the past years has shown. "I will not have a wicked child," said the strong-willed, devoted woman; and she would pray in their presence that they might be laid in an early grave rather than do evil. "They must be taught implicit, uncomprising obedience," she used to say.

Her daughter Emma says, "I remember how she would gather us round her and pray with us. I used to wear a low frock, and her hot tears would often drop upon my neck, sending a thrill through me which I can never forget."

Mr. Booth had long felt anxious to do evangelistic work again, and hoped that at the next meeting of Conference, in 1861, this would be permitted; but the same old opposition was manifested by a few, not only toward Mr. Booth, but toward all revival work. Several large Wesleyan chapels were closed both to them and to other evangelists. After much prayer and thought, Mr. Booth resigned his connection with Conference, and without means or place to preach, like John Wesley, made "the world his parish."

Mrs. Booth, who had strongly favored this step, wrote to her mother: "I have promised him to keep a brave heart. At times it appears to me that God may have something very glorious in store for us, and when he has tried us he will bring us forth as gold. It will not be the first time I have taken a leap in the dark, humanly speaking, for conscience' sake."

Mrs. Booth and the children went to her mother's house in London, making the journey from Newcastle by sea, for economy's sake. While in London Mr. Booth conferred with several evangelists, looking for an open door. An invitation soon came from Cornwall, for both Mr. and Mrs. Booth, which they gladly accepted, leaving the children for a time with their grandparents. They expected to stay in Cornwall for six or seven weeks only, but remained for eighteen months, the revival being in progress all that time.

She wrote home: "William preached in the largest Wesleyan chapel, about half a mile from the other. It was crammed out into the street. I should think there were eighteen hundred people inside, and I never witnessed such a scene in my life as the prayer-meeting presented. The rail was filled in a few minutes with great, strong men, who cried aloud for mercy."

The confusion did not please Mr. Booth, who believed in everything being done "decently and in order;" but Mrs. Booth, quiet though she was, liked it better, she said, than the "stoical indifference" in many places of worship.

The revival interest spread from town to town in Cornwall. Miners and mine owners, fishermen, and business men, indeed all classes, were profoundly moved. Many saloons closed from lack of patronage. Sometimes the after-meetings for prayer lasted till three in the morning. Some persons walked *all night* after the Sunday service to be at their work on Monday morning.

Besides preaching to mixed audiences, Mrs. Booth held especial services for women, sometimes speaking to twenty-five hundred. Her words about rearing their children, following the fashions, and living a more consecrated life, were never forgotten.

"We were very much affected by Mrs. Booth's domestic graces, as well as by her public gifts," said the "King of the Wesleyans," a very rich and prominent Christian worker. "I remember calling upon her one day and finding her busy ironing, with all the dexterity and confidence of an experienced hand."

As a result of their eighteen months of labor, about seven thousand persons professed conversion. A large proportion joined the churches, and lived exemplary lives afterwards. It is probable that a large number of these would never have been aroused to their need of religion except through the enthusiasm of a revival.

Early in 1863 Mr. and Mrs. Booth went to Cardiff in Wales. As so many chapels had been closed to them, they resolved to use public and sectarian buildings, and thus were enabled to reach thousands who would not go inside a church. A circus was obtained for their meetings. When Mrs. Booth spoke in it, she said, " The sight of it overwhelmed her at first," but she was helped to overcome all timidity. Night after night both she and her husband went home exhausted, after the inquiry meetings; but their frail bodies were wonderfully sustained. "It is killing work," she wrote her mother, "although an infinitely blessed one."

"I have every reason to think that the people receive me gladly everywhere, and that prejudice against female ministry melts away before me like snow in the sun," she wrote her parents.

At Cardiff about five hundred professed conversion. Several helpful friends for life were made there: Messrs. John and Richard Cory, the latter a Baptist, rich ship and colliery owners, who have helped to support the work for thirty years, a contractor, Mr. Billups, and his talented wife, and others. The latter invited them to Weston-super-Mare for a season of rest and change, which was most welcome to the weary evangelists.

After Cardiff, they spent eight weeks at Walsall, near

Birmingham. Here, in the children's meetings, their little son Bramwell, aged seven, was one of the converts. Mrs. Booth thought he had been unusually interested at Cardiff, — their children were now all with them, — and asked him then to give her a definite answer as " to whether he would accept the offer of salvation." Looking his mother calmly in the face, with something of her own will and decision of character, he answered, " No."

In 1864 Marian, Mrs. Booth's sixth child, was born; Herbert, the fifth, having been born in 1862. This year, 1864, it was decided, as the calls were so numerous and the work so great, that Mrs. Booth should conduct the meetings in several towns alone, while her husband labored elsewhere. The results proved that Mrs. Booth was equal to her chosen work.

Finally an invitation came from London, which they accepted, as Mrs. Booth had long desired to return there. A house was engaged in Shaftesbury Road, Hammersmith, and thither the children were brought. Mr. Booth began his labors, July 2, 1865, in a large tent erected in the Quakers' burying-ground, Whitechapel. Nearly every night two meetings were held, first an open-air service on the Mile-end Road, and then a service in the tent. In the fall, the tent having blown down, the meetings were held in a dancing-saloon.

A motley crowd gathered at the services; ragged, wicked, sunk in the depths of poverty and wretchedness. No wonder Mr. Booth told his wife that he seemed to hear a voice saying, " Where can you go and find such heathen as these, and where is there so great a need for your labors ? " Whitechapel has long been the scene of murder and theft, of drunkenness and all manner of sorrow and sin. Here nobody would close a chapel door to Mr. Booth or his wife, for ninety per cent of these people never entered a chapel or would allow one in their midst.

Heretofore the family had been decently provided for by the contributions at the meetings, but now where would their support come from? Certainly not from these poor people, who could not keep soul and body together without charity.

"If you feel you ought to stay, stay," said Mrs. Booth. "We have trusted the Lord *once* for our support, and we can trust him *again!*" Then they gave up the Conference to go among the respectable and well-to-do in the great towns of England; now they had come to the lowest, and who would stand by them?

Fortunately there are always some noble men and women who realize that those who have been blest with wealth should use it for the good of humanity, for in this world we must needs be "our brother's keeper." Samuel Morley, a member of Parliament, a rich manufacturer at Nottingham, and a Christian gentleman, heard of the East End meetings, and wrote a letter from Scotland saying that he would like to meet Mr. Booth on his return. A month later Mr. Morley sent for him.

He listened with great sympathy to the report of open-air meetings, processions marching along the street, singing as they went, while mud and garbage were thrown at them, and of many cases of conversion. And then, with practical Christianity, he asked Mr. Booth of his family, and offered to provide a large part of their support. Mr. Booth hastened to his wife to tell the good news, and together they knelt in thankful prayer. Years later Mr. Morley called himself a "sleeping partner," in the Salvation Army, and in the time of the purity agitation gave Mrs. Booth two thousand pounds to help carry on the rescue work of the army. He never gave grudgingly, but, says Commissioner Booth-Tucker in his eloquent life of Mrs. Booth, "with a graceful generosity that made his gifts so peculiarly acceptable, adding that she must call and see him again."

While Mr. Booth was working in the poor East End of London, through Mr. Morley's arranging Mrs. Booth was speaking in the aristocratic West End. She spoke fearlessly about fox-hunting in words that ought to have weight in this country as well as England.

"Observe," she said, "the delight of all the gentlemen and noble ladies when a whole pack of strong dogs is let loose in pursuit, and then behold the noble chase! The regiment of well-mounted cavalry and the pack of hounds all charge at full gallop after the poor frightened little creature. It will be a great disappointment if by any means it should escape, or be killed within as short a time as an hour. The sport will be excellent in proportion to the time during which the poor thing's agony is prolonged, and the number of miles it is able to run in terror of its life.

"Brutality! I tell you that, in my judgment, at any rate, you can find nothing in the vilest back slums more utterly, more deliberately, more savagely, cruel than *that!*"

At another time she said, "O friends! give up the sentimental hypocrisy of singing, —

"Rescue the perishing,
Care for the dying,"

in the drawing-room, to the accompaniment of the piano, without ever dreaming of going outside to do it; such idle words will prove only a mockery and a sham in the great day of account."

Early in 1866 Mrs. Booth was very ill for a long time from over-exertion; but as soon as she was partially recovered she began work at Margate, a fashionable seaside resort, taking her family with her. The meetings were crowded from the beginning, and many prominent persons were converted.

Mr. Knight, the well-known publisher, offered to report and publish her sermons, giving her the profits; but her modesty made her decline, which she afterwards regretted, as few of them were ever reduced to writing, and therefore not preserved. Her notes for her sermons were usually made on odd scraps of paper, sometimes while nursing a child, or in the intervals of household labor. Her early life, however, by its wise and full reading, had partially prepared her for these busy years.

In London, some wealthy men wished to build a church for her, larger than Spurgeon's Tabernacle; but she declined, as she felt called to evangelistic work. Mrs. Booth was now thirty-eight years old, the mother of eight children, Eva having been born on Christmas Day, 1865, and Lucy in April, 1867.

After the meetings at Margate, Mrs Booth was called to another seaside resort even more fashionable, — Brighton, a delightful resting-place from London smoke and bustle. She spoke in the Dome, erected by

George IV., a handsome hall accommodating three thousand persons.

About nine hundred remained to the prayer-meeting. Satan seemed to whisper to her, "You will never ask such people as these to come out and kneel down here. You will only make a fool of yourself if you do!" But answered Mrs Booth to herself, "Yes, I shall. I shall not make it any easier for them than for others. If they do not sufficiently realize their sins to be willing to come and kneel here and confess them, they are not likely to be of much use to the kingdom of God."

A fashionable life seemed to Mrs. Booth worse than useless. "Living in pleasure," she said, "eating, drinking, dressing, riding, sight-seeing! Spending their precious gifts all on self, self, self!"

In December, 1869, Mrs. Booth's mother died. With a radiance of expression unearthly, she whispered, "We shall all meet again!" and passed away in triumph. Mr. Mumford, her father, in his daughter's first public meetings, had come back to his former faith and joy in religion, and with childlike humility and tenderness helped her meetings in every way possible.

In 1870, besides work in various places, Mrs. Booth spent three months at Hastings, England, in gospel labors. At first several Christians doubted the propriety of having a woman preach; but her work in reaching souls had been so blessed already, that they did not dare take upon themselves the responsibility of refusing her. They were soon convinced of her power and her acceptability, when three hundred professed conversion, and church-members themselves were awakened by her zeal and self-sacrifice.

The following year at Easter the first Whitechapel anniversary was held, with a free tea for a thousand of the "missioners." There were as usual wonderful testimonies from those who showed by their lives that they were reformed in heart. One poor gypsy, with tears running down his cheeks, said, "I belong to one of the lowest class of people that ever was born. . . . My face is nearly black; but my heart is washed white by the precious blood of Christ. . . . My heart is so full, that instead of crying out in the street, '*Chairs* to mend!' I have forgot what I was doing, and called out '*Souls* to mend!'"

In March, 1873, Mrs. Booth began some meetings in Portsmouth, a large military and naval centre, with over a hundred and twenty thousand inhabitants. Desiring to reach the neglected, she engaged a hall or theatre seating three thousand, in the worst part of the city, where soldiers, sailors, and their low companions gathered. From the first night, when the hall was packed, to the end of the seventeen weeks which she spent in Portsmouth, there seemed never to be a vacant seat in her meetings, and hundreds were turned away.

Writing to a friend of the sea of faces, she said: "The sight almost overwhelmed me. With its two galleries, its dome-like roof, and vast proportions, when crammed with people, it presents a most imposing appearance. The top gallery is ten or twelve seats deep in front, and it was full of men. . . . Oh, how I yearned over them! I felt as if it would be a small thing to die *there* and *then*, if that would have brought them to Jesus. Oh, if we realized as we *ought* the value of souls, we should not live long under it! . . .

"It seems to me God's time to visit this place; and whoever had been the instrument he had sent, he would have blessed them. I adore him for sending me."

In October of the same year she began a series of meetings at Chatham. The Press had already recognized her wonderful influence. The *News* said: "Mrs. Booth possesses remarkable powers as a preacher. With a pleasing voice, distinct in all its tones, now colloquial, now persuasive, she can rise to the height of a great argument with an impassioned force and fervor that thrills her hearers. Quiet in her demeanor, her looks, her words, her actions, are peculiarly emphatic. . . . And yet there is no ranting — nothing to offend the most fastidious taste."

Mrs. Booth was seized on the third Sunday at Chatham, at the close of the service, with a severe heart attack, and carried unconscious from the room; but in two weeks she was in her place again. As soon as the meetings were concluded, the results being such as to cause thanksgiving, the children became ill with whooping-cough, and received all the tender attention that one of the most devoted mothers could give them.

Every kind of disease seemed to find its way into the Booth family. Neither children nor parents were ever rugged, and did not seem fitted to cope with hardships; but coming continually in contact with the most wretched poverty, they could not escape the diseases incident to crowded tenement houses and half-starved inmates.

The ages of the eight children ranged from five to sixteen years. Many mothers would have felt that their cares were so great at home that they could do nothing for the poor and the sorrowing outside; but Mrs. Booth knew there were other children to be cared for besides her own, and other homes to be brightened and saved. She had learned that the benevolent work, or indeed any great work for humanity, is done by those who are already busy. The idle and the indolent are those who "never have time."

When little Marian Booth was seven years old she had small-pox; and the other children were obliged to go into the country under the care of the eldest son, Bramwell, then fifteen. His good mother wrote him while she stayed and watched by the sick one: "I hope you will, in this emergency, show yourself to be a true son of your mother, and a consistent disciple of the Lord Jesus."

After the hard work of the day, far into the night, Mrs. Booth would write to her children; now to Catherine, afterwards called the Maréchale, who at twelve years of age was holding meetings among her companions; now to Ballington, who, through the kindness of a friend, was absent at school: "Don't neglect prayer. Be watchful; mind that copy about talking. Too much talk ruins heaps of people. It is a fine attainment to be able to hold one's tongue. Wise people are seldom great talkers. Mind this. . . .

"I do hope you are industrious. . . . Remember, Satan steals his marches on us by *littles*. A minute now and a minute then; be on the lookout, and don't be cheated by him! Your time is flying; one-quarter will soon be gone! . . . I will send you a few stamps for extra letters; but you must do without any *other* extras. . . .

"Never forget my advice about listening to secrets! . . . Never allow any boy to approach you with a secret which you would not like me to hear. Then you are safe. . . . Don't hear anything that needs to be whispered; it is SURE TO BE BAD. . . . You must try not to worry; do your best in the day, and then lay your head on your pillow at night in peace, and sleep in Jesus."

All the children began their Christian work early in life. Bramwell was but twelve when he led his first meeting at Bethnal Green. His mother wrote him: "If you begin with the children, you will gain self-possession, which is all that is necessary in your case to make speaking easy. You see, you can talk to three or four hundred in the same time, and nearly as easily, as you can talk to one, and always with more effect in the form of an address." Catherine was about the same age when she started her children's meetings. At first Mrs. Booth was scarcely willing that her little daughter, then fourteen, should speak on the street corners to a rough crowd in the East End of London; but Bramwell said, "Mamma dear, you will have to settle this question with God; for Katie is as surely called and inspired by him for this particular work as yourself."

Recognizing her talents, several friends urged Mrs. Booth to give Catherine a superior education. The principal of a lady's college offered to receive and educate her gratuitously.

Mrs. Booth went to the school; but the fashionable dress of the pupils and their worldliness made her afraid to place her daughter there. Catherine longed for the education, but submitted to the will of her mother, which was always law to the children.

Mrs. Booth wrote her: "I never loved you so deeply; not when you were my first baby girl, as pure and beautiful as a snowdrop; but oh! I do so want you and all my children to live supremely for God. I do so deeply deplore my own failure, compared with what my life might have been, that I feel as though I could die to save any of you from making a mistake. . . . You must not think we do not rightly value education, or that we are indifferent on the subject. We have denied ourselves the common necessaries of life to give you the best in our power. . . . But we make God and righteousness *first*, and education second."

Catherine devoted all the time possible to books. In French she became especially proficient, which proved invaluable to her in later work. Before she was seventeen she had held evangelistic meetings lasting three weeks or a month in many of the largest cities of England. Her brother Bramwell, two years older than herself, always accompanied her.

He relates an instance of her great power over her audiences. At a large theatre where their meetings were in progress, one Sunday evening a crowd of the lowest and roughest people forced their way past the doorkeepers into the gallery, where they sat with hats on, smoking, laughing, and indulging in coarse jests, all through the opening exercises.

When Catherine arose and stood before the little table, she began to sing, —

"The rocks and the mountains will all flee away,
And you will need a hiding-place that day."

At once there was perfect quiet in the turbulent house. Hats were removed, and for forty minutes it seemed as though no one moved. Her text was, "Let me die the death of the righteous, and let my last end be like his."

As she closed, she asked for volunteers to begin a new life. "I'll make one," said a big man, rising in the gallery, scarcely able to speak for sobbing. Thirty others rose also, and dated their reformation from that hour. Much of this time Catherine was suffering from threatened curvature of the spine; but she finally recovered. Like her mother, however, she seemed to put all physical obstacles under her feet, and go forward to victory.

From Stockton-on-Tees, Mrs. Booth wrote of Catherine: "I was astonished at the advance she had made. . . . It was sweet, tender, forcible, and divine. I could only adore and weep. She looked like an angel, and the people were melted and spell-bound, like children. . . . She plays the harmonium out-of-doors at noon every day, and crowds stand round to hear her sing, and many a rough son of toil pays her the tribute of his tears. . . . Pray that she may be deaf alike to the voice of flattery and of condemnation."

To one of her sons she wrote: "If I know my own heart, I would rather that you should work for the salvation of souls, . . . if you only get bread and cheese all your life, than that you should fill any other capacity with ten thousand pounds per year. *I* believe in eternal distinction. 'They that turn many to righteousness shall shine as the stars, for ever and ever.' . . . This is what the world wants, — men of one idea; that of getting people saved. There are plenty of men of one idea, — *gold*-getting."

Sickness had again forced its way into their home,

Mrs. Booth had been ill for several weeks from heart trouble; and now Bramwell, just twenty, was breaking down from heart and throat affection. A friend invited him to Scotland, where he eventually recovered.

While there, his mother, who was a great admirer of the works of the Rev. Charles G. Finney, the American evangelist, sent him a large volume of Finney's "Theological Lectures." His "Autobiography" and "Revival Lectures" seem to have been household words in the Booth home.

The husband now came very near to death's door from overwork. Mrs. Booth wrote a friend, "My soul seems dumb before the Lord. A horror of great darkness comes over me at times. But in the midst of it all, I believe he will do all things well. . . . My beloved says I am to tell you he is in the furnace, but has perfect peace." From constant watching Mrs. Booth became prostrated, and together they were removed to Tunbridge Wells for change of air. Scarcely were they settled when they heard the distressing news that their daughter Lucy, eight years of age, had small-pox. The stricken parents returned as soon as possible, sent the other children into the country, and cared for the little sufferer.

In January, 1877, the evangelistic work of Mr. and Mrs. Booth, which had resulted in the establishment of many "Christian Missions," took a new name and some new methods. Among the converts was Elijah Cadman, "a chimney-sweep by profession," says Commander Booth-Tucker, in his life of Mrs. Booth; "a pugilist for recreation, a good customer at the public-house, a desperate handful for the police, a ringleader in every sort of mischief. . . . His conversion fell like a thunder-clap upon his old associates. It was as complete as it was sudden. . . . He loved his Bible so passionately that he carried it with him wherever he went by day, and slept with it under his pillow by night, although he was so unlettered that he could not tell whether he was holding it right side up or wrong! But he soon learned to read, on purpose to be able to master its contents."

When appointed to take charge, later, of a mission, he called it in his circular a "Hallelujah Army." Mr. Booth, in preparing his annual Christmas appeal, asked, "What is the Christian Mission?"—"A Volunteer Army," was the answer written in his circular. Mr. Booth, leaning over the shoulder of his secretary, crossed out the word Volunteer, and wrote Salvation; and in this way the "Salvation Army" took its name.

The Rev. William Booth, the general superintendent, became general of the army, others captains and majors, and the stations received the name of "corps." A flag was soon adopted, the blue border typifying holiness, the scarlet ground the blood of Christ, the yellow star in the centre the baptism of the Holy Spirit, and "Blood and Fire," the motto across the star, the blood of the Saviour and the fire of the Holy Ghost. A uniform was soon chosen for the men, and a plain garb for the women, designed by Mrs. Booth.

These novel methods caused the crowds to become greater than ever when the procession of Salvationists appeared on the street. There was opposition even in their own ranks, and fears that the work would be crippled. Mrs. Booth wrote to a friend, "The rich and respectable are giving us up on every hand, as they did our Master when he got nearer the vulgar cross; but we hear him saying, 'I will show them greater things than these.' And, money or no money, we must go on."

The Salvation Army now began to receive its baptism of fire. The press jeered, and the pulpit condemned; the mob, encouraged by such high authority, stoned and shot at and cursed men and women whose only offence was singing gospel hymns while clad in the garb of soldiers.

Sir Arthur Blackwood, distinguished in the Crimea, said at one of the army meetings, speaking of a convert who, when he rose to speak, pulled off his coat, "Of course he was like a workman. Why is it more strange than that a man should put a surplice on? And if a man tucks up his shirt-sleeves to do some hot work, why is it more thought of than the lawn sleeves that our good bishops are accustomed to wear? I don't find fault with the one. It is in harmony with our education and ways. But do not let us find fault with the other. . . . Time is too short for us to be quibbling and quarrelling about *methods* of warfare."

Magistrates imprisoned them for obstructing the streets and disturbing the peace. In Lancashire a mob trampled on one of the leaders, tore her bonnet from her head and her shoes from her feet; but marching on in her stockings, with her hair streaming down her back, she took her place on the platform as though nothing had happened. The hall was packed to suffocation, and many were converted that night.

"Take no notice of them! March straight on!" were the words which General Booth always addressed to his soldiers. In rain and sleet, in heat and cold, reviled, kicked, killed even, those who remained obeyed orders and marched on, always returning good for evil.

If John Wesley and the early Methodists had not received the same treatment, if Christianity itself had had no dens of lions, and catacombs in which to hide away in the early days, if history were not replete with illustrations of those who have suffered for opinions' sake, then it would be almost impossible to believe that the Salvation Army could be so treated, especially so in the nineteenth century.

With all this reviling, the worst and the poorest were reached as they had never been before. General Booth had once replied, when asked where he would get his helpers, "From the public-houses and gin-palaces." A "Drunkard's Brigade" was organized in almost every corps; and thousands gave up the drink habit, and prevailed upon their comrades to join the ranks. Rough men lived the religion they professed, and died happy. "Tell them all's well," were the words of an old sailor in one of his last messages to his comrades. "John Smith's packed up and ready to go." And as he waited for the last summons, he said, "Let me go! I be a child of God! Let me go! Bless ye! *I be happy!*"

A ringleader in sin came to one of the meetings with her comrades, to make sport. Her father, when she was a child, had attempted while in a drunken rage to kill her mother. The girl sprang at him, seized his knife, and ran. Falling upon the blade, she put out an eye. This sad experience did not deter her from evil. She was to make a signal on this night at the meeting to her comrades to begin the disturbance. The signal was never given. She was broken in heart over her sins, lived two years a consistent life in the factory where she worked, and then entered the Woman's Training Home, and became a most successful worker in the army.

One of the first to be imprisoned was Ballington Booth, "for upholding," as he says, "my Master's name to the perishing multitudes in the streets of Manchester. I was placed with the common felons, lived on a few ounces of bread and a little *skilly*, scrubbed my cell, and slept on a plank. But in all my life I never felt more blessed and encouraged than whilst there!"

At Basingstroke, where the mayor was a brewer, a drunken mob treated most cruelly two girl-officers and several in the procession. In one year, 1881, six hundred and sixty-nine persons in the army "were knocked down or otherwise brutally assaulted;" of these two hundred and fifty-one were women. The complaints that the army obstructed the highway were most often made by saloon-keepers, whose business was injured through decrease of patronage.

Several wealthy persons withdrew their support from General Booth and his wife. She wrote to a friend that she would be willing to live in a whitewashed cottage, and eat potatoes and cabbage, "and we have come almost to that!" She began to write to a person who was abundantly able to help; but, heartsick and worn, threw down the pen, and gave way to grief. Human nature could not always bear up under the heavy load of care and privation. Their necessities were relieved later when a friend invested five thousand pounds in trust for Mrs. Booth and her family. The profits from their hymn-books, and from all their periodicals, have gone into the army fund.

The Salvation Army grew beyond all expectation, certainly beyond the expectation of all save that wonderful woman of faith, Mrs. Booth. She wrote: "We see now that God has been shaping it to become a great power in the country, perhaps *in the world!*"

In 1879 General Booth arranged for a conference, or "Council of War," at Newcastle. Mrs. Booth wrote her daughter Emma to come and see the great meetings and help. This girl of nineteen, naturally shy, had already shown herself a power in the work. "Try and get the children," writes the careful mother, "into a good state of soul before you leave them. The mayor was at the meeting the other night. When shaking hands with me, he said, ' This is a most wonderful movement!' . . .

"Hundreds of the greatest roughs have been converted. And all through the instrumentality of six young women, — humble, simple souls, full of love and zeal. Truly, God hath chosen the weak things! Oh, my dear child, it makes me long to see you *all* at it in some way or other! Tell Eva and Lucy to get on and to get ready, but, above all, to keep their souls right. It is not to the clever or talented or educated that these things are given, but to the *whole-hearted* and *spiritual.*"

On Saturday, May 17, Mrs. Booth presented flags to nine of the newly formed corps, in the presence of about four thousand persons. Her address, as usual, was simple yet eloquent. On the next day, Sunday, some twenty thousand people gathered in the open air for service; and in the evening twelve thousand were crowded into the various buildings in which the meetings were held. The council closed Monday with an all night of prayer.

During this year, 1879, Mrs. Booth addressed large gatherings in fifty-nine towns. She was then fifty years of age, in the full vigor of her able mind and all-embracing sympathy. Besides laboring among the very poor and the outcasts, she spoke at several West End meetings to the rich and the aristocratic, explaining and defending the Salvation Army. Mr. T. A. Denny, one of London's wealthy givers, helped to arrange these meetings. He wrote the general: "Your blessed wife will affect the West of London, and do more good to the cause than any other machinery that I know of. God is with her, of a truth!"

Lords and ladies and princes gathered to hear her. She wrote one of her sons, "Pray for me! You may, perhaps, be wanted to stand amongst princes to do battle for the Lord." One lady in high circles said, "We never heard this sort of gospel before." Clergymen of all denominations thanked her for coming. The Rev. Dr. Dale of Birmingham, one of the grand men of England, was hearty in his commendation. Invitations to hold drawing-room meetings poured in upon her, fourfold more than she could accept.

Sometimes she grew despondent, and said, "If I dared to give up working I should do so a hundred times over, but I *dare not*. . . . The obtuseness, indifference, and heartlessness of professed Christians is the greatest trial of my life." After this she preached to crowded houses in Edinburgh, Glasgow, and other cities in Scotland.

In 1880 the Salvation Army work was carried over

the sea. Nearly eight years before, in 1872, James Jermy, from England, had started a Christian mission in Cleveland, Ohio. "Canada and America," he wrote, "are full of backsliders. . . . When I got here [Cleveland], I found thousands going the way of death." The mission was successful, but was given up when Jermy returned to England.

In 1879 the foreman of a silk factory, Amos Shirley, from England, started the work in Philadelphia, in an abandoned chair-factory, which "savored more of a stable than a place of worship." He wrote to General Booth for help; and George S. Railton, with a party of seven "Hallelujah Lasses," sailed Jan. 14, 1880, for America. Mrs. Booth was deeply interested in this work across the ocean, believing great things would come of it. She sent two flags, one to the first New York corps, the other to the first Philadelphia.

"To some people," said Mrs. Booth, addressing the young women, "you may appear insignificant; but so do we all. So did those women who stood grouped round the cross of Christ to the proud Pharisees who walked mocking past. But their names have been handed down to us, while those of the Pharisees have been forgotten."

Great crowds watched them depart from their native soil, to meet in the New World the same buffetings and jeerings as in the Old. Who would have believed then that a dozen years later Boston's great Music Hall would be packed with its best people, not out of curiosity, but to listen in sympathetic earnestness to Mrs. Booth's son Ballington, and his able and lovely wife.

In January, 1881, another little company sailed for

Australia, without money or friends, to carry the gospel to the poor twelve thousand miles away. Ten years afterwards General Booth spoke in a magnificent hall in Australia to five thousand people, hundreds of them eager to begin a Christian life. He was accorded such a welcome as could never be forgotten. The Wesleyan ministers gathered round him, and they prayed and wept together. How different from the old days when they would not permit him to be an evangelist! The Y. M. C. A. building in Melbourne has just been purchased for ninety-five thousand dollars, for the army headquarters.

Scarcely had delegations gone to America and Australia, before Mrs. Booth's daughter Catherine, who was speaking to crowded houses in England, was asked to go to France. "It seemed as though the Lord was asking of me more than I could perform," said Mrs. Booth; but the daughter, twenty-three years of age, and a little band of girl-warriors, started for the Continent.

The meetings were first held in an upper room at the end of an alley, in the communistic quarter of Paris. A rough crowd gathered, and night after night Catherine spoke, with little effect apparently. A Christian Frenchman said in kindness, "You had better go home to your mother. The Salvation Army cannot possibly succeed here." — "If I cannot save France, I can die for it," was the reply of the consecrated girl.

The way to their hearts was opened through suffering. Truly said Mrs. Booth, the mother, "The whole work of saving men is a *work of suffering* from the beginning to the end." Catherine had attempted to hold meetings also in Switzerland. There were no processions in the streets or brass bands, but the mob broke open and pillaged the places of meeting, and the authorities ordered the halls closed. When Catherine held a service in the woods, she was sought out, and hurried away to Neuchâtel prison, because, like John Bunyan, she "was about her Master's business, and must rather obey the Lord's voice than that of man."

The sorrowing mother wrote her, " Oh, if it were only I who could go to prison (poorly as I am)! I feel I could bear it better than you. . . . I am almost worn out, but you have life before you, and who knows how much is involved to this poor lost world ?"

Before this letter was received, Catherine had written her from prison, " All my anxiety yesterday was about *you*. As to the work and myself, all is well. I have a mattress, a blanket, and a shawl. The food is very decent, and the bread is not hard. . . . This is all right. God is in it." Catherine and her assistants were acquitted at the trial, but as they left the court they were kicked and stoned by the mob.

On their return from prison to Paris, the crowds were eager to see them, and thus the way was opened to address both high and low. A fashionable ballroom was hired in the Boulevard des Capucines, where ladies and gentlemen came in evening dress to hear a little company of women preach salvation.

Herbert, Catherine's brother, came over to aid her, and a young Quaker minister, an excellent French and German scholar, Arthur Clibborn. After helping Catherine for six years in the work, during which time he was often stoned and imprisoned, he married her, and took the Booth name, Arthur Booth-Clibborn. They have four children, Evangeline, Victoria, Samuel, and Augustine, whose pretty baby face is in the *Conqueror* for January, 1895.

A most valuable and brave helper in the French work was Miss Florence Soper, the daughter of a physician in Wales. While receiving her education in London, she attended Mrs. Booth's West End meetings, and gave up a life of luxury to join the ranks of the Salvation Army. She was married to Mr. Bramwell Booth in 1882.

Notwithstanding the buffetings in France and Switzerland, the work grew to such an extent that in one year three hundred thousand meetings were held in the two countries, and nearly eight hundred thousand copies of the *War Cry* were sold.

In May, 1880, a training-home for women was opened in London, with Mrs. Booth's second daughter, Emma, in charge, and later in the year a similar one for men, under her son Ballington. The cadets, as they were called, were taught history, geography, and the like, with more time given to the Bible and the especial work to which they would probably devote their lives. The usual term of instruction was from four to six months, with the practical work of going among the depraved or destitute daily.

In 1881, at Easter, the first Salvation Army meeting was held at Exeter Hall, with a crowded audience. Already the army was gaining a strong position in London. They had bought a theatre and a public-house for £16,000, an orphanage which had cost originally £60,000, for £15,000, and rented a large rink for £1,000 a year.

The next year, 1882, when a council of war was held

at Sheffield, the procession of Salvationists was attacked by a mob; mud, clubs, and stones were thrown; some were made unconscious by the blows, their faces gashed, and clothing torn. General Booth and his wife, the former standing in a carriage giving orders to his men, escaped injury as by a miracle. John Bright wrote Mrs. Booth a sympathetic letter, saying, "The people who mob you would doubtless have mobbed the apostles. Your faith and patience will prevail."

Others high in authority appreciated their work. The Queen sent Mrs. Booth a message, that "she learns with much satisfaction that you have, with the other members of your society, been successful in your efforts to win many thousands to the ways of temperance, virtue, and religion."

Canon Farrar spoke of Mrs. Booth as "the remarkable lady whose quiet yet burning zeal, masculine understanding, feminine tenderness, and perfect faith, have rendered such invaluable service to the great work of his [General Booth's] life." Father Ignatius said, "What a glorious woman! What 'a mother of giants in Israel'! What an astounding *fact* is the Salvation Army! What a shame and what a glory to the churches!" Cardinal Manning was one of the earliest to rejoice in the work.

Year after year Mrs. Booth continued her labors, preaching at Cambridge, Rugby, Portsmouth, Leamington, — indeed, all over England, and in France also. In 1886 General Booth visited Canada and the United States, holding two hundred meetings during his three months' absence; but Mrs. Booth was too frail to accompany him. All her life she had suffered from ill-health. " It seems to have been my special lot to suffer," she said in her last illness. " I can scarcely remember a day in my life which has been free from some kind of pain or other."

At the great International Council held in 1886 in London, four of its largest halls were packed with people for five days. At the next anniversary meeting in 1887, at the Alexandra Palace, fifty thousand passed the turnstiles. What an amazing change from the tent in the Quaker burying-ground in 1865!

During this year, 1886, Mrs. Booth's second son, Ballington, was married to Maud Charlesworth, the daughter of the Rev. Samuel Charlesworth. Finely educated, extremely pretty, and most winsome in voice and manner, she had left a home of comfort to accept the privation and hardship of army work in France with Catherine, and in Sweden and England. At Upsala she spoke to nearly two thousand students of the University, none others being admitted to the barracks. It was said that they were unreachable by the church; but they came willingly to hear Miss Charlesworth, and many were greatly blessed by coming. Soon after her marriage, Commander and Mrs. Ballington Booth were appointed to take charge of the work in the United States, and they have been most successful.

Two years later, in 1888, Mrs. Booth's second daughter, Emma, was married to Frederik de L. Tucker, and went to India with her husband, who had already introduced the work into that far-off land. Mrs. Booth spoke tenderly at the wedding service. " When this marriage came before me, and I saw at a glance what it involved . . . I staggered. Then I remembered : 'But she is not yours; you gave her at her birth, and you have given her ever since. . . . Are you going to draw back?' I looked up to heaven, and said, 'No, Lord; she is thine, whatever it may cost; thou shalt have her for this particular service if thou dost want her."

Mr. Tucker was a young judge in the Indian civil service, receiving £1000 a year, but resigned to give his life to Christian work. In less than ten years, through his efforts and other Salvationists, ten thousand people in India professed conversion, nine out of every ten being natives.

The year of Emma's marriage Mrs. Booth was warned, by a small tumor of the cancerous type in the breast, that her days were numbered. When told by her physician that she had only a few months to live, she said her first thought was that "she should not be at her husband's bedside when his last hour came." General Booth was speechless. He says, "I felt as if the whole world were coming to a standstill. . . . She talked like a heroine, like an angel to me. . . . It seemed as though a hand were laid upon my very heart-strings. I could only kneel with her and try to pray."

To her children, who had idolized the strong yet tender woman, the news was crushing. "We look at one another through our tears, and cannot speak," wrote Emma from Reading. "My heart stood still," said Bramwell, when he heard the sad tidings. "She had been so much more than a mother, — had been so much of a leader, adviser, and counsellor, — that it seemed impossible to spare her." He had written her years before: "You do not know how I love and look up to you more and more every day I live."

She spoke yet a few times more with her fast-failing strength. Her last address was for Dr. Parker in the City Temple, June 21, 1888. She spoke for more than an hour with all the old-time persuasion, fervor, and eloquence. When she had concluded she was so exhausted that she could not be removed from the pulpit for nearly an hour.

"When we come to face eternity," she said, "and look back upon the past, what will be our regret? That we have done so much? Oh, no! That we have done so little . . . that we have not let God and eternity be the all-absorbing theme of our lives; that we have wasted any energy, time, or strength on less important things."

Her last message to the fifty thousand gathered at the anniversary at the Crystal Palace was, "Make the people good; inspire them with the Spirit of Jesus Christ. Love one another; help your comrades in dark hours. I am dying under the army flag; it is yours to live and fight under. God is my salvation and refuge in the storm."

In 1889 Mrs. Booth was removed to Clacton-on-Sea, about seventy miles east of London, near the mouth of the Thames, to a Home of Rest which had been provided for the staff officers of the army. Here General Booth, by the bedside of his suffering wife, and with her prayerful and constant co-operation in thought and suggestion, wrote that soul-stirring book, "In Darkest England, and the Way Out." Not till the last chapters had been sent to the press did the summons come to depart.

General Booth's book aroused the thinking people of two hemispheres. He showed that three millions, or one-tenth of the whole population of great Britain, exclusive of Ireland, are pauperized and degraded.

Mrs. Booth had often said, "The day is coming when these masses will require to be dealt with. Will it not be better to face them with the gospel than the sword? Let us beware lest we have a repetition of the Revolution scenes they had in France. What can you do with them? You can leave them alone, as you have left them alone. You may leave them to the 'penny dreadful' and the *Police Gazette* for their Bible, and the public-house for their sanctuary. But surely there is a better way!"

About two of these three millions, "or the submerged tenth," are homeless and starving. While much of this poverty comes through drink, much of it also comes from inability to get work.

The Rev. Josiah Strong, in his book "The New Era," writes: "It would appear from Mr. Charles Booth's investigations in East London that fifty-five per cent of the very poor, and fully sixty-eight per cent of the other poor, are not so through any fault of their own, but because they lack employment. . . . It is estimated that the suffering of fifty-three per cent of the needy in New York is for lack of work."

General Booth knew the uselessness of asking men to be saved when they were starving. He believed there were noble persons who would give money if it could be rightly used. The United Kingdom already paid about ten million pounds for poor law and charitable relief. He asked for one-tenth of this, one million pounds, or five million dollars for his scheme, to remedy some of this destitution and despair. He could begin the work with one hundred thousand pounds.

He proposed three colonies, — the City Colony, the Farm Colony, and the Over-Sea Colony. The City Colony should supply temporary needs, with its cheap food depots, shelters, and rescue homes. The Farm Colony, with hundreds of acres of land, should provide a self-supporting home, and the surplus population find over the seas in New South Wales, in South Africa, or elsewhere, a place to begin life anew.

The one hundred thousand pounds was soon subscribed. In the Cheap Food Depots, food was given at nearly cost price: soup one cent a basin, bread and coffee one cent, potatoes one cent, rice one cent. In one year nearly three million meals were supplied by the Food Depots: 100,000 breakfasts at a farthing, or half a cent each, to poor children; one cent meals to 1,200,000 persons.

At the Shelters, some for men and some for women, a clean bed, and warm room with coffee and bread for supper and breakfast, was given for eight cents, which the recipients could pay for in work, if they were able to work. Nearly 400,000 lodgings were provided the first year in these Christian Shelters, where there was an army meeting held each night, the girls from the Training Homes coming to sing.

The *Conqueror* for January, 1895, a magazine published by the Salvation Army, says: "Since the launching of the Darkest England scheme at St. James's Hall, London, in 1891, over 11,500,000 meals have been sold to the poorest of the people, and more than 3,500,000 homeless men and women have been sheltered; 9,853 men have been received into the workshops."

At the Industrial Factory at Whitechapel, men out of

employment found work for eight hours a day, with board and small wages, till better places were obtained. Some made mats, others benches for the Army, others cut fire-wood, etc. Nothing was sold below market prices.

Many such factories have already been started for making matches, mattresses, binding books, knitting, carpentry, painting, laundry-work, teaching boys trades, and the like. Work can be taken home by needy women and children. Labor Bureaus have also been most useful. Farm Colonies were soon in operation in England, India, Australia, South Africa, Ceylon, and elsewhere. These farms will be used to train the people in agriculture; food be produced for the Cheap Food Depots, bees be kept, houses built, with plenty of work for the dwellers. Farms of from three to five acres, with a cottage, a cow, tools, and seed, are to be let permanently for an annual rent, or land-tax.

For the Farm Colony at Hadleigh-on-Thames fifteen hundred acres of land were purchased. Two hundred of these acres are used for growing fruit and vegetables. There are twenty-seven dwelling-houses and cottages on this property; seven dormitories accommodating three hundred and fifty men, a bakery, a store, a reading room, and an Army hall for meetings. Of the twelve hundred and seventy-eight colonists up to June, 1894, two hundred and seven were sent to situations obtained for them, five hundred and ten after satisfactory conduct left with situations in view, and forty-eight emigrated or enlisted in the Royal Army. About one-fourth were discharged. The remaining have earned and received, besides their board, over fifteen thousand dollars.

General Booth proposes to utilize the waste of London; to gather up the old boots and shoes and make them over; the useless tins to be made into toys for children — the toys of France are made largely from sardine tins; food from the houses of the wealthy to be used for men and women and animals; bones for enriching the soil; paper and rags for a paper-mill — the Salvation Army uses thirty tons of paper per week; and bottles cleansed and used anew. The Over-Sea Colonies have not yet been attempted.

The work done by the Salvation Army is marvellous, and yet perhaps only in its beginning. There are about four thousand corps or societies, with about twelve thousand officers in forty-two countries and colonies, speaking nearly as many different languages. Over two million meetings are held annually, with nearly three million visits from house to house. In the United States seventeen million persons attend meetings at the plain Salvation Army halls each year.

Its army papers, such as the *War Cry* have a circulation of over forty-three millions yearly. The army owns over four million dollars worth of property, and has an annual income from all sources, of about the same amount.

Its work in the slums, both in Europe and in the United States, deserves all praise. The slum sisters are everywhere honored for their self-sacrificing work. They live among the depraved, visiting the sick, the outcasts, and the dying, scrubbing filthy houses, and preaching in saloons and hovels a gospel which Mrs. Booth so nobly preached before them. In some of the tenement houses in New York City, Mrs. Ballington

Booth found seven families in one room! There are four slum posts in New York, two in Boston, two in Philadelphia, and two in Chicago.

The army does great good in its Prison Gate Homes, taking prisoners when discharged, who have neither home nor work, and caring for them till work is found, or until somebody is willing to trust them.

General Booth's suggestion of a poor man's bank, where philanthropists with capital loan small sums on security with a fair rate of interest, has happily been followed in some cities. It is well known that most pawn-brokers charge exorbitantly, and make wrecks of many a poor, deserving family. Homes of rest, and places of entertainment for the poor, with parks, playgrounds, music, and boats, without the usual evil accompaniments, are included in the general's scheme.

Dr. Albert Shaw, of the *Review of Reviews* says: "One may criticise the Salvation Army from every point of view; but when he has said all that can be said, it remains true that there exists to-day no other organization that can compare with it for economical and efficient work among the poor of the English-speaking cities."

Mrs. Booth helped to plan all this with her husband, and though she did not live to see the results, she saw the "Light coming over the waters!" Through long months she waited and suffered. "Pray that the Lord may speedily finish his work and take me home," was her oft-repeated request to those who stood beside her.

By her wish, the marriage of her son Herbert took place at this time, that she might witness it before death. The bride was Miss Coriline Schoch of Holland, daughter of an officer in the Dutch Army, who, with his family, had joined heartily in the Salvation Army work.

All through the weary days of pain, the noble woman who had preached trust and hope to others, trusted and found joy in believing. "Have faith, faith, mighty faith!" she said to those who stood about her dying bed. "I am going into the dark valley *believing*. . . . I am ashamed of the little I have achieved, and if I had only had more faith I might have achieved *so much!* . . . I trust Him. He will carry me through. Though my heart and my flesh fail — and mine is *such* a heart! Oh!" she said, realizing how hard it was to part with those we love, "it seems as if my heart had got its roots all round the world, clutching on to one and to another, and as if it will not let them go!"

To the army she sent this message: "The waters are rising, but so am I. I am not going under, but over. Don't be concerned about your dying; only go on living well, and the dying will be all right. . . . The only consolation for a Salvationist on his dying bed is to feel he has been a soul-winner. . . . Redeem the time, for we can do but little at our best." To her son Herbert, she said, "Let the coffin be plain — such as will be in keeping with the life I have lived."

On the night of Friday, Oct. 3, 1890, it was evident that the suffering was almost over. With trembling voices her children knelt about the bed singing, —

"We shall walk through the valley of the shadow of death!
　We shall walk through the valley in peace!
　For Jesus himself will be our Leader, —
　We shall walk through the valley in peace!"

Each time the word "peace" was reached, she raised her hand, though unable to join them.

They sang again, —

> "We are waiting by the river,
> We are watching by the shore;
> Only waiting for the angels,
> Soon they'll come to bear us o'er."

"Rock of Ages," and "Jesus, Lover of my Soul," were sung, and then she said brokenly, "Go — on!" Almost the last words were, "Lord — let the end be easy — for Emma's sake."

Saturday afternoon came, and the sun was sinking in a cloudless sky, after a severe storm the previous night. With illumined face she seemed to have a vision. "I see," she whispered, but could say no more. Each one present kissed her forehead, and holding the hand of her husband, with one deep sigh she passed into "the valley of the shadow of death."

In a plain coffin of oak, covered by the army flag under which she died, her body was carried to Clapton Congress Hall, London, where she had so often spoken to thousands. On the coffin-lid were her well-worn Bible, her bonnet, and her cloak.

All around were touching mementoes, especially from the poor; little bunches of flowers; a quaint wreath of cotton rosettes with "Victory" in tinsel letters; a wreath from a servant-girl "in memory of Mrs. Booth's goodness to her sister."

For five days, from early morning till ten o'clock at night, thousands upon thousands passed by that glass-covered coffin. Some were rich, some ragged; ministers and lawyers; laborers and outcasts. "She lived for the likes o' me!" sobbed one poor girl with dishevelled hair and torn hat.

An old woman, who stood so long that she was gently urged to move on, said, "No, no! Let others move on! I've a right to stop. I've come sixty miles to see her again. She was the means of saving my two sons."

On October 13, the body of Mrs. Booth was removed to the Olympia Skating Rink, with a capacity of twelve thousand persons, for the funeral services. Thirty-six thousand persons passed the turn-stiles, and then it became necessary to shut out the thousands who could find no room to stand.

At six o'clock in the afternoon the service began with the hymn, —

> " When I survey the wondrous cross
> On which the Prince of glory died."

Later in the exercises the bereaved family sang one of their mother's favorite hymns : —

> "We shall walk through the valley of the shadow of death!"

The day following, the body was borne to Abney Park Cemetery, through four miles of crowded human beings. Business for the time was almost suspended. England has rarely witnessed such a scene.

The authorities had limited the admission to the cemetery to ten thousand, and these had been waiting there for some hours for the coming of the procession. After "Rock of Ages" had been sung, several of Mrs. Booth's children spoke beside the open grave; and then her husband, as the twilight came on, made a touching and beautiful address to the assembled thousands. He spoke of her "who for forty years had stood by his side in the battle's front, ever willing to interpose herself between him and the enemy, and ever the strongest when the battle was fiercest.

"There has been taken away from me the delight of my eyes," he said, "the inspiration of my soul, and we are about to lay all that remains of her in the grave. I have been looking right at the bottom of it here, and calculating how soon they may bring and lay me alongside of her, and my cry to God has been that every remaining hour of my life may make me readier to come and join her in death, to go and embrace her in life in the Eternal City!"

As Charles Wesley said, "God buries his workmen, but he carries on his work." Beside Mrs. Booth's grave the Salvation Army pledged "to devote themselves to the great end of saving souls," and they are keeping their pledge.

LUCY STONE.

WHEN Lucy Stone died at Dorchester, Mass., Oct. 18, 1893, the press of the whole country spoke in her praise. The *Boston Herald* said, "She goes to her grave honored and beloved and mourned by the American people." The *Boston Daily Advertiser:* "Her death is an irreparable loss."

The New York *Independent:* "The death of Lucy Stone removes one of the world's great benefactors. . . . She dies full of honor, paid to one of the most gracious of womanly women that ever lived."

The Boston *Congregationalist:* "Small in stature, dainty in dress, with a voice of singular sweetness, sympathetic in manner, all who came in contact with her admitted the charm of her personality. . . . Mrs. Stone's public life was closely identified with the two interests of securing equal rights for negroes and women. . . . The essential womanliness of her nature never became the least impaired or obscured by being constantly before the world as the champion of these two causes. She died, preserving to the end the same serenity of soul and heroic patience in suffering which endeared her while living to so many hearts.

The *New York Sun* said: "As a pioneer in the movement for the legal and political elevation of women, she

LUCY STONE.

had lived through ridicule, obloquy, and even persecution, until at last she was honored and reverenced as the heroine of a great, beneficent, and actually accomplished revolution. Lucy Stone's name must be enrolled on the list of illustrious Americans." *Harper's Bazaar* added its testimony to a long and able list of journals: "Her life was full of earnestness, goodness, and blessedness, and the world is better that she lived."

Lucy Stone's life will always be an inspiration to every man or woman who is struggling for a principle; to every youth, who, poor and unaided, is working for an education; to every boy or girl who learns, through her history, the secret of that persistent, cheerful, indomitable courage and energy which bring success.

Lucy Stone was born in the town of West Brookfield, Mass., Aug. 13, 1818. Her father, Francis Stone, a farmer, as strong in character as the rocks he lived among, was, says Mr. Blackwell, the husband of Lucy Stone, "well-intentioned and honest, a 'good provider,' who always kept his family well supplied with food, clothing, fuel, and such advantages as he thought appropriate. Like most New England farmers on rocky farms, a hundred years ago, he was necessarily a hard worker and a close economist. He expected his wife and children to be the same."

The mother of Lucy Stone, Hannah Matthews, was a gentle and beautiful woman, greatly beloved by her neighbors, and perhaps not more ruled over by her husband than other wives of the place. Mr. Stone was, indeed, better than some; for when at his marriage his wife received twenty dollars from her father's estate, instead of keeping it as his own, as the common law allowed him to do, he bought her a set of silver spoons and a side-saddle. In these days, when a wife has a right to her own property, a gift to her bought with her money would not seem so generous.

Mrs. Stone worked hard, as was necessary for the mother of nine children. When her eighth child, Lucy, was born — she had milked eight cows the night before the birth of her child — she said, "Oh, dear! I am sorry it is a girl. A woman's life is so hard!"

Lucy's childhood was spent in useful work in the house and on the farm. As soon as she could count, she was taught to drop pumpkin-seeds in the hills, and corn in the furrows. She drove the cows in the morning starlight, before the sun was up, and her little bare feet often ached with the cold. She learned how to make butter and soap, to be a good cook, and seemed to be preparing herself for a helper of some industrious and saving farmer.

During these early years the girl was thinking of matters seemingly beyond her age. Why was her sweet mother obliged to yield, like the children, to the stern will of the father? Why, after all the hard years of united labor, was the money all his? Why did she, who lived a devoted Christian life, never take part in the church services, as he did? Why were there no opportunities for girls to earn a living like their brothers? Why did men go to college, while women were offered only the simplest rudiments of an education?

Feeling that the laws of the country were wrong on such matters, she determined to ascertain from the Bible that her mother loved, whether that book did not favor equality for all. Coming upon some of St. Paul's words to the local churches of that day, she was so discouraged that she " wanted to die." Soon, however, she had another desire — to go to college, study Greek and Hebrew, and learn for herself whether the true spirit had been translated from the original text.

Years afterwards, when she had become an excellent student in those two languages, and her love and reverence for the Bible had increased with her study of it, she found to her comfort and joy that Paul himself wrote to the Galatians (iii. 28), "There is neither bond nor free, there is neither male nor female; for ye are all one in Christ Jesus."

She learned also from reading history how women like Hypatia taught philosophy in the schools of ancient Egypt; how Aspasia, herself an orator, had made, according to Plato, "many good orators, and one eminent over all the Greeks, Pericles;" how Hortensia argued in the Roman forum; how Laura Caterina Bassi held the chair of physics for twenty-eight years at the University of Bologna, after taking her degree in 1732; and Maria Agnesi, born at Milan in 1718, the chair of mathematics.

"As early as the thirteenth century," says Dr. H. Carrington Bolton, in the *Journal of Science* for February, 1881, on the "Early Practice of Medicine for Women," "two women were numbered among the eminent professors of the University of Bologna, Accorsa Accorso and Bettisia Gozzadini: the former held the chair of philosophy, the latter that of jurisprudence.

"The rival university of Padua, founded in 1228, had also its female representatives. Of these the most distinguished was Elena Lucrezia Cornaro. . . . She was familiar with French, Spanish, Latin, Greek, and Hebrew, besides her native Italian, and had some acquaintance with Arabic. While endowed by nature with poetical and unusual talents, she possessed at the same time great perseverance and capacity for serious studies, and discoursed eloquently on abstruse topics in philosophy, mathematics, astronomy, and theology. At the age of thirty-two the University of Padua conferred upon her the degree of Doctor of Philosophy." Bishop Dupanloup's " Studious Women " also gives a goodly list of noted scholars.

Lucy Stone became all the more eager for an education. Her two elder brothers, with that love of learning which is characteristic of the New England home, were assisted by the father to go to college. Then Lucy asked to be helped also. Mr. Stone was astonished. He said to his wife, " Is the child crazy ? "

To Lucy he said, with dignity and the voice of one accustomed to control, " Your mother only learned to read, write, and cipher; if that was enough for her, it should be enough for you." But it was not enough, and the girl determined to fight the battle of poverty alone. However the mother might have sympathized, she had no money with which to help her child. What she earned by daily toil and care found its way into the pockets of the husband, who spent it as seemed wise to himself.

Years after, in 1887, when Miss Anthony spoke of " the failure of the law to give a wife any share of the accumulations of the marriage partnership " as a great injustice, Lucy Stone, perhaps remembering the case of her mother, told a story of the boy who said of his mother, "She works for us all, but there ain't any money into it."

Mr. Stone voiced the common feeling about the education of women. Mrs. Livermore said, in 1893, "When about seventeen years of age, I went in company with five or six other like-minded young ladies, to visit President Quincy of Harvard College, and we asked the privilege of attending lectures in the college. President Quincy replied, 'You don't want this sort of education. This is for boys. You would be a disgrace to your friends if you came here. What you need to learn is to make bread, and sew, and keep house.'"

"All these domestic accomplishments," said these girls, "we have learned already from our mothers at home. We ask now for something else."

"The time will never come," rejoined President Quincy, "when Harvard will open its doors to women."

The disappointed young women withdrew to the old burial-ground on Copp's Hill, and pledged to work together till women received equal educational advantages with men. A half century later, there were forty thousand women in the colleges.

Lucy Stone, despite her father's opposition, began to earn money for the far-off college course. She picked berries in the hot sun in summer, sold them, and hoarded up the pittance which they brought. In the autumn she gathered chestnuts, and with the money obtained by their sale she bought books.

As soon as she was old enough she taught school. "I remember being a teacher," she said in 1891, in her address, "The Gains of Forty Years." "My first teaching was done for a dollar a week; and later, when I had sixteen dollars a month, a person said to me, 'Why, what a good salary that is for a woman!' When my brother, who was receiving thirty dollars a month, fell ill, and I took his school for two weeks, the committee gave me sixteen dollars a month, because that was 'enough for a woman.'"

It was not customary to hire a woman to teach a winter school, as then the older boys were released from farm work, and could attend to lessons, and it was supposed that a woman could not govern them. Lucy, however, had become so successful through her winsomeness, allied to firmness, that she was engaged to teach a winter school which had been broken up because the big boys had thrown an offensive master head-foremost out of a window into a deep snowdrift.

As perhaps might have been expected, the chivalric boys determined to help the young teacher by their good manners and well-learned lessons, and the term was a most successful one.

While a girl, Lucy Stone had joined the Orthodox Congregational Church in West Brookfield, Mass. One of the deacons, Mr. Henshaw, was brought before the church, in trial, for having entertained anti-slavery speakers at his house, and otherwise aided to stir up the people against human bondage. Finally the vote was taken with regard to the offending deacon.

"At this time," said Lucy Stone, "I was very young. I was a church member, but I did not know that women did not vote in the church; and so, when an important vote was taken, in the innocence and ignorance of my heart, I held up my hand to vote with the rest, supposing it was all right. But the minister, tall and large, pointing over to me, said to the man counting the votes, 'Don't you count her.' And the man counting the votes looked a little surprised himself, and said, 'Isn't she a member?' 'Oh, yes,' he said, 'she is a member, but she isn't a voting member!' And the scorn that was in his tones! I felt it to the tips of my toes. That afternoon they took six other votes, and every time I held my hand up high; every time they did not count it. All the same I held my hand up."

In 1837, when Lucy was nineteen, she was teaching school in North Brookfield. There had been much excitement over the public speaking of Angelina and Sarah Grimké and Abby Kelley. The sisters Grimké, daughters of Judge Grimké of Charleston, S. C., becoming convinced that slavery was sinful, emancipated their slaves, came North, joined the Friends in Philadelphia in 1828, and spoke under the auspices of the Anti-Slavery Society. Angelina married Theodore D. Weld, a lecturer and reformer, May 14, 1838.

The Association of Congregational ministers were so disturbed on account of such public speaking by women that they issued a "Pastoral Letter" in 1857, against "the danger which threatened the female character with wide-spread and permanent injury."

"We cannot therefore," said this document, "but regret the mistaken conduct of those who encourage females to bear an obtrusive and ostentatious part in measures of reform, and countenance any of that sex who so far forget themselves as to itinerate in the character of public lecturers and teachers."

Lucy attended this meeting of the Association, now become famous through Whittier's well-known poem : —

> "And what are ye who strive with God,
>   Against the ark of his salvation,
> Moved by the breath of prayer abroad,
>   With blessings for a dying nation?
> What, but the stubble and the hay
>   To perish, even as flax consuming,
> With all that bars his glorious way,
>   Before the brightness of his coming?"

While the "Pastoral Letter" was being read, Lucy, who sat with her cousin among the laymen and women who filled the galleries to look upon the ministers assembled in the body of the house, was greatly moved. "I was young enough then so that my indignation blazed," she said years afterward; "and I told my cousin that, if I ever had anything to say in public, I should say it, and all the more because of that 'Pastoral Letter!'"

When Lucy was twenty, in 1838, she studied for a time at Mt. Holyoke Seminary. Instead of keeping a mite-box to hold her savings for foreign missions, which was the custom among the students, she kept in her room one of the little yellow collection boxes of the Anti-Slavery Society, with the picture of a manacled slave upon it, kneeling with uplifted hands, with the words, "Am I not a man and a brother?"

Poor as she was, she found the means to put William Lloyd Garrison's *Liberator* into the reading-room. It was long a secret who could place such a firebrand among innocent girls, unaccustomed to think upon the evils of the time. Even good Mary Lyon, the principal, doubted the wisdom of allowing the paper to remain, and said to Lucy, who confessed that she was the offender as soon as she was asked, "The slavery question is a very grave question, and a question upon which the best people are divided."

In 1840 Lucy was a student at Wilbraham Academy. She wrote to her brother, Mr. W. B. Stone, Warren, Mass.: "I am well, and get along well with my studies. . . . Miss Adams and I walked out to Springfield last Saturday, and back again, the whole distance being nearly twenty-five miles. . . . It was decided by a large majority in our literary society the other day that ladies ought to mingle in politics, go to Congress, etc., etc. What do you think of that?"

When Lucy was twenty-five she had earned enough money to enter Oberlin College, Ohio, then the only college in the country willing to admit women. It is claimed that Antioch College, Ohio, was the first to give women *equal* privileges with men. It was dedicated by the Hon. Horace Mann, its first president, in September, 1852. "Crossing Lake Erie from Buffalo to Cleveland, as she could not afford a stateroom," says her daughter, Alice Stone Blackwell, "she slept on deck on a pile of grain-sacks, among horses and freight, with a few other women, who, like herself, could only pay for a 'deck passage.'"

While at Oberlin, Lucy paid her way by teaching in the preparatory department of the college, and by doing housework in the Ladies' Boarding Hall at three cents an hour. She could have obtained board at one dollar a week at the college, but this she could not afford. She cooked her own scanty supply, making it cost her less than fifty cents a week. She had only one new dress during the whole four college years, and that was a calico. Of course there was no money with which to return home for a visit during all this time.

"She had an experience," truly said Mrs. Livermore, "that would naturally make one bitter, hard, sour, and unlovely; but it did not make her so. When asked if she did not feel hardly toward the memory of her father, who objected to her going to college, she said, 'Oh, no, it was only the narrowness of the times.'" He said to Lucy before he died, "You were right and I was wrong."

When any one remarked in her hearing that she "wished she had never been born," Lucy Stone always made reply, "You must not say that. It is a great thing to be born. To be born is to have a hold upon immortality. To be born is never to die. For that one can afford to endure some physical pain and earthly afflictions."

While in Oberlin, having severe sick headaches on Sunday afternoons from keeping her bonnet on during the long Sunday morning sermons of those times, Lucy took her bonnet off, and was brought before the Ladies' Board for an action so contrary to custom. When told that St. Paul said that it was a shame for a woman to appear in church with her head uncovered, she replied, "Then, on the Day of Judgment, how shall I account to God for my wasted Sunday afternoons?" This being an unthought-of sin, she was permitted to sit in the back pew under the gallery, and remove her bonnet during part of the service.

Lucy Stone and a few others, being interested in prominent questions of the day, asked to be allowed to take part in the exercises of the college debating society; but this was refused. The girls therefore assembled at the house of an aged colored woman whom Lucy had taught to read, and here, very quietly, they carried on their debates.

Oberlin, from the first, had been the friend of the slave. A school was started among the colored people, and Lucy was asked to teach it. Humble as was their own condition, they did not wish to be taught by a woman, so inferior was the sex considered in intellect. A very tall and very black man spoke for the class, saying that they had nothing against Miss Stone personally. With her usual winsomeness she persuaded them that it would be wise to learn to read, whoever taught them. They consented, and soon became greatly attached to her. When, during a brief absence, the Ladies' Boarding Hall took fire, a whole line of colored men appeared at the place, breathlessly asking, "Where is Miss Stone's trunk?" that they might save it for her.

Her first public speech was made for the colored people while she was in college. On the anniversary of the West Indian emancipation, she was asked to be one of the speakers and accepted. The next day, after the meeting, she was called before the Ladies' Board, who desired to reason with her for public speaking, which they considered unwomanly and unscriptural.

"Did you not feel yourself very much out of place up there on the platform among all those men?" asked the wife of the President. "Were you not embarrassed and frightened?"

"Why, no, Mrs. Mahan," was the answer. "Those men were President Mahan and my professors, whom I meet every day in the class-room. I was not afraid of them at all!" And yet, in spite of all these supposed misdemeanors, the young woman was beloved for her truthfulness, her good sense, and her unselfish character. "You know we alway loved you, Lucy!" said one of the professors, years after she had left college.

Lucy stood well in her lessons, and was awarded one of the honors at commencement. She was notified that the essay she was to prepare would be read for her by one of the professors, as it was not proper that a woman should read in public. Seeing that the honor was hedged about by these conditions, she declined to write the essay. Nearly forty years after this, when public opinion had changed, and largely through her instrumentality, she was invited to be one of the speakers at the great Oberlin semi-centennial, where thousands were gathered to listen, instead of the few hundreds who assembled at the Commencement in 1847, when she graduated.

William Lloyd Garrison wrote from Oberlin to his wife, Aug. 28, 1847, "Among others with whom I have become acquainted is Miss Lucy Stone, who has just graduated, and yesterday left for her home in Brookfield, Mass. She is a very superior young woman, and has a soul as free as the air, and is preparing to go forth as a lecturer, particularly in vindication of the rights of woman."

Forty-six years after her graduation, Feb. 2, 1893, Lucy Stone wrote to President Charles F. Thwing, of Western Reserve University, Cleveland, Ohio, in reply to questions asked of thirteen hundred collegiate Alumnæ, concerning the amount of intellectual work done in a day by women, etc.,—

"I was a student four years at Oberlin. I never lost

a day from ill-health. I took the college course with the men, and held a fair rank as a student. The same was true of the other girls in college. But nearly every one of us worked. We were poor. We earned our way through college. We did our own cooking (most of the time), and our washing and ironing all the time. Some of the girls paid their way by washing for the male students. . . .

"I should never think of making a course of special study for those who may be mothers, any more than for those who may be fathers. The college training is to put him in possession and command of himself. After that he chooses his profession, and with his tools ready to prepare for it. Human beings are much alike. I grew up with four brothers, and have all my life had more or less to do with men. . . . My idea is that colleges should give boys and girls the same drill, the same courses of study, and after that it is at their option what they will choose."

Lucy Stone's first woman suffrage lecture was given in the pulpit of her brother, the Rev. William B. Stone, in Gardner, Mass., the same year in which she graduated. She was soon engaged to lecture for the Anti-Slavery Society. When a meeting was held in Malden, Mass., under the auspices of this society, of which Garrison and Wendell Phillips were officers, the minister of the Congregational Church was asked to give a notice concerning it, which he did in these words: "I am requested by Mr. Mowry to say that a hen will undertake to crow like a cock at the Town Hall this afternoon at five o'clock. Anybody who wants to hear that kind of music will, of course, attend."

Notwithstanding words so ungentlemanly from the pulpit, "I had" says Mrs. Stone, "a very large meeting. Everybody came, and Mr. Mowry was asked what kind of a hen it was, and all about it; and altogether it was a very good advertisement of the meeting."

From this time onward for many years Lucy Stone travelled over a large part of the United States, speaking for woman suffrage or for the colored people. She suffered the same persecutions as Garrison, Phillips, and the Grimké sisters. Once, in winter, a pane of glass was removed from behind the speaker, a hose was put through it, and the slight girlish lecturer was deluged with ice-cold water. She put on a shawl, and continued her address. Sometimes pepper was burned. Once when Parker Pillsbury was speaking, a hymn-book was thrown, which hit Lucy on the back of the neck.

Lillie B. Chace Wyman, in the *New England Magazine* for December, 1891, quotes from Miss Bremer's "Homes in the New World," an interesting picture of Lucy Stone as she appeared in Faneuil Hall, Boston, in January, 1850.

"A young, fair lady, in a simple white dress, and hair without any ornament, stepped forward, leading a dark mulatto woman by the hand. She had been a slave, and had lately escaped from slavery on board a vessel, where she had been concealed. Her owners, who suspected her place of concealment, obtained a warrant for searching the vessel, which they did thoroughly, burning brimstone in order to compel her to come forth. But she endured it all, and succeeded in making her escape.

"It was a beautiful sight when the young white woman, Miss Lucy Stone, placed her hand upon the head of the black woman and called her sister, before the assembled crowd. . . . She then related the history of the late slave, and talked about slavery for a full hour, with perfect self-possession, perspicuity, and propriety of tone and gesture."

This slave girl was nineteen years old, and " came to the cold North half-starved and half-frozen, leaving behind her own baby, who could not have survived the hardships of her way of escape."

Once in New York, at a woman suffrage meeting, William Henry Channing advised Lucretia Mott, who was presiding, to adjourn on account of the clamor of the mob. She answered in her mild and gracious manner, "When the hour fixed for adjournment comes, I will adjourn the meeting, not before."

At last Lucy Stone was introduced. Her lovely face and "the sweetest voice ever possessed by a public speaker" at once quieted the mob. As soon as she had ceased speaking, the howling began again, as the mob surged into the dressing-rooms. Lucy reproached them, when they replied, "Oh, come, you needn't say anything; we kept still for *you!*"

At an anti-slavery meeting on Cape Cod, in a grove, the mob surrounded the speakers, roughly handled Stephen Foster, tearing his coat from top to bottom, and intimidated all save Mr. Foster and Lucy Stone. The latter so won the admiration of one of the leaders of the mob on account of her bravery, that he defended her with his club, and stood by her while she, from a stump, addressed the multitude. They were so moved by her speech that they became quiet, and took up a collection of twenty dollars to pay Stephen Foster for his coat!

These days were as clouded by poverty as the days in college. "In Hanover Street, Boston," she once said, "was a boarding-house kept by a very respectable retired sea-captain and his wife, where I could get meals for twelve and a half cents, and lodging for six and a quarter cents. I slept in the same bed with two of the daughters, in the attic occupied by the servants, and separated from them only by a curtain. I had some small handbills printed; and as I could not pay for posting them, I bought a paper of tacks and put up bills myself, using a stone for a hammer. A collection was taken at the close, and I went around with the hat myself. There was no one else to do it."

Sometimes when she tacked up the posters, the boys in the street followed her, shouting and jeering and preparing to tear them down. Then she would call the boys about her, and talk to them kindly, till they were won into good feeling and courtesy.

Once, when Lucy was in great need of a new cloak, the Hutchinson family, who were to sing at Salem, Mass., the same evening on which she was to lecture, proposed to unite the entertainments and divide the proceeds. This was done, and the cloak was purchased with the money.

Mrs. Livermore thus describes Lucy Stone as she was in those years. "The first time I ever saw her was at an anti-slavery bazaar in Boston. She could not have weighed more than a hundred pounds at that time, a tiny creature with the prettiest pink color, and her girl-look was just as sweet as the look of her later years. I thought at the time she was the sweetest thing I had ever seen in my life. . . .

"I remember asking Wendell Phillips once if he did

not think that Lucy Stone might lose sight of woman suffrage a little in her work against slavery, and he exclaimed that with her it was always women first. She thought most, cared most, to help and uplift women. Wendell Phillips said he told his wife that he must tell Lucy that in this anti-slavery work she must not talk so much about women. . . . But Mrs. Phillips told him to let Lucy alone; for she knew what she wanted, and what she was about."

Lucy finally arranged to speak Saturday evenings and Sundays for the anti-slavery association, and the rest of the time for woman suffrage, though the former society could not bear to lose her services. She said to Samuel J. May, the agent of the society, "I was a woman before I was an abolitionist, and I *must* speak for the women."

Lucy Stone had determined never to marry, but to devote her life to the best interests of woman. When Mr. Henry B. Blackwell, a hardware merchant in Cincinnati, Ohio, and a worker with voice and means in the anti-slavery cause, fell in love with her, Mr. Garrison told him that "he would never win Lucy for a wife, for many had tried it and failed."

For a long time she refused him, quoting to him, says her daughter, a verse from a favorite poem written by Anne Whitney, the sculptor, referring to the aloe, which blossoms only once in a century: —

> "If the aloe wait an hundred years,
>   And God's times are so long, indeed,
>   For single things, as flower and weed,
>   That gather only the light and gloom,
>   For what great treasures of joy and dole,
>   Of life, and death perchance, must the soul
>   Ere it flower in heavenly peace, find room!"

This verse was often on her lips in the latter part of her life, and she repeated it to her daughter when on her death-bed. Another favorite poem to her who seemed to stand almost alone through these early years, was that of Bryant, "To a Water-fowl;"—

> "He who from zone to zone,
> Guides through the boundless sky thy certain flight,
> In the long way that I must tread alone,
> Will lead my steps aright."

Mr. Blackwell's love for Lucy, and his devotion to her purposes in life, won her consent to their marriage, when she was nearly thirty-seven, which took place at the home of her parents at West Brookfield, Mass., May 1, 1855. The Rev. Thomas Wentworth Higginson, then a preacher in Worcester, the well-known author and leader in our Civil War, married them.

Before marriage Mr. Blackwell and Lucy Stone signed a "protest," May 1, against the then existing laws which gave the husband the control of the wife's property, person, and children. They said, "We believe that personal independence and equal human rights can never be forfeited, except for crime; that marriage should be an equal and permanent partnership, and so recognized by law."

Lucy Stone retained her maiden name as a symbol of individuality, and with her husband's approval, having been assured by such eminent lawyers as Ellis Gray Loring and Samuel E. Sewall that there was no law requiring a wife to take her husband's name; it was done simply as a matter of convenience and custom.

"I always thought it," says Colonel Higginson, "a

great tribute to her transparent simplicity and directness of character that people took all that so quietly, and accepted it in her as they do in the case of singers and actresses, with whom it proceeds from a different motive.

The *Springfield Republican* said, after Mrs. Stone's death, "Lucy Stone's protest against the traditional idea of the marriage relation, by which the woman has been regarded as the mere appendage of the man, and which has been the root of all the evil laws that during thousands of years had given all the rights to the husband, and to the wife such privileges as he might allow, was one of the signal advances toward the true idea of marriage and the real position of women, not only in domestic matters, but in the body politic. Out of that protest, jointly signed, has proceeded more courageous progress toward the rights of man and woman as individuals than from any other single incident."

About two years after her marriage, in 1857, their only child, Alice, was born. She became not only a helper during the life of her mother, but an able upholder of her principles after her death. With an ardent love for children, Lucy Stone devoted herself wholly to her child. Miss Anthony said to her, "Lucy, I believe you have lost your power as a speaker for the cause since you married." She replied, "I have lost it since my Alice came, but it will come back." A little girl was adopted to be a sister to Alice; but she died about ten years later, before she reached womanhood.

For nearly forty years after her marriage, till her death, Lucy Stone's life was one untiring, continuous effort for humanity. She once said to Mrs. Livermore,

"When I began to work for woman suffrage, it was so hard and so difficult that, if I had been put at the foot of the loftiest peak of the Rocky Mountains, with a jack-knife in hand, and had been told, 'Hew your way up,' it would have been pastime, compared to my task."

In 1866 Mrs. Stone helped to organize the American Equal Rights Association, which worked for both women and negroes, and was chairman of its executive committee. Three years later, Nov. 14, 1869, a convention was called at Cleveland, Ohio, which resulted in the organization of the American Woman Suffrage Association, of whose executive committee Mrs. Stone was chairman for nearly twenty years. Garrison, George William Curtis, Colonel Higginson, Mrs. Julia Ward Howe, and others joined in the work.

Of that convention in Cleveland, Mr. Blackwell wrote: "That beautiful city, never less beautiful externally than then, showed its internal nobility of character by crowding the vast hall with an audience equal to any similar body we ever beheld. The assembly entered into the spirit of the occasion with what might almost be termed a religious enthusiasm. . . . The temper of the convention was as magnanimous and noble as its object was dignified and sublime. The result will be shown by time and chronicled in history."

At this convention I heard Lucy Stone for the first time; and I shall never forget her winsome manner, her simple, eloquent words which never antagonized, her unusually sweet voice, her womanly face beaming with good-will to everybody, her delicate tact and grace, and her common-sense.

One can well imagine the incident which Colonel

Higginson relates of Helen Hunt going to a suffrage meeting in New York to write a burlesque of it for a paper, and saying to him on her way home in answer to his query if she had plenty of material for her letter, "Do you suppose I would ever write a word against anything that a woman with such a voice as Lucy Stone's wants to have done?"

The year following the Cleveland convention, January, 1870, the *Woman's Journal* was established, Mrs. Stone raising most of the money for it, and for more than twenty years she was its senior editor. The *Revolution* was started two years previously, in 1868, by Susan B. Anthony. Elizabeth Cady Stanton, one of the earliest workers for woman suffrage, was chosen editor.

For years Lucy Stone was the President of the New England Woman Suffrage Association; she was a power in the Massachusetts association; she spoke at every annual hearing before the Legislature of Massachusetts and other States; she aided in campaigns for the suffrage amendments in Kansas, Vermont, Michigan, Nebraska, Colorado, and Rhode Island; she spoke before almost numberless clubs and societies; she wrote articles for the press; she studied the law carefully, and she had an accurate knowledge of its injustice to women in various states.

Colonel Higginson tells how he once went with her before the Judiciary Committee of the Rhode Island Legislature, and she spoke of the law of that State. Judge Green of Providence, Chairman of the Judiciary Committee, said, after she had finished speaking, "Mrs. Stone, you put me to shame by the discovery that all these wrongs exist under cover of Rhode Island law. It is perfectly true; you have not made a single mistake. And yet I, the chairman of this Judiciary Committee for years, have done nothing to remove them." "From that moment," says Colonel Higginson, "Judge Green was her friend and our friend."

Judge Green was not the only one persuaded by the arguments or the knowledge of Lucy Stone. Susan B. Anthony said, at the National Convention in 1891, that Mrs. Stone decided her for woman suffrage. She had been dissatisfied with her unequal pay for work as a teacher; and after reading Lucy Stone's speech before the Worcester Convention in 1850, as reported in the *New York Tribune*, she became perfectly clear on the subject, and had remained so ever since.

Julia Ward Howe said, in 1893, at the Lucy Stone memorial meeting of the New England Women's Press Association, "I remember when I thought it unworthy of her to speak in public as she did, because I thought it was hardly proper for a woman to be so conspicuous. . . . But I was only one of many, and we should be thankful that our horizon has broadened to its present circumference. If Mrs. Stone were to start again to-day, she would not find, as she did then, that nearly the whole world was against her."

Again Mrs. Howe said, at the Woman's Congress in Memphis, Tenn., after speaking of the time when she was opposed to woman suffrage, and at last attended a meeting where Lucy Stone was presiding, "As I heard the arguments, and still more as I felt the calm, dignified, and noble atmosphere of that convention, and looked upon the faces of Phillips, Garrison, and Higginson, I found that I had got into very high company, and all the arguments seemed to go over to the other side. Although my beautiful youth lies back of that period, the part of my life since I began to work with the suffragists seems to me bright with a hope and a glory unknown before."

In the autumn of 1877 Mrs. Stone and Mr. Blackwell went to Colorado to work for woman suffrage in that State. Each wrote back interesting letters to the daily press of Boston.

On the journey, Mrs. Stone, as ever, found opportunities to do good. A delicate young wife was holding a baby in her arms. Mrs. Stone entered into conversation with her, asking about her child and the young father beside her.

"Let his strong arms take the baby, and rest your weak and tired ones," said the kindly woman. "I want to take him," said the young man, who had been absent from his wife for a few weeks, while at work, "but he is afraid. He don't know me, and he won't come to me."

"Oh, yes, he will! This is the way," and Mrs. Stone reached out her hands to the baby, who enjoyed being carried about, and then gave him into the arms of the father.

"You must teach your husband to help you with the child," said Mrs. Stone. "Have you had any breakfast?" as it was early morning.

"No," for she could not put the baby down to get any.

"Well, now, while he is content with his father, come and get a glass of milk, and some bread and butter; you will feel ever so much better."

From Southern Colorado Mrs. Stone wrote, in 1877:

"Here you ride by railroad mile after mile, alongside of huge piles of rocks, sometimes so near that you can almost touch them with your hands, or can gather the eggs from the nests of the chimney swallows, which hang by millions all up and down these bare rocky walls.

"You ride on and on, sometimes looking up with terror at overhanging rocks, which the beckoning of a finger would call down, or moved to mirth by the fantastic shapes which great masses of red or white sandstone have assumed when they tumbled out from the common mass ages ago, down into the level plateau below. . . . You pass the rocks and you come upon plains barren, sandy, with no inhabitants but rabbits and prairie dogs, with no trees but only sage brush, grease-wood bushes and prickly pears. You can ride all day and not vary this desolate scene. You will find parks without a fence or boundary except mountains. I crossed one of these, into which the whole State of Massachusetts might be set down, with a large margin all around it. On these parks vast herds of cattle feed, enough of them, it would seem, to supply the markets of all the world. We passed to-day the house of one man who has fourteen thousand head of cattle. In other ranges are flocks of sheep to match."

The seed sown by Mrs. Stone, Miss Anthony, Mrs. Margaret W. Campbell, and others in Colorado in 1877, bore fruit sixteen years later, in the fall of 1893, when by popular vote the state carried the constitutional amendment for woman suffrage — giving to women "exactly the same rights as men in exercising the elective franchise" — by a majority of about six thousand votes.

Ministers very generally preached in its favor, and prominent editors, lawyers, and politicians helped to win the victory.

The Hon. James S. Clarkson, assistant postmaster-general under President Harrison, thus writes of the election in Denver: "I had felt, in my judgment, passive resistance to woman suffrage, only from fear that participation in public affairs might in some degree be hurtful to the delicacy and tenderness of refined womanhood. . . . Having seen them in the activities of a very exciting political campaign, one in which at least ninety per cent of all good and intelligent and refined women of this city and State were taking a part, not merely passively, but actively, and having spent the whole day Tuesday visiting the polls in this city, where probably thirty thousand voted, and not only voted, but bore their part in the party and public duties of the day, I am left to the frank and manly duty of saying that even this last feeling of fear as to woman suffrage on my part is gone. . . . The American woman is clearly as much of a queen at the polls, in her own bearing and the deference paid her, as in the drawing-room or at the opera. . . . There is more chance of a lady seeing or hearing something unpleasant in passing through a crowd to the average theatre or opera than there was in any lady going to these voting places yesterday. . . .

"It must be remembered, too, by the sceptical people in the East . . . that the people of this State are largely from the Eastern States themselves, and that the women here are as refined and accomplished and well-educated as in any city or State in the East. . . . For my part, I believe that woman suffrage is inevitable in every American State; and that, as it comes, it will bring good to every State, to every city especially, and to the nation. . . . The profoundest problem in government is municipal government, and it will never be solved successfully until woman and her moral conscience and quick intelligence are brought to the help of its solution." And thus thought Abraham Lincoln, Charles Sumner, Phillips Brooks, Longfellow, Whittier, and a host of others. Mr. Gladstone has said that the voting of women in England and Scotland has been "without detriment and with great advantage."

Lucy Stone did not live to see the successful issue in Colorado; but she lived long enough to see school suffrage gained in twenty-two States, municipal suffrage in Kansas, full suffrage in Wyoming, and wonderful changes brought about by herself and a few other brave and devoted women.

At the fortieth anniversary of the First National Woman's Rights Convention, held in Boston, Jan. 27–28, 1891, Mrs. Stone told of the gains of forty years. When she began to speak in public, only a few occupations were open to women. "The attempt to open other occupations," said Mrs. Stone, "was met by the fiercest opposition. Printers' unions were formed, with the pledge that they would not work for any man who employed women. A dry-goods store in Maine, which employed a woman, was boycotted by the men, and good women of the neighborhood warned the merchant of his sin in taking women out of their sphere." Now the Hon. Carroll D. Wright, in his labor reports, shows that three hundred occupations are open to women.

Wages to women were very small. A dressmaker

commanded thirty-three cents a day, while a tailoress, going from house to house, was given fifty cents a day. A teacher in the summer school received a dollar a week and "boarded round." A man received four times as much as a woman or even more.

Women had almost no opportunity for higher education. "Oberlin then," said Mrs. Stone, "was the only college open to women. It admitted women and negroes on the same terms as white men, and bore its share of odium for it. But after these forty years we now have Boston University, and Wellesley and Smith and Bryn Mawr, and Vassar and Cornell in New York, and Michigan University, and the Western colleges everywhere, welcoming women. The great Chicago University not only has its pick of the best professors, but it wins sympathy and favor because it is coeducational. Pennsylvania University, Yale and Tufts Colleges, catch the spirit of the times and move on."

Women could not enter the professions. When Elizabeth Blackwell, her father having lost his fortune, decided to study medicine, "she was met on all sides," says her sister, Dr. Emily Blackwell of New York, "by incredulous and contemptuous amazement and discouragement." She wrote letters to medical colleges, but most returned no answer; others declined. At the Geneva Medical College, New York, where there were one hundred and fifty students, the dean read a letter to the students, from a Philadelphia physician, asking for Miss Blackwell's admission. If a single student were opposed, she was not to be received. To the astonishment of the dean, the class voted "Yes" in the most hilarious manner. She came in 1848, was cordially received, and graduated with honor. But all hospitals were closed to her, and she was obliged to go to Paris to carry forward her work.

For many years the medical schools determined that no incident, similar to that at Geneva, should happen in future; but gradually the predjudice was overcome, until "in 1891," says Dr. Emily Blackwell, "there are forty-nine medical colleges admitting women in the United States and Canada, nine being separate women's schools. . . . Over two hundred and fifty women are studying this winter in the schools of Philadelphia and New York alone. In England women physicians are nearly as numerous. . . . In China several hospitals and centres of practice have been established by women. From India, China, and Persia, native women have been sent to be educated in American colleges."

Entrance into law and theology has been just as difficult for women. Not until 1870, in Chicago, was a degree given in law to a woman. Washington University, St. Louis, was the first to admit women to its law school. Twenty years after, in 1891, twenty-three States admitted women to their bars. In several denominations women have been ordained to the ministry.

One of the greatest changes in the last forty years has been in the betterment of laws with regard to women. Our forefathers accepted the Common Law of England. Mrs. Stone says, in *The Chautauquan* for April, 1891, "No wife had any right to herself. She had no right to her children. She could own nothing that she earned. If a woman earned a dollar by scrubbing, she brought it home, and her husband had the right to take the dollar and go and get drunk with it and beat her afterwards. If a woman wrote a book, the copyright belonged to her husband, not to her. All her personal property was given to her husband. The right to her real estate was taken from her, and given to her husband for his life, if she had a child born alive. She could not make a will. . . . The wife who washed and ironed and cooked and spun and wove, who made the clothes for the family and sat up nights to knit stockings and mend the family wardrobe, was regarded by her husband as supported by him, and she, too, considered herself supported."

In most of the States the laws are greatly improved. "The wife now retains the personal property she had before marriage. She may earn whatever she can outside of the family. She may make a will disposing of at least a part of her property."

In the summer of 1893, Lucy Stone, worn with the constant labor of an unusual life, was at Gardner, in the home of her sister, taking a needed rest. On her birthday, Aug. 13, Mrs. Livermore, just recovering from illness, wrote her, " There is nothing for us to do, Lucy, but to put away all thoughts of sickness, and gird ourselves up, and keep on together with the procession to the end; " and the gentle woman wrote back, " Thank you for that. We will do it. We will keep together, and be good comrades straight to the end."

On her return to her home in Dorchester, she was unable to attend the conventions as she and Mrs. Livermore had planned. "I have dropped out," she said, "and you will go on without me. . . . Good-by! If we don't meet again, never mind. We shall meet sometime, somewhere; be sure of that. We shall be busy together again in some good work somewhere; and we will be good comrades again somewhere."

At their last interview she said, "You have often called Alice the daughter of the regiment; don't forget her; help her; be good to Alice!"

During the autumn days, at Pope's Hill, Dorchester, she sat on the piazza on the east of the house, looking out on the beautiful bay, and the Blue Hills of Milton. She watched the two elms in front of her home with increased pleasure; and when she could look at nature no longer except from her chamber window, the leaves of the great maple outside gave her "a wealth of music" as they fluttered in the wind. She had always longed to see the mountains in Switzerland, but she had been too busy. "But I have done what I wanted to," she said, "I have helped the women." Another day she said, "I am so glad to have lived, and to have lived at a time when I could work!"

To a friend who expressed the wish that she might have lived to see woman suffrage granted, she replied, "Oh, I shall know it. I think I shall know it on the other side. And if I do not, the people on this side will know it."

She talked with her family about the preparations for her funeral, asking that it be cheerful and simple, and telling them, as she saw them in tears, not to be so grieved. "It is a part of the great order, and I am glad to help you about these things."

To a friend she said, "I have not the smallest apprehension. . . . I look forward to the other side as the brighter side, and I expect to be busy for good things."

Toward the end she longed for death, partly on account of weakness, but more especially because she disliked to tire others. "You will be all worn out," she said. To a neighbor she remarked, "I am hoping to pass away very soon." The friend replied that she must keep up courage. "Oh, it isn't a question of courage," said the dying woman, with a smile lighting up her face. "I *like* to go to the other side; and I have not the least fear of it."

On the afternoon of Wednesday, Oct. 18, 1893, for the first time her mind wandered, and it was difficult for her to speak. She seemed to wish to say something to her daughter Alice, who, putting her ear close to the moving lips, heard her parting words, "Make the world better." Her last articulate word "Papa," was to the man who had been her devoted companion in a happy union of almost forty years. She soon became insensible, and at forty-five minutes past ten, in the evening of Oct. 18, passed away as if in sleep. After all was over, Mr. Blackwell said to his daughter, as they sorrowed together, "We must try to keep mamma's flag flying;" and she could have had no stronger wish than that.

On Saturday, Oct. 21, at 2 P.M., the funeral was held in the Church of the Disciples, corner of West Brookline Street and Warren Avenue, Boston. People began to assemble at noon; and when the doors were opened, the church was soon crowded. "An immense audience was present," says *The Christian Register*. "Never have we seen in Boston a more representative gathering of people interested in social, philanthropic, and political reform."

On the wall, behind the pulpit, a great heart of red oak leaves enclosed a cross of autumn leaves. At the left was the bust of Lucy Stone by Anne Whitney, and on the right a life-sized portrait of Wendell Phillips, both bust and picture draped with autumn leaves.

The coffin was covered with flowers. The Massachusetts Woman Suffrage Association sent seventy-five yellow roses, one for each year of her life, with ferns; other suffrage leagues from all over the country sent white chrysanthemums, roses, palms, and other flowers; Julia Ward Howe sent a large wreath of pansies. A bunch of lilies of the valley, a favorite flower of Mrs. Stone's, was placed in her hand.

The Rev. Charles G. Ames, pastor of the church, conducted the services, reading, as Mrs. Stone had requested before death, from two of Whittier's most beautiful hymns, one, "The Eternal Goodness:" —

> "I know not what the future hath
> Of marvel or surprise,
> Assured alone that life and death
> His mercy underlies.
>
> And so, beside the silent sea,
> I wait the muffled oar;
> No harm from Him can come to me
> On ocean or on shore.
>
> I know not where His islands lift
> Their fronded palms in air;
> I only know I cannot drift
> Beyond His love and care."

Also, "My Soul and I:" —

> "Know well, my soul, God's hand controls
> Whate'er thou fearest;
> Round Him in calmest music rolls
> Whate'er thou hearest.

> What to us is shadow, to Him is day,
> And the end He knoweth;
> And not on a blind and aimless way
> The spirit goeth."

Colonel T. W. Higginson, Mrs. Mary A. Livermore, Miss Mary Grew of Philadelphia, Mr. William Lloyd Garrison, the Rev. Samuel J. Barrows, Mrs. Edna D. Cheney, and others, made addresses. Mrs. Howe sent a poem to be read in her absence. The pall-bearers were twelve in number, six women and six men. The body was taken to the receiving-tomb at Forest Hills Cemetery to await cremation, in accordance with Mrs. Stone's request. Memorial services were held by various associations East and West, and many pulpits made the noble life of Mrs. Stone the theme of their discourses.

Lucy Stone was a woman of great courage. "I have heard her say," says her daughter, "that in the mobs and other dangers of the anti-slavery times, she was never conscious of a quickened heart-beat."

Once, when the house was on fire from some clothes hung too near a gas-stove, with great presence of mind and calmness, she extinguished the flames, though burning her hand severely.

Her modesty and unselfishness were as great as her courage. When before her death it was suggested that the funeral be held in a church rather than at the house, as many friends would wish to come, she felt sure that the number would be small, and advised against it, but said her family might do as they pleased. The Rev. Dr. L. A. Banks tells of a meeting where Mrs. Howe, himself, and others were to speak. Mrs. Stone was asked if she would not speak also. She answered,

"Only for a few minutes. They will want to hear the new voices, and I am only a plain brown wren anyway." To which Mrs. Howe quickly replied, "If I remember correctly, the little brown wren has a most exquisite song of her own."

When she found that her daughter, at the request of many friends, had published a sketch of her, she hid it away under a pile of magazines.

Mrs. Stone had remarkable self-possession. "She was calm amid all distractions," says Mr. Ames, "self-possessed, because having a sound mind happily encased in a sound body. And self-possession means so much!" "She was calm as well as impassioned," says Mrs. Howe; "soaring above mean irony, and meeting rude argument with a sweet humanity!"

Notwithstanding all the obstacles in Mrs. Stone's pathway through life, she was cheerful and optimistic. From her sick bed she dictated, perhaps her last words for the press, an answer to the question of *The Independent*, for its symposium, "Is the world growing better?"

"I believe the world grows better, because I believe that in the eternal order there is always a movement, swift or slow, toward what is right and true — a tendency toward higher things, stronger than the impulses of evil."

She was a woman of great kindness of heart. She did not keep herself shut away from anyone in need, although her life was so crowded with duties. Flowers and fruits were sent from her garden, and boxes of clothing, west, north, and south. "I remember, on one occasion," says Mrs. Livermore, "she was about to take up and help a poor woman for whom I believed little or nothing could be done, — a woman I had been through the mill with, and had not succeeded in helping as I wished. I told Lucy Stone all I could tell her. I begged her not to burden herself. She had cares enough. She heard me through; and then she said in her soft voice, 'I believe all you say, but I shall do what I intended for her just the same.'"

She was a lover of children. She said, "I wish that parents could see that hope of praise and reward is a much greater incentive to faithful effort than is fear of blame and punishment." No wonder that some one said, "You look like the lovely grandmother of all good children."

She was the friend of all dumb animals. By the desk where she sat and wrote in her lovely home, looking out on the grape arbor and large green spruce-tree, was the window-ledge where she fed the birds all the long winter, calling them her "little boarders." A black cat was also an especial pet. His maltese mother now purrs to the visitors who enter the Blackwell home.

Lucy Stone's home life was as restful and happy as her public life was laborious and trying. For twenty-six years she and her husband and daughter lived in Dorchester in a three-story, cream-colored house, overlooking the bay, surrounded by seven acres of fruit-trees, lawn, and garden. Her garden was a great delight to her. She loved flowers, especially yellow ones, such as buttercups, marigolds, and golden-rod.

In the house a broad hall divides the drawing-room on the east from the library and dining-room on the west. Here many a noted guest has been welcomed and entertained. All is refined and restful, as was the gracious woman who once presided over it. Golden brown predominates in carpet and furnishings. Over the parlor mantle hangs the picture of Lucy Stone and her baby. In the library are the Dickens, Gibbon, Scott, and many Lives, which she enjoyed, before her open fire, whenever her busy life permitted.

"She was as fond of a love-story as any girl of sixteen," says her daughter, "that is, if it were a simple and innocent love-story; for she had no patience with that class of modern novels which turn upon the flirtations of married people."

Her black walnut writing-desk is in the dining-room, where she could be near her kitchen to superintend the daily needs of her household. Over it hang the pictures of Salmon P. Chase of Ohio, his gift to her, Theodore Parker, Gerritt Smith, and William Lloyd Garrison. At the left hangs a little picture, a blacksmith with his dog, mending a boy's hoop, which she used to say rested her. Church's "Heart of the Andes," and Bierstadt's "Rocky Mountains," were favorite pictures of hers.

Above this room is the chamber where she died. Books and newspapers are here, the latter having been her daily companions as long as she was able to read, or to hear reading. She liked to know what was taking place in the great world, in which she had been such an active worker.

Colonel Higginson truly said of Lucy Stone, that she was "a remarkable woman in many ways, in no way more so than in her ability to keep and make friends, while scarcely making an enemy."

She has given the world an example of persistent purpose, united with great gentleness and loveliness of character. She won her way without harshness; she was as good a listener as speaker; she led without seeming to lead; she was ever the natural, kindly, helpful woman, attractive in face, and persuasive and charming in manner. She gave her talents unselfishly to make the world better. "She rests from her labors, and her works do follow her."

LADY HENRY SOMERSET.

In February, 1895, in Boston, through the courtesy of Frances E. Willard, one of the best beloved women in America, I met the gifted Lady Henry Somerset, a woman of fine presence, gracious manner, and handsome face. Her dark eyes brighten as she speaks, and her smile is winsome and kindly.

Why have thousands crowded to hear her every time she has spoken in public? Why has her face been pictured in papers and magazines? Why have her words been copied from one end of the country to the other?

Not alone because she is rich, or titled, or attractive. It is not a new thing to see English nobility in America. But it is a rare thing to see a woman reared in the circle of royalty, giving her life to the poor and the despised, leaving fashionable society that she may have time to work for reforms, forgetting the ease of luxury and rank to accept the hardships of a devoted leader in the uplifting of the race.

Lady Henry Somerset is the daughter of the third Earl Somers, who was a man of great refinement, scholarly tastes, and noble character. Much of his life was spent in travel, with his friend Sir Henry Layard, in making excavations in ancient Nineveh, for which he provided the means largely, or in other archæological expeditions,

LADY HENRY SOMERSET.

or with the Earl of Warwick in collecting from old castles and out-of-the-way places, treasures of great value. He was the friend of Turner and Ruskin, as well as of the great men of Italy, — Cavour, Garibaldi, and Mazzini.

"He accompanied Mr. Robert Curzon in his explorations of the unknown treasures of the Greek monasteries," writes his daughter, Lady Henry, in the *Union Signal*, April 14, 1892. "The results of their study are given in Mr. Curzon's famous book, the 'Monasteries of the Levant.' . . . He made drawings of Athos, Pergamos, and many other well-known centres of early Christian influence."

Earl Somers passed some time at Windsor, Osborne, and Balmoral, as Lord-in-waiting to the Queen, but resigned to give himself to books and art. He sat in the House of Lords for over thirty years. It was his daily practice to translate from his Greek Bible, which he loved.

Devoted to art, it was not strange that he should have fallen in love with a beautiful face. When Mr. G. F. Watts, the royal academician, was a young man, he painted a portrait of Miss Virginia Pattle, the daughter of Mr. James Pattle, a director of the East India Company. Virginia's grandmother, one of the ladies-in-waiting to Marie Antoinette, and her grandfather, one of the courtiers of Louis XVI., had fled from France to the East Indies to avoid the guillotine. Their beautiful daughter had married Mr. Pattle, at whose death Mrs. Pattle and her six daughters repaired to England. Crowds came to see the picture of Virginia, the most beautiful, among them Viscount Eastnor, afterwards Earl Somers.

He determined to know the beauty, met her soon after at a reception given by Lady Palmerston, and married her within a year. She was artistic, imaginative, elegant, and a social queen.

Two daughters were born to Earl and Countess Somers, Lady Isabel and Lady Adeline. Having no sons, every attention was bestowed upon the education of these daughters, who were to inherit the great estates of their father.

Lady Isabel from childhood was as familiar with the French language as with the English, and almost equally so with German and Italian. She was, however, left almost entirely to the charge of governesses, who were changed so often, that before her education was considered complete, twenty different women had filled that position. No wonder that Lady Isabel, at five, replied to Sir Henry Layard, when he asked her if she had a good time in the world, " Yes, I should enjoy life very much if it were not that I have too many parents."

When Lady Isabel was six or seven years of age, she was taken by her parents to a ball given by the Queen. When Victoria and Prince Albert quitted the dais where they had been seated during the early part of the ball, and went into the banqueting-room, the child, dressed in white with a wreath of daisies about her head, quietly seated herself in her Majesty's chair. When the Queen returned, she said, smiling, "This is little Isabel." With an offended air, the daughter of an earl replied, "*Lady* Isabel!"

A dozen years later, when she was presented at court, dressed in white and wearing a daisy wreath, the queen had not forgotten the incident, and said, as her hand was kissed, "*Lady* Isabel!"

The two daughters, either from reading "Uncle Tom's Cabin," or from an innate love of freedom, though children at the time of our Civil War, were warm partisans of the North. One day when Lord Palmerston was dining at their house, he spoke of the "mechanics" of the North, and hoped the South would succeed in the war. Lady Isabel and her sister were so annoyed at the great man, that they went up-stairs and turned his portrait against the wall.

Lady Isabel read the Christian fathers before she was eleven years old, and John Stuart Mill's "Subjection of Women," and "Essay on Liberty," when very young.

Among the many suitors for the hand of the rich and attractive Lady Isabel was Lord Henry Somerset, a younger son of the Duke of Beaufort, of a very distinguished family, in direct descent from the Plantagenets. The armor worn by Edward the Black Prince, son of Edward III., is one of the treasures at Badminton, the princely home of the Duke of Beaufort. The older son, the brother of Lord Henry, the Marquis of Worcester, is unmarried. Lord Henry was a member of the House of Commons, and a Privy Councillor. Lady Isabel did not at first accept him, but finally acceded to the wishes of her mother, and married him in 1872. Tennyson sent her, on her bridal day, a basket of snowdrops gathered with his own hands.

Two years later, in 1874, her only son, Henry Charles Somers Augustus Somerset, was born. The marriage proved an unhappy one, their tastes and habits being unlike; and an amicable separation was arranged, the courts giving her the guardianship of her boy.

Already Lady Isabel had found comfort in her sorrow in caring for the poor. " I first saw Lady Henry," says one of her devoted servants, " when she was lighting a fire in my mother's empty hearth in a London slum." Though, of course, much in society at this time from her high social position, she says of herself, " Though I was a woman of the world, I have never been a worldly woman. I have never seen the day that I would not gladly have left parks and palaces for fields and woods."

Her sister, Lady Adeline, had married the Marquis of Tavistock, afterward Duke of Bedford, and is now a widow; her father was much abroad, and the life at her favorite seat, Reigate Priory, was a quiet and somewhat lonely one. This estate, with the Priory, twenty miles from London, indeed the whole town of Reigate, was a portion of the gift made by William of Orange to Lady Henry's ancestor, Lord Chancellor Somers, for his help in expelling the Stuarts, and securing the throne to William and Mary. John, Lord Somers, was an eminent statesman, knighted in 1689, made lord-keeper of the great seal in 1693, and lord chancellor, and raised to the peerage as Baron Somers of Evesham in 1697. He was in Parliament fifty-nine years; "in some respects," says Macaulay, "the greatest man of that age, equally eminent as a jurist and as a politician, as an orator, and as a writer." He was noted also for his powers of conversation, and for his invariable good temper.

The Priory of Reigate, in Surrey, long antedates the time of Chancellor Somers. It was familiar to the Pilgrims who went to the shrine of Thomas à Becket at Canterbury, centuries before. Evelyn planted its groves, as he tells in his diary. It is said that the draft of Magna Charta was made there, which King John was forced to sign. A large brick building at the rear of the house is a relic of the monastic institutions which Henry VIII. destroyed.

Lady Henry lived at the Priory, and found her happiness in caring for her only child, and in reading books, theological, sceptical, scientific, and poetical. One day in June, seated under a grand old elm, her mind disturbed by doubt, she seemed to hear a voice saying, "My child, *act as if I were*, and *thou shalt know I am!*" That message changed her whole life. She went to her room early that night, and read through the Gospel of St. John. The next morning she told the friends who were visiting her that she had decided to retire from society; and as soon as they had departed she hastened with her son to Eastnor Castle, among the Malvern Hills in Herefordshire, about one hundred miles from London.

"Beautiful for situation," says Mr. Stead in the September, 1893, *Review of Reviews*, "the joy of the whole country-side, the castle rises high above one of the most lovely miniature lakes that ever gladdened a landscape. The view from the terrace over the lake, which fills the wooded basin, is like a scene in fairyland. As the swan sails stately across the mere, making long ripples across the glassy water in which the foliage of a hundred trees is reflected as in a burnished mirror, you seem to be transported to the region which the bards of chivalry have made their own."

The Eastnor estates are fifteen miles in length, and comprise twenty-five thousand acres. After a three miles' drive from the lodge-gate through Eastnor Park, with its great oaks, the castle is reached. This was built by John, first Earl Somers, in 1812, in the style of a Norman baronial castle. "The grand entrance," says Sarah Lee Teetor, "is through a lofty arched porch, leading through great doors up a flight of stone steps to the entrance hall. The decorations of this hall are Romanesque. Over the entrance is a trophy, consisting of a shield of hippopotamus skin, spears, and a Greek helmet. Near the door is an old Italian walnut cabinet, inlaid with imperial arms and other figures, with cupboards beneath. Above is the musicians' gallery. Of the arms arranged on each side of the stairs leading to the grand hall, on the left, is a large Venetian halberd of great beauty, probably used by the body-guard of the Doge on state occasions, engraved with the Lion of St. Mark, dated 1525.

"The grand or main hall is sixty feet long by thirty feet wide, and is sixty-eight feet high. The decorations are in perfect harmony, and on one wall is the inscription in ancient Arabic letters meaning, 'A perfect benediction.' From the upper part of the hall, the long shafts of the columns are Languedoc marble. The lower columns are of jasper, gray and Purbeck marble inlaid with porphyry. The spaces over the doors are filled in with onyx. In this hall is placed the principal part of the rare collection of arms and armor found by Charles, Earl Somers, one of chief interest being that of the body-guard of the Emperor Charles I., preserved in Milan for many years, and purchased by Lord Somers in 1853." This Earl, the father of Lady Isabel, was born in 1819, and died in 1883. In the dining-room are portraits of the Cocks family, which, with its great wealth, became allied to the Somers family by marriage. "From the walls of the dining-room hang shields containing arms and quarterings, showing the alliances made by the Cocks family from the reign of Henry VII. to the present day." Richard Cocks, the first settler at Castleditch, who died in 1623, is buried in Somers Chapel in Eastnor Church.

"The gothic drawing-room," says Mrs. Teetor, "the library, the inner hall with the great staircase and corridors, are all worthy of special description; but we pass on to the state bedroom, where is the state bedstead. It is Italian of the seventeenth century, and belonged to Cardinal Bellarmin. The posts and cornices are richly carved with figures, masks, and arabesques. Of the tapestry in this room, in three panels are represented the triumphs of Religion, Death, and Industry."

Eastnor Castle is open to the public on Mondays and Fridays from eleven o'clock till four, throughout the year. A shilling is paid for admission, and this is given to charity.

In this beautiful abode Lady Henry lived for some years her studious, quiet life. The Bible was her chief solace and companion. She found her work close at hand among her thousands of tenants. She soon learned what everybody learns who studies the causes of poverty and crime, that liquor drinking and liquor selling are for the most part responsible. She took the total abstinence pledge with several of her tenants, and started a small temperance society, making her first public address fifteen minutes long in a little school-room close to the castle gates.

Soon after she held Bible readings in the kitchens of the farmers on her estate, then mothers' meetings in the castle itself, and then, the world outside learning of her eloquence and power, inherited, perhaps, in part from the self-poised, learned Chancellor Somers, and vivified by an earnestness born of the spirit, urged her to speak in distant cities. At first she was timid and nervous, but this was gradually overcome. She learned to moderate her voice by practice, stationing her maid in the gallery of the castle, to raise a handkerchief whenever her tones were too low to be heard.

In deep sympathy with the poor, she visited the miners of South Wales, hired halls or erected tents, and securing lodgings in the family of some workingman, held "a ten or twelve days' mission" among them. Sometimes in the black darkness of the pits she held meetings among the colliers during their dinner-hour, and hundreds of sooty men listened with tearful faces in amazement and gratitude to the Christian words of this daughter of an earl. No wonder it seemed to them like a celestial visitation; like a dream rather than a reality. There was no more doubt. She had learned the truth of the divine voice, "Act as if I were, and *thou shalt know I am*," and she knew now in her own heart.

Once, when Lady Henry was seeking for a lodging in a great iron manufacturing town, she was directed to the house of a coal weigher. Telling the wife that she wished a room for a lady who was going to hold religious meetings, the woman replied, "If it was for you I would not mind, but ladies give so much trouble."

She finally consented; and when, to her surprise, Lady

Henry returned, saying, " You see I have come instead of the lady, but I will not give you any trouble," the good woman was greatly pleased.

Unmindful of fatigue, Lady Henry, called from town to town, has spoken in not less than two hundred villages and cities of Great Britain. In 1890 she was urged to become the president of the British Women's Temperance Association, succeeding Mrs. Margaret Bright Lucas, the sister of John Bright.

A year and a half later Lady Henry visited America by invitation of the National W. C. T. U., to attend the World's Woman's Christian Temperance Union held that year in Boston, representing half a million of women. The charming, unaffected manner, the persuasive eloquence, the devoted life, of one from the highest circles of Great Britain, won all hearts. Lady Henry spoke to crowded houses, always a great host not being able to gain admittance. She visited our poets, Whittier and Holmes; both high and low were alike anxious to do her honor.

Soon after she went to Chicago, and for some months assisted Miss Willard in editing the *Union Signal.* These two brilliant and noble women, Miss Willard and Lady Henry, became, as was natural, most devoted friends.

" My first visit to America," said Lady Henry, "was as much to see and know Miss Willard as for any other purpose, and to understand from her the principle upon which she had worked the marvellous organization of which she has long been president. It was a rainy Sunday some seven years ago, that I went down as usual at the castle to have tea with my capable and faithful housekeeper. We usually sat together on Sunday afternoon, and discussed the affairs of the village and the wants of the people, as she conducted large mothers' meetings for me in the village. I saw on her table a little blue book, and taking it up, read the title, 'Nineteen Beautiful Years.' It was the well-known memorial volume written by Frances E. Willard after the death of her sister Mary. I sat down by the fire, and soon became so engrossed that my old housekeeper could get nothing out of me that day, nor did I move until I had finished the little volume.

"From that time on I was impressed by that personality that has meant so much to so many women. The simplicity, the quaint candor, and the delicate touches of humor and pathos, were a revelation to me of a character that remained on my mind as belonging to one whom I placed in a niche among the ideal lives of whom I hoped to know more, and at whose shrines I worshipped."

The mother of Miss Willard became very fond of the English lady. "She has the unobtrusiveness of perfect culture," said Mrs. Willard; "she shall be loved always for her sweet ways." Lady Henry attended Mr. Moody's training-school for Christian workers, and in April, 1892, her son meantime having travelled in the Yellowstone and the great Northwest, returned to England.

Just before her departure, a farewell meeting was held in Tremont Temple, Boston, at which Lady Henry was presented with various gifts, perhaps none more useful than a rocking-chair, the women having heard that Eastnor Castle, with all its elegance, did not possess this American article of comfort. A poem for the occasion by Julia Ward Howe, and an address from the Mass.

W. C. T. U. were written on vellum, bound in white satin, and tied with a silver bow.

During the summer in England, Lady Henry took an active part in the Liberal elections, giving thirty-six addresses in fourteen days. Sometimes she met the yells and curses of the mob, while beer-mugs crashed through the windows of her carriage. Alas! that men and women have experienced the same treatment in America in the time of slavery and in the "crusade" against the liquor traffic. Those who fight wickedness in high places are accustomed, like Stephen, to being stoned.

In the autumn of 1892 Lady Henry returned to America to be present at the National Convention at Denver, Colo., taking Miss Willard back to England with her, where the English people gave our own temperance leader as grand a welcome at Exeter Hall and elsewhere as our country had given Lady Somerset. At Lady Henry's town house in London, at Reigate Priory, and at Eastnor Castle, Miss Willard, frail in health from her unselfish devotion to humanitarian work, found the rest and companionship she so richly deserved.

When she returned to America, Lady Henry said, "Our deepest love and gratitude go with her; and we feel that we are bound to those whom the great ocean separates with a tie that neither time nor space can dim, for their leader has done more to unify the women of England and America than the Atlantic cables that coil their lengths beneath the tossing billows, or the ocean greyhounds that bear us swiftly from shore to shore."

Lady Henry's three homes are kept open the year round, well supplied with servants, for herself and her friends. Her London home, in Gordon Square, is an old-fashioned, roomy abode. "The drawing-room," says Annie Wakeman Lathrop, "is a square, lofty apartment, fitted up in a style of quiet elegance. . . . The sofas are wide, and covered with down cushions, and there are easy-chairs and footstools in plenty. On the walls hang engravings of quiet, restful scenes, with several framed photographs of Lady Henry's friends." There is one of Miss Willard, and one of Whittier. There are many books, and vases of fresh flowers in every possible place.

The subsequent years for Lady Henry have been full to overflowing with hard work. "Letters come to her," says Miss Willard, in *The Outlook*, "from every nook and corner of the earth, urging her presence and help in the foundation of national and local unions. From seventy-five to one hundred letters a day, and from a dozen to twenty telegrams, must be taken care of as a mere incident of her greatly preoccupied life. . . . She reads her innumerable letters as rapidly as they come, unless they are purely routine letters, when they go to her secretary. Lady Henry sits with stenographers all day long, unless she is obliged, which is usually the case, to attend committees or fulfil engagements. Her greatest deprivation is the lack of time to read, for she has always been devoted to books; it is pathetic to see her put a copy of Tennyson, Wordsworth, Drummond, or Matthew Arnold in her travelling-bag, hoping to get a few minutes to read on the train or in the intervals of meetings. She works as busily on the cars as in her office, and has immense power of concentration, so that she throws off letters, articles, paragraphs, speeches, with remarkable facility."

Lady Henry is one of the editors of *The Woman's Herald*, and of the *Woman's Signal*, published in London. " I have always thought editorial work a most fascinating occupation," she says. "There is nothing I like better, and I only regret that I cannot devote more time to it than I do. My many speaking engagements interfere and make the work rather toilsome. But then, what a happiness work is! there is nothing so satisfactory as having an object in life." She does not live for herself. " Sacrifice," she says, " is the foundation of all real success."

Lady Henry writes much for the magazines, giving to charity the compensation which she receives. Her gifts are many and constant. At Reigate she has for many years sustained an industrial home for girls from the workhouse schools, " impressed," she says, " with the paramount necessity of providing such girls with surroundings that shall mean to them throughout their lives a memory of home."

" She has made her seats at Eastnor and at Reigate," says Mr. Stead, "into guest-houses for the recruiting of the weary and heavy laden of every rank, but chiefly of the poorest. Hundreds of convalescents from the most squalid regions of London have found themselves, through her bounty, treated as the guests of a peeress in castle or in priory."

Fêtes are frequently given to thousands of working people. " My greatest desire," she says, " is that a day spent at Eastnor may be a happy memory to tired and hard-working men and women, and that they may retain some recollections of its peace and beauty in the midst of their toiling lives."

In Somers Town, a tract in London given to her ancestor, the Chancellor, by William III., on which a hundred and twenty-five thousand persons now live, Lady Henry has made many improvements. "Old buildings are disappearing," says a writer, "disreputable houses are being removed; and in their places are being built comfortable homes at low rentals, baths and coffee-houses for men, nurseries for children, comforts for the sick, and protection agencies for the workingman." She has built chapels among her tenantry, and provided reading-rooms and restaurants. The trustees of her estates have tried through the courts to restrain her from closing the liquor-saloons in buildings owned by her. Some of these, inherited from her father, having long leases, she has not yet been able to close.

In her report for 1894 before the British Woman's Temperance Association, Lady Henry says, "Much fine sentiment is expended in descanting on the 'happy homes of England;' talk of country lanes, and pleasant wayside cottages nestling amid green fields and flowering orchards; but it is not only in the city slum that blots our civilization that we find want and misery. The history of the tillers of the soil in their old age is well-nigh as desolate."

She said to a friend, "The wage-earners, men and women alike, have our profoundest sympathy. We shall give our support to all measures for the amelioration of the lives of our toiling sisters and brothers." She believes the "eight-hours" measure is sure to become a law within the next few years. When persons of wealth and power thus realize their responsibility, and accept their fortune as a trust to be used for the betterment of the world, we may look forward happily with James Russell Lowell: —

> "Down the happy future runs a flood
> Of prophesying light;
> It shows an earth no longer stained with blood,
> Blossom and fruit where now we see the bud
> Of Brotherhood and Right."

Lady Henry is an ardent advocate of universal peace. " So deluded and demoralized," she says, " are women by the scarlet, the tinsel, and the sword, that they present the anomaly of being the most ardent admirers of their own greatest scourge. If there is to be a change in the pernicious estimate of war, it must come by the awakening of those who suffer most from its results. And if women are to bring this about, the leaders of women must be willing to endure the sneer which will be raised by the exposure of the shams, the wickedness, and cruelty that invariably accompany the march of military banners. When women understand that to be a trained destroyer of human life is a degrading, even if it be a necessary vocation, war will cease. Nothing happens in this world; we must set causes in motion if we expect results, and for this each one is equally responsible."

Lady Henry is a firm believer in suffrage for women. She says, " I shall always fearlessly declare my settled purpose to work for this cause whenever and wherever I have the opportunity, until our brothers place us side by side with themselves upon the throne of government, that they and we, and the homes of which we are the equal and mutual guardians, may be first pure, then peaceable." She has always said, "We recognize no difference in the moral standard for man from that ordained for woman."

"I believe," she writes, "that, as in the home circle two hearts are needed at the hearth, and as two hands must be clasped along the ways of life, so in the larger home circle which we call a nation, no government is complete in which the woman's voice is not heard in council with the man's."

She thinks "the gaining of the rights of citizenship is the most effective means by which women can obtain redress for their own wrongs and assist in the redressing of all wrongs, whether done to man, woman, or child. The life-giver ought also to be the law-giver. . . . We are equally grateful to an advanced radical like John Burns, or to a conservative like Mr. Balfour, for voting and speaking in favor of Woman's Suffrage."

Lady Henry, in *The Arena* for October, 1894, says of woman: "You entrust her with the most sacred duty on earth; you ask her first to give the nation her children; you ask her to nurture and care for them; you ask her to instil into their minds the holiest aspirations that are to be their guide in after life; you ask her, with all her experience and her judgment, to look upon the world with its many social evils that her mother's eyes are swift to see while yours are blinded; and then you ask her to believe that it is 'justice' that her voice should be silent, her action powerless to guard the interests of her girls whom you declare that men, and men alone, must represent. You ask her to sit through long weary nights rocking the cradle, but, when the child grows up to manhood, you say that she has no right to deal with those questions that make for the weal or woe of his future life."

Lady Henry, with her great wealth, sets an example of simplicity in dress. If she wears any ornament, it is apt to be a small diamond crescent at her throat. She says she "would like very much to make a crusade against the eighteen-inch waist which the poor shop-girls labor with, and every other unnatural distortion of the body. In fact, I think some of the fashion plates which are exhibited positively wicked." Lady Henry urges out-door life for women. "There is nothing," she says, "that weighs upon our spirits more, or is fitted to arouse more gloomy forebodings for the future of our country, than the stooping, narrow-chested, anæmic-looking girls who crowd the offices, factories, and shops of all our cities. An outing into the pure country air once a year has hitherto been the summit of their hopes, but a revolution is being slowly wrought that will entirely change the aspect of life for working-girls. The country with all its recreative charms will soon be at their doors. The privilege hitherto belonging only to the rich — a Saturday to Monday in the country, when the sultry air makes town intolerable — is fast becoming possible to them; and the new friend that brings with it these fresh hopes is none other than that swift steed of steel, the bicycle." Lady Henry is president of a cycling association.

Lady Henry is fond of horses, and may be seen, in those rare intervals of leisure at Eastnor, "in the great park, or along the blooming highways, driving with skill and grace her favorite pair; going up the Monument hill, where like a sentinel stands the obelisk in memory of her brave ancestor; gathering the doves around her from their cote on the lodge-gate; speaking a friendly word to faithful servants all their lifetime in the family, asking after their ailments, promising to see them in their cottages; and when night falls, and the Castle bell is heard summoning the family to the chapel, Lady Henry is at the reading-desk to conduct the evening devotions."

While in America Lady Henry labored constantly, not sparing herself in any good work. When the women who made shoes at Haverhill, Mass., had a grievance, she spoke in their behalf. When some of the boys of Melrose, Mass., formed an anti-tobacco society, Lady Henry, as a tribute of esteem for Mary A. Livermore, whose home is at Melrose, gave a lecture to fifteen hundred persons, the proceeds to be used in providing headquarters for the boys. The W. C. T. U. of Massachusetts gave Lady Henry a grand banquet at Music Hall, Boston, when the flags of the two nations were intertwined, and an immense audience rose to welcome the distinguished visitor, as they sang " God save the Queen."

Lady Henry is fond of America. She thinks American women " in the aggregate are better educated than English women, though the best intellectual women in England are unsurpassed anywhere. . . . To the magnificent public schools of America is undoubtedly due their educational position. It is the early training and discipline that tell through life. The educational system of America provides these, and makes solid women."

She said in her farewell in *The Union Signal*, April,

1892, "In some respects my own dear land excels yours, even in the particular that is your most striking quality — progressive thought. I make no plea for the superiority of our own government; but I merely state that it has given us a far more rapid and accurate postal service, and railways much less destructive to human life, although they do not provide the comfort and the luxury that I find in this country. The smoking-car on your trains seems to me a degradation. . . . The fact that our telegraph system is under government control is of inestimable value to our people. We can send twelve words for twelve cents to any part of the United Kingdom. Our civil service, being wholly divorced from politics, is in every way more satisfactory. It is inconceivable to me that any people so intelligent as the Americans should patiently put up with changing every local postmaster with every change of President."

While Lady Henry's work lies along many lines, a large part of her time is given to the temperance reform. During seven months of 1894 in England, she held one hundred and fifteen meetings, and twenty-seven conferences, addressing nearly two hundred thousand persons.

With all these varied labors, she has found time to be a companion for her only son, who is as devoted to her as she to him. She has been his almost constant companion, the bright, cheerful sharer of his boyish plans and hopes. The story is told of her that when he was six or seven years old, a titled lady called upon her at Reigate, found her on the lawn " with the butler, two footmen, the nurse, and a maid, all busy making hay." Her son, like his mother, loves the country, and she was adding to his pleasure.

This year, 1895, May 18, he became twenty-one years of age, an event duly celebrated at the Priory. He resembles his mother in looks and manner. Like her he also writes well, and has a book in press concerning his travels in the Northwest. He has recently been in Central America with Mr. Richard Harding Davis, evidently possessing the love of exploration which characterized his grandfather, Earl Somers.

After the summer of 1895, spent in Norway, and the autumn in the United States, Lady Henry and Miss Willard propose to make the tour of the world, presenting to the various governments the Polyglot Petition with three million names in fifty languages, asking for the prohibition of the liquor and opium traffic in every land. The attention of hundreds of thousands will thus be called to the subject.

Lady Henry is in early middle life, with the enthusiasm of earnest womanhood, and the hopefulness of a devoted Christian. "The altruistic spirit is abroad in the world," she says, "and nothing can stop its onward march; born in the heart of Christ, its radiations continually sweep wider circles, and shall enclose all the tribes and races of men. The sweet south wind of the Spirit shall blow over the poppy fields of the East and blight them; shall sweep unobserved into the dismal Zenana homes and fill them full of sunshine; shall penetrate and purify every habitation of cruelty; shall stamp on every face the image of God, and touch every brow with the glory of a heavenly hope."

Lady Henry's remarkable gifts as a speaker have won for her wide recognition on both sides of the Atlantic. Miss Willard says, "There is not another woman in

England who has such sympathetic power over an audience. Her gentle presence, tender tones, and wide hospitality of thought win every heart. She has the mind of a statesman; its scope and grasp are altogether beyond those of most women; and she unites in her thinking and character the best powers of a capable man and a thoughtful and highly educated woman."

Lady Henry is also an artist, her water colors being highly praised. Her Christmas card of last year, "A Nineteenth Century Nativity," was artistic and beautiful. A woman with a sleeping babe in her arms, is seated on a doorstep asking alms. These words are in gold letters, —

> " Who gives me alms feeds three —
> Himself, the hungry one, and ME."

Best of all, Lady Henry's life is an example to the women of society and wealth, of the way to use time and influence, and a comfort to the poor in showing that the religion of Christ does really mean human brotherhood.

JULIA WARD HOWE.

LIKE Lady Henry Somerset in England, Julia Ward Howe has used her high social position and brilliant talents for the good of the world. She was born May 27, 1819, in a handsome home in Bowling Green, at that time the fashionable part of New York City. Her father, Samuel Ward, was a merchant and banker of New York, of the firm of Prime, Ward, & King.

"He was a majestic person," says Mrs. Howe, "of somewhat severe aspect and reserved manners, but with a vein of true genialty and a great benevolence of heart. His great gravity, and the absence of a mother, naturally subdued the tone of the whole household; and though a greatly cherished set of children, we were not a very merry one."

Her grandfather, Samuel Ward, a graduate of Brown University, was a lieutenant-colonel in the Revolutionary War; was at Peekskill, Valley Forge, and Red Bank, and wrote an official account of the last-named battle. He was a scholar, as well as a brave soldier, and all through his campaigns carried with him a diamond edition of the Latin classics. He was the son of Gov. Samuel Ward of Rhode Island, Mrs. Howe's great-grandfather. The mother of Gov. Samuel Ward was a great-granddaughter of Roger Williams. Four of Mrs.

Howe's ancestors were governors of Rhode Island, two Wards and two Greens. On her mother's side her ancestors were the Marions of South Carolina, her mother being a grand-niece of General Marion.

This mother, Julia Cutler Ward, was a woman of much beauty and intellect. She died at the early age of twenty-eight, leaving six little children, the fourth Julia, only five years of age.

The blow was a distressing one to the banker and his children. For weeks he lay prostrated on a bed of sickness. Finally his wife's sister, Miss Eliza Cutler, came into the home to bring up the children as best she could. She was a witty and talented woman, and helped to develop them in mind as well as in body.

Mrs. Laura E. Richards, the daughter of Julia Ward Howe, in her book, "When I was Your Age," published by Estes & Lauriat, says of Miss Cutler, "A very good aunt she was, and devoted to the motherless children; but sometimes she did funny things. They went out to ride every day — the children, I mean — in a great yellow chariot lined with fine blue cloth. Now, it occurred to their kind aunt that it would have a charming effect if the children were dressed to match the chariot. So thought, so done! Dressmakers and milliners plied their art; and one day Broadway was electrified by the sight of the little Misses Ward, seated in uneasy state on the blue cushions, clad in wonderful raiment of yellow and blue. They had blue pelisses and yellow satin bonnets.

"And this was all very well for the two younger ones, with their dark eyes and hair, and their rosy cheeks; but Julia, young as she was, felt dimly that blue and yellow was not the combination to set off her tawny locks and exquisite sea-shell complexion. It is not probable, however, that she sorrowed deeply over the funny clothes; for her mind was never set on clothes, either in childhood or in later life. Did not her sister meet her one day coming home from school with one blue shoe and one green?"

The little Julia showed great fondness for books. When nine years old she was studying Paley's "Moral Philosophy" with girls twice her age. Yet with a love for studies beyond her years, she was a child at heart, and grieved when at this age her dolls were taken from her, and she was told that "Miss Ward was too old to play with dolls any longer." "This heart-rending separation took place on her ninth birthday," writes Mrs. Howe's daughter Maud.

For Julia, as well as for all his children, the father provided the best teachers in music and in German and Italian. One of these teachers was Dr. Joseph Greene Cogswell, late librarian of the Astor Library.

When Julia was fourteen, her father bought a large house on the corner of Broadway and Bond Street, — red brick, with white marble columns and steps. Here every Thursday evening eminent musicians came to accept the Ward hospitality, and to return the courtesy by displaying their talents. So well did Julia play and sing, that her friends urged her to devote her life to music.

Two years after the large home was purchased, Samuel Ward, Jr., returned from Germany, where he had been studying. Sharing his sister's love of music and literature, Julia's life became happier than ever in this close affection of two superior minds. Samuel had travelled with the poet Longfellow, and their warm friendship lasted as long as they lived.

Distinguished authors gathered at the Ward home, and stimulated the young girl in her love for books. When she was sixteen she wrote, "The Ill-cut Mantell; a Romaunt of the Time of Kynge Arthur," and gave the manuscript to her youngest sister, who relates this incident : —

"One day the young poet chanced upon her two younger sisters busy in some childish game. She upbraided them for their frivolous pursuit, and insisted that they should occupy themselves, as she did, in the composition of verses. Louisa, the elder of the two, flatly refused to make the effort; but the little Annie dutifully obeyed the elder sister, and, after a long and and resolute struggle, produced some stanzas, of which the following lines have always been remembered, —

> 'He hears the ravens when they call,
> And stands them in a pleasant hall.'"

Although brilliant and witty in conversation, society did not satisfy Julia. "In the large rooms of my father's house," she says, "I walked up and down, perpetually alone, dreaming of extraordinary things that I should see and do. I now began to read Shakespeare and Byron, and to try my hand at poems and plays." She is glad these were not published then, as, she says, "A little praise or a little censure would have been a much more disturbing element in those days than in these."

The girl did not tell her father of these desires for

authorship, lest he should be disturbed by such an unusual wish on the part of a young woman. Though he loved her devotedly, and while eating his meals would hold in his left hand the hand of this daughter who sat next to him at table, she always stood somewhat in awe of him.

Mrs. Howe recently told Mr. John D. Barry, that her first published work, when she was seventeen, was "a review of a poem of Lamartine's called 'Jocelyn,' together with a translation of parts of it." She said, "The Rev. Leonard Woods, editor of one of the theological reviews, published it. Then, not long afterward, I wrote an article on a translation that had just appeared of some of the minor poems of Goethe and Schiller. This was printed in the *American Review*, edited by Charles King, afterward President of Columbia College. Both of these articles attracted attention, and encouraged me very much."

Artists as well as musicians and authors, came to the Ward mansion to visit its picture-gallery, where the father had collected many foreign works of art. It was not strange, therefore, that a sister of Julia should marry the well-known artist, Thomas Crawford of Rome, the father of Marion Crawford, the novelist.

Besides all this study and intercourse with scholarly people, there were times of merry-making at the banker's home. Mrs. Howe, in the *Forum* for July, 1893, in an article, "How the Fourth of July should be Celebrated," speaks of the laughing faces of her young brothers, who, she says, "were allowed to arrange a small table, for their greater convenience, on the pavement of ancient Bond Street, a very quiet by-way in those days. From this spot went forth a perpetual popping and fizzing, varied by the occasional thud of a double-headed fire-cracker. Shouts of merriment followed those explosions. The girls within-doors enjoyed the fracas from the open windows; and in the evening our good elders brought forth a store of Roman candles, blue lights, and rockets. I remember a year, early in the thirties, in which good Gideon Lee, a Democratic mayor of New York, issued an edict prohibitive of all home fireworks. Just as we had settled ourselves in the determination to regard him thenceforth as our natural enemy, the old gentleman's heart failed him; and, living next door to us, he called to say that he would make a few exceptions to the rule for the day, and that we should count among these."

While in the prime of life, Mr. Samuel Ward, the father, died, and the family moved out of the Bond Street home, and went to live with an uncle, Mr. John Ward. Not long after, Julia, who was now a very attractive young woman, went to Boston on a visit. There she met Margaret Fuller, Horace Mann, Charles Sumner, Ralph Waldo Emerson, and other distinguished people. They were pleased with the intellectual and charming girl from New York; and she, in turn, revered the friends who gave her such a cordial welcome.

Among this band of thinkers was Dr. Samuel Gridley Howe, already noted as a philanthropist and reformer. Born in Boston in 1801, a graduate from Brown University in 1821, he espoused the cause of Greek independence in 1824, and sailed for Greece. At first he was a surgeon, and attempted to organize hospitals; then he took an active part in the war, and for two years suffered all the hardships and dangers of the conflict.

When he saw that the Greeks were starving, he hastened to America, eloquently pleaded their cause, procured money, clothing, and provisions, and went back with a full vessel for their relief. He personally superintended the distribution, and famishing women and children looked upon him as an angel from heaven. Though idolized by the Greeks, he was obliged to leave them in 1830, having contracted swamp-fever.

The Greeks never forgot the tall and handsome young soldier, with black hair and large blue eyes, whose face beamed with love for the oppressed. "Once," says his daughter Laura, " he saved the life of a wounded Greek at the risk of his own, and the rescued man followed him afterward like a dog, and would even sleep at his feet at night." Whittier, in his poem "The Hero," has told of this incident, —

> " Oh, for a knight like Bayard,
> Without reproach or fear!
> My light glove on his casque of steel,
> My love-knot on his spear!
>
> Oh, for the white plume floating
> Sad Zutphen's field above, —
> The lion heart in battle,
> The woman's heart in love!
>
> . . . .
>
> Smile not, fair unbeliever!
> One man at least I know
> Who might wear the crest of Bayard,
> Or Sidney's plume of snow.
>
> . . . .

Last to fly and first to rally,
 Rode he of whom I speak,
When, groaning in his bridle-path,
 Sank down a wounded Greek, —

With the rich Albanian costume
 Wet with many a ghastly stain,
Gazing on earth and sky as one
 Who might not gaze again!

He looked forward to the mountains,
 Back on foes that never spare;
Then flung him from his saddle,
 And placed the stranger there.

'Alla! hu!' Through flashing sabres,
 Through a stormy hail of lead,
The good Thessalian charger
 Up the slopes of olives sped.

Hot spurred the turbaned riders, —
 He almost felt their breath,
Where a mountain stream rolled darkly down
 Between the hills and death.

One brave and manful struggle, —
 He gained the solid land,
And the cover of the mountains,
 And the carbines of his band."

After leaving Greece, Dr. Howe travelled in France and Switzerland, attended a course of lectures in Paris in the winter of 1831, and in 1832 returned to America.

Such a young man could not rest without helping somebody. He and a friend became interested in the blind, for whom there were no schools in our country; and Dr. Howe took several blind children to his home and taught them. Others took an interest, Colonel Perkins gave a fine house for the school, and Dr. Howe became the valuable head of the Perkins Institution for the Blind.

He at once went to Europe to make further investigations in the schools of France and England. While in Paris, his sympathy for oppressed Poland led him to carry relief to the Polish army which had crossed into Prussia. He was arrested and imprisoned for several weeks, and regained his liberty only after repeated demands made by the American minister. Dr. Howe was taken over the French frontier by night, and told never to enter Prussia again.

After the school for the blind had been carried on a few years, Dr. Howe took into his heart and care a little girl eight years old, deaf, dumb, and blind, Laura Bridgman, born at Hanover, N.H., in 1829. When two years old the child lost sight, hearing, speech, and the senses of taste and smell, through a severe sickness. Her case seemed hopeless to all save Dr. Howe.

With a patience that seemed inexhaustible, and a wisdom that constantly thought out new expedients, the child was taught to read, to write, to do needlework, to play on the piano, to be a joy to herself, and an honor to the institution. Not satisfied to confine his labors to the blind, Dr. Howe took up the cause of idiotic and weak-minded children, and was abundantly rewarded by the results.

When Julia Ward met Dr. Howe, who was eighteen years older than herself, it was not strange that among many admirers he won her heart and hand. "' Chev' was the name by which she always called our father," says her daughter Laura: " it was an abbreviation of

Chevalier; for he was always to her the 'knight without reproach or fear.'"

Dr. Howe and Julia Ward were married in 1843, when she was in her twenty-fourth year. Her two youngest sisters had prepared the wedding garments; and "it was with difficulty," says her daughter Maud, "that the bride-elect could be induced to express a preference as to the material of her wedding-dress, so little was her mind occupied with the concerns of the wardrobe."

Soon after the wedding, Dr. and Mrs. Howe made an extended journey in Europe, taking with them the bride's youngest sister, Annie, who had written in her childhood the unique poem on the ravens in the hall.

Charles Dickens had told the story of Laura Bridgman in his "American Notes," and many were eager to see Dr. Howe and his gifted young wife. They received much attention from Dickens, Carlyle, the Duchess of Sutherland, the poet Rogers, Sydney Smith, Monckton Milnes, and others.

In their own carriage, with the sister Annie, they travelled through the Netherlands and along the Rhine. Switzerland, the Tyrol, and Germany were greatly enjoyed. They spent a month at Milan, and five months in Rome, where Mrs. Howe's first child was born, and named Julia Romana, after the city of her birth.

On their return to Boston, Dr. and Mrs. Howe found a warm welcome. Soon an estate was purchased near the Institution for the Blind, of which Dr. Howe always remained the director, which the young mother, on account of its great garden and conservatories, called, half in sport, "Green Peace."

It was a roomy old house, with a large dining-room. "On the floor," says the daughter Laura, "was a wonderful carpet, all in one piece, which was made in France, and had belonged to Joseph Bonaparte, a brother of the great emperor. In the middle was a medallion of Napoleon and Marie Louise, with sun-rays about them; then came a great circle, with strange beasts on it ramping and roaring (only they roared silently); and then a plain space; and in the corners birds and fishes such as never were seen in air or sea. Yes, that *was* a carpet! It was here we danced the wonderful dances."

Into this happy home came six children, five besides the Julia born in Rome,—Florence, Harry, Laura, and Maud. A beautiful boy died in 1863. Mrs. Howe refers to him in an exquisite poem, "Little One," in her "Later Lyrics," published in 1866, —

> "My dearest boy, my sweetest!
> For paradise the meetest;
> The child that never grieves me;
> The love that never leaves me;
> The lamb of Jésu tended;
> The shadow, star befriended;
> In Winter's woe and straining,
> The blossom still remaining.
>
> . . . . . .
>
> If men would garlands give me,
> If steadfast hearts receive me,
> Their homage I'd surrender
> For one embrace most tender;
> One kiss, with sorrow in it,
> To hold thee but one minute,
> One word, one tie recalling,
> Beyond the gulf appalling.
>
> . . . . . .

> I mourn in simpler praying,
> More work and less delaying,
> In hope enforced that mellows
> The crudeness of thy fellows,
> Who, past thy lovely season,
> Attempt the wars of Reason;
> I mourn thee with endeavor
> That loves and grieves forever."

"Green Peace" was a home where the literary mother and the philanthropic father found their greatest comfort. Dr. Howe played with his children, took them with him in his morning walks, told them stories, or read to them from his favorite poets, Scott and Byron.

Mrs. Howe, with her beautiful voice, sang to the children the German songs which she and her brother had sung together after he came back from Heidelberg, or pretty French and Italian airs. When the little ones wanted a change she wrote songs of her own, composing both the music and the words, such as "Baby's Shoes," published in "Later Lyrics," —

> "Little feet, pretty feet,
>   Feet of fairy Maud,
> Fair and fleet, trim and neat,
>   Carry her abroad!
>
> Be as wings, tiny things,
>   To my butterfly:
> In the flowers, hours on hours,
>   Let my darling lie.
>
> . . . .
>
> Like a charm which doth arm
>   Some poor mother's pain
> For the child dream-beguiled
>   She shall know again,

> By the pet amulet
> Kept through lonely years;
> Little shoe, I and you
> Would not part for tears."

There was no end of happy times provided by the devoted mother for the children. Now they had a party or a delightful picnic, which was never complete unless the mother was present; now they had "Blue Beard" acted, or they pored over Shakespeare illustrated, or listened to the famous exploits in the Trojan War. "It was worth while to have measles and things of that sort," writes Laura, "not because we had stewed prunes and cream-toast — oh, no! — but because our mother sat by us and sang 'Lord Thomas and Fair Elinor,' or some mystic ballad."

With all this merry-making for the loved ones, Mrs. Howe found time for much study and writing, especially when they were at their charming summer-home at Lawton's Valley, in Newport, with its old mill and waterfall which Mrs. Laura Richards has so beautifully described in her "Queen Hildegarde."

Here Mrs. Howe read the Latin poets, especially Horace, and the Latin historians; also Spinoza, Hegel, Kant, and other German philosophers. In recent years she has often lectured upon the latter. Here she wrote many of her essays and poems for various magazines.

Mrs. Maud Howe Elliott thus describes their life at Oak Glen, the Newport home, in the *Critic* for June 11, 1887, —

"The day's routine is something in this order: breakfast in the American fashion, at eight o'clock; and then a stroll about the place, after which the household duties are attended to; and then a long morning of work. Letter-writing, a heavy burden, is attended to first; and then whatever literary work there is on the anvil is labored at steadily and uninterruptedly until one o'clock, when the great event of the day occurs. This is the arrival of the mail. . . .

"After the newspapers and the letters have been digested, comes the early dinner, followed by coffee served in the green parlor, which is quite the most important apartment of the establishment. It is an open-air parlor, in the shape of a semi-circle, set about with a close tall green hedge, and shaded by the spreading boughs of an ancient mulberry-tree. Its inmates are completely shielded from the sight of any chance passers-by. . . . It was in this small paradise that 'Mr. Isaacs' was written, and read aloud to Mrs. Howe, chapter by chapter, as it was written by her nephew, Mr. Crawford. Sometimes there is reading aloud from the newspapers and reviews here; and then the busiest woman in all Newport goes back to her sanctum for two more working-hours, after which she either drives or walks till sunset. . . . In these sunset rambles Mrs. Howe is sure to be accompanied by one or more of her grandchildren, four of whom, with their mother, Mrs. Hall, pass the summer, at Oak Glen. . . . After supper, when the children are at last quiet and tucked up in their little beds, there is more music, either with the piano in the drawing-room, or, if it is a warm night, on the piazza with the guitar. . . .

"Behind the house there is a grove of trees, — oaks, willows, maples, and pines, — which is the haunt of many singing-birds. . . . There are lotus-trees at Oak

Glen; but its mistress cannot be said to eat thereof, for she is never idle, and what she calls rest would be thought by many people to be very hard work. She rests herself, after the work of the day, by reading her Greek books, which have given her the greatest intellectual enjoyment of the later years of her life. Last summer she studied Plato in the original, and this year she is reading the plays of Sophocles."

In 1854, when Mrs. Howe was thirty-five, her first volume of poems, "Passion Flowers," was published anonymously, though the authorship was soon guessed by Emerson, Longfellow, Holmes, and others.

The following year, 1855, "The World's Own," a five-act tragedy in blank verse, was played at Wallack's Theatre in New York, Mathilda Heron and Edwin Sothern taking part in it. Two years later, 1857, a second volume of poems appeared, "Words for the Hour," full of the spirit of the sad and earnest years which preceded our Civil War.

Both Dr. Howe and his wife were ardent workers in the anti-slavery cause. They edited an anti-slavery paper, the *Boston Commonwealth*, established by the patriotic and ever generous Mr. Stearns, and were leaders with Garrison, Sumner, Phillips, Higginson, and Theodore Parker. "It was my husband," says Mrs. Howe, " who suggested the holding of meetings in Boston for the discussion of the problem with Abolitionists on one side, and pro-slavery men on the other. Robert Toombs, who boasted that he would hold his slaves under the shadow of the Bunker Hill Monument, and Colonel Houston, I remember, came, and we had lively times."

In 1858 "Hippolytus," a tragedy, was written for

Edwin Booth by Mrs. Howe. "A Trip to Cuba" was published in 1860, giving an account of a winter spent by Dr. Howe and herself in the tropics. The next year was written the world-famed, "Battle Hymn of the Republic." She has told how it came to be written.

"In the late autumn of the year 1861 I visited the national capital, in company with my husband, Dr. Howe, and a party of friends, among whom were Governor and Mrs. Andrew, Mr. and Mrs. E. P. Whipple, and my dear pastor, Rev. James Freeman Clarke.

"One day we drove out to attend a review of troops, appointed to take place some distance from the city. In the carriage with me were James Freeman Clarke and Mr. and Mrs. Whipple. The day was fine, and everything promised well; but a sudden surprise on the part of the enemy interrupted the proceedings before they were well begun. A small body of our men had been surrounded and cut off from their companions; re-enforcements were sent to their assistance, and the expected pageant was necessarily given up. The troops who were to have taken part in it were ordered back to their quarters, and we also turned our horses' heads homeward.

"For a long distance the foot-soldiers nearly filled the road. They were before and behind, and we were obliged to drive very slowly. We presently began to sing some of the well-known songs of the war, and among them, —

'John Brown's body lies a-mouldering in the grave.'

"This seemed to please the soldiers, who cried, 'Good for you!' and themselves took up the strain. Mr.

Clarke said to me, 'You ought to write some new words to that tune.' I replied that I had often wished to do so.

"In spite of the excitement of the day, I went to bed and slept as usual, but awoke next morning in the gray of the early dawn, and to my astonishment found that the wished-for lines were arranging themselves in my brain. I lay quite still until the last verse had completed itself in my thoughts, then hastily rose, saying to myself, 'I shall lose this if I don't write it down immediately.' I searched for a sheet of paper and an old stump of a pen which I had had the night before, and began to scrawl the lines almost without looking, as I had learned to do by often scratching down verses in the darkened room where my little children were sleeping. Having completed this, I lay down again and fell asleep, but not without feeling that something of importance had happened to me." The poem was written at Willard's Hotel.

"One of my friends," says Mrs. Howe, "now has the original 'scrawl' of the 'Battle Hymn.' It is almost indecipherable; if I hadn't copied it the day after it was written, I should probably have lost it."

The poem was published early in 1862, in the *Atlantic Monthly*. While in Libby Prison, Chaplain McCabe and his fellow-prisoners in some way obtained the words of the hymn, and sang it with rejoicing upon learning of a Union victory. After his release he lectured in Washington, and told of the incident. The verses soon came to be known and loved everywhere.

The same year, in the winter of 1862, in Mrs. Howe's home on Chestnut Street, Boston, she gave a series of parlor lectures, each of ten personal friends being privileged to invite a specified number to attend. The subjects were, "Liberty, Equality, Fraternity," "Doubt and Belief," "Proteus; or, The Secret of Success," "Duality of Character," and others. These essays were so greatly enjoyed, that she was soon asked to read them in public. She wrote about this time three papers for the *Christian Examiner* on "The Name and Existence of God," "The Ideal State," and "The Ideal Church."

In 1867 Mrs. Howe made her third journey across the Atlantic, with her husband and two of her children, Julia Romana and Laura. Dr. Howe, although sixty-six years old, was as earnest as ever in behalf of the struggling Greeks, and at this time went to carry aid to the little island of Crete. After a long sojourn in England, France, Germany, and Italy, they returned, and Mrs. Howe published, in 1868, a book of travel, "From the Oak to the Olive."

About this time Mrs. Howe became interested in Woman Suffrage. In a memorial address, after the death of Lucy Stone, Oct. 18, 1893, Mrs. Howe said, "I think it may have been in 1869 that Colonel Higginson wrote to me, earnestly requesting that I would sign, with others, a call for a woman's suffrage convention, to be held in Boston. The war had then brought many of us out of the ruts of established ways. It had changed the aspect of our social world, and, will ye, nill ye, had forced us to take a larger outlook into the possibilities of the future than it had been our wont to do. I not only signed the call just mentioned, but actually found my way into the assemblage, where Lucy Stone, Wendell Phillips, Colonel Higginson, and William Lloyd Garrison occupied the platform. As I entered and shyly seated myself, a messenger sought me out, and invited me to sit with the friends of suffrage.

"The speeches to which I listened were calm, even, and convincing; and when I, in turn, was requested to say a few words, I gave in my adherence to the cause. From that time forth I marched to the music of a new hope; and all the years that have passed since then I have never had occasion to regret the departure which I made then and there."

In 1869 Mrs. Howe helped to establish the New England Women's Club, composed of several hundred able and cultured women, who meet weekly to listen to some paper or discussion on educational or other useful topic. They have parlors in Park Street, Boston. Mrs. Howe was the second president of the club, and its members have never been willing that she should resign.

She also founded the Boston Saturday Morning Club. With Colonel Higginson, she founded the Town and Country Club of Newport, and is its president. For many years Mrs. Howe has been president of the Association for the Advancement of Women, of which she was an original member, and to whose annual congresses she has contributed valuable papers.

"In 1870," says Mrs. Howe, "the horrors of the Franco-Russian war moved me to write an epistle 'to womanhood throughout the world,' asserting the right of women to prevent the waste of life, of which they alone knew the cost. This document was translated into several languages, and was quite widely distributed and read."

In the year 1872 Dr. and Mrs. Howe, with their

daughter Maud and a party of friends, spent three winter months in the island of San Domingo. President Grant appointed Dr. Howe a member of the commission which was sent to investigate the advisability of annexation to the United States. Dr. Howe was heartily in favor of the union.

From San Domingo, Mrs. Howe went abroad as a delegate to the World's Prison Reform Congress in London, before which body she spoke earnestly against the flogging of prisoners. She had also the hope of uniting the women of Europe and America in a society advocating peace in place of war, and the settlement of international difficulties by arbitration. In London she spoke to large audiences Sunday evenings, on "The Mission of Christianity in Relation to the Pacification of the World." At one of the large public meetings held by Mrs. Howe, Sir John Bowring, the noted author and linguist, Mrs. Ernestine L. Rose, and others took part.

Mrs. Howe may not live to see the fulfilment of her hopes in this respect; but she rendered great service to humanity when she turned the thoughts of women to the horrors of war, rather than to its glitter and glory.

In 1873 Dr. Howe and his wife again visited San Domingo, and became deeply attached to the people. The health of the former had become much impaired by his severe labors; and on Jan. 9, 1876, he died after a brief illness. Dr. James Freeman Clarke says of Dr. Howe, in his volume of "Memorial Sketches," "To me it seems that his last work was far greater than his first, and that the chivalry of his youth was crowned by the diviner and more gallant endeavors and successes of his manhood and age."

Mr. Anagnos, a Greek, who started the first kindergarten for the blind at the Institution, had married the eldest daughter, Julia Romana Howe, a young woman of superior mind and character, whose early death brought sorrow to a great many hearts. Her fair face and gentle presence among the blind children who loved her linger in my memory as an exquisite picture. Mr. Anagnos succeeded Dr. Howe.

The year after Dr. Howe's death, Mrs. Howe took her daughter Maud to Europe, and remained abroad two years, visiting England, France, Holland, Switzerland, Germany, Egypt, Syria, Italy, Turkey, and Greece.

Since that time she has devoted herself untiringly to everything that elevates humanity. She has lectured in all parts of the United States, and has always shown herself the elegant, well-bred, highly educated woman. Some of her best-known lectures are, "Is Polite Society Polite?" "Greece Revisited," "Women in the Greek Drama," and "Reminiscences of Longfellow and Emerson."

She has lectured before the Parisians in the French language, on the education and condition of women in the United States, also in Florence, Italy, and Athens. During her last visit to Rome she preached two sermons.

In her own country she has preached in many pulpits. "I well remember," she says, "the astonishment of people when, a great many years ago, I preached a sermon in a Boston church. Yet at the time I did not think of the criticism that would be passed upon me for doing it. I simply felt the desire to preach, so I preached; and I have preached a great many times since in churches. . . . I have seen the barriers against women slowly broken down during the past quarter of the century; and I feel sure that the time is coming when women will have all the political and industrial privileges of men."

"I have great faith," says Mrs. Howe, "in the ministerial ability of women, and was one of a committee which held the first convention of women ministers in Boston, late in the seventies."

Mrs. Howe has written for the *North American Review*, the *Forum*, the *Atlantic Monthly*, *Youth's Companion*, and many other periodicals. For some time she was an associate editor of the *Woman's Journal*. Besides all this, she has published several books, "Modern Society" in 1881, a "Life of Margaret Fuller" in 1883, and edited some others.

When the women's department of the Cotton Centennial Exhibition at New Orleans, in the winter of 1885, needed at its head a woman of energy, brain, and polished manners, Mrs. Howe was at once chosen, and filled the position to the satisfaction of all. She was none the less warmly welcomed because she had adhered to principle in the anti-slavery days.

Her homes on Beacon Street, Boston, and at Newport, R. I., are centres where the cultivated love to gather, and where all are received with that courtesy and grace which mark the kindly woman in the able leader.

As the birthdays of Julia Ward Howe come and go, she is fittingly remembered by the many who honor and love her. Her seventieth birthday, May 27, 1889, was celebrated by a reception at the New England Woman's Club, attended by the leading people of Boston. Oliver

Wendell Holmes, then eighty years of age, said, "Better be seventy years young than forty years old."

On her seventy-fifth birthday, 1894, a reception was given Mrs. Howe by her son, Henry M. Howe, a noted mining engineer, at his home on Marlborough Street, Boston. The *New York Critic* of June 2, said: "Notable men and women gathered to honor her. To repeat their names would be to repeat the names of the leaders of the social and literary circles. That Mrs. Howe herself enters into the last quarter of her century with the same strong physical and mental powers which have distinguished her in the past is shown by her active work on the days preceding her birthday. Last week she delivered a most interesting address before the High School Alumni, and yesterday she presided at a meeting of the woman suffragists of New England."

At the high school "she gave some very sensible advice to the women. While she held emphatically that a good appearance is not to be despised, and that its neglect is reprehensible, yet she wished to warn earnestly against the tendency of the times, which threatens to carry this attention to a demoralizing extreme. 'A woman who dresses beyond her means is a fraud,' she said; 'and a woman who sacrifices her health to dress is a sinner.' . . . She gave some sound advice regarding the formation of a truly substantial character."

In an article in the *Forum* for May, 1887, Mrs. Howe has given her opinions on "Dress and Undress." "Good women," she says, "are bound to maintain the best traditions of their sex. Refinement and good sense are foremost among these, and neither of them will permit either the dressing or the acting down to a low level of attraction. There is an admiration which dishonors. There is homage which exalts. Any training which allows women to mistake the one for the other is demoralizing, and should be so recognized and set aside."

Again she says, "Tight lacing and high heels may kill as surely as cholera, though not so swiftly. . . . By the general consent of society, such follies are deemed amiable ones; and as self-sacrifice is especially preached to women, I fear that the sacrifice of their bodily health to appearance is looked upon even by good men with a sort of acquiescence. Here, I think, religion should intervene. This wonderful body is a sacred gift which women, equally with men, should receive as a value to be accounted for."

The demands upon Mrs. Howe are constant. At the celebration of William Cullen Bryant's sixtieth birthday by the Century Club of New York, Mrs. Howe read a poem "A Leaf for the Bryant Chaplet." Dr. Holmes and Emerson also took part. In 1894, at the celebration of the centenary of Bryant's birth, at his native place, Cummington, Mass., Mrs. Howe was again invited to read a poem, and did so. At the unveiling of the Columbus statue in Central Park, New York, Mrs. Howe delivered the poem, Bishop Henry Potter offered the prayer, Vice-president Stevenson withdrew the covering from the statue, and Chauncey Depew made the principal address.

At the World's Columbian Exposition in Chicago, 1893, Mrs. Howe spoke before the Woman's Congress, twice at the Parliament of Religions, at the Congress of Social Purity, following Archbishop Ireland, and twice in the Woman's Building.

Mrs. Howe read a beautiful poem at the dedication in April, 1893, of the new gymnasium for the kindergarten for the blind, at Jamaica Plain, a suburb of Boston, —

> "There is a kindergarten of the mind
> More regal than the realm of sight,
> Richer than gold or gems combined,
> Man's true inheritance and right.
>
> Dark ignorance doth wall it round,
> And watchful guardians keep the key
> By which the entrance may be found
> To their domain of mystery.
>
> * * * * * * *
>
> There dwell great sages of the past,
> The leaders and the saints of old,
> Souls in such noble features cast
> As have succeeding times controlled.
>
> These little ones, whose darkened eyes
> Afford no lesson of the day,
> Stand waiting in a mute surprise
> Till we shall ope to them the way."
>
> * * * * * * *

Invited to Des Moines, Iowa, in the spring of 1894, the Legislature, then in session, sent Mrs. Howe an official invitation to visit both houses at a stated time. They sent a carriage to bring her to the State House, where the Governor received her, and conducted her first to the Senate and then to the House of Representatives. In each of these her entrance was officially announced, the whole body standing until she had taken her seat beside the Speaker, who made her an address of welcome, to which she responded.

Mrs. Howe has often spoken before the Massachusetts

Legislature on suffrage for women. In Paris she was made lady president of a large suffrage convention, there being also a president of the other sex, who addressed her as "Madame la Presidente." She has read several essays before the Summer School of Philosophy at Concord, Mass.

Mrs. Howe's friends have been the eminent of two hemispheres. Kossuth was given a great reception at Green Peace. Agassiz was a loved and frequent visitor there. Charles Sumner found the Howe home one of rest and congeniality. Edwin Booth came to a party given in his honor; and Mrs. Richards tells how "instead of talking to all the fine people who were dying for a word with him, he spent nearly the whole evening in a corner with little Maud, who enjoyed herself immensely. What wonder, when he made dolls for her out of handkerchiefs, and danced them with dramatic fervor?"

But not to the great only has Mrs. Howe been a friend. Her daughter Laura says, "Our mother's hospitality was boundless. She loved to fill the little house to overflowing, in summer days, when every one was glad to get out into the fresh, green country. Often the beds were all filled, and we children had to take to sofas and cots. Once, I remember, Harry slept on a mattress laid on top of the piano, there being no other vacant spot."

One stormy night, at Newport, two men came to the door of Mrs. Howe's home, and asked lodging. They had been refused at a farmhouse near by. Doctor Howe was absent, the old coachman slept some distance away, in the barn, and the eldest child, Julia,

was ill. For a moment Mrs. Howe hesitated, as well
she might; and then she gave the strangers food, and
showed them to an upper room to sleep for the night.
Fortunately the men proved worthy of her kindness.

She has shown her belief in helpfulness from one
of her "Parables" in "Later Lyrics:" —

"'I sent a child of mine to-day;
  I hope you used him well.'
'Now, Lord, no visitor of yours
  Has waited at my bell.

The children of the millionaire
  Run up and down our street;
I glory in their well-combed hair,
  Their dress and trim complete.

But yours would in a chariot come
  With thorough-breds so gay,
And little merry maids and men,
  To cheer him on his way.'

'Stood, then, no child before your door?'
  The Lord, persistent, said.
'Only a ragged beggar-boy,
  With rough and frowzy head.

The dirt was crusted on his skin,
  His muddy feet were bare;
The cook gave victuals from within;
  I cursed his coming there.'

What sorrow silvered with a smile,
  Glides o'er the face divine?
What tenderest whisper thrills rebuke?
  'The beggar-boy was mine!'"

Mrs. Howe has always been the friend of the unfortunate. Blind Laura Bridgman loved her, and wrote her when she was in Rome: "I think of you very, very often. When you come home, I shall shake your hands and hug and kiss you very hard, because I love you and am your dear friend. . . . Please to kiss the baby for me many times a day, every day. My best friend, good-by."

"One of Mrs. Howe's most cherished recollections," writes a friend, "is of the Sunday services which she and her husband conducted in San Domingo for the colored people, whose place of meeting was a dilapidated little church with a mud floor."

Though Mrs. Howe is a Unitarian by profession, she is tolerant of other creeds. In the *North American Review* for January, 1889, in an article entitled "Robert Elsmere's Mental Struggles," she says, "On our way to our own place of worship, we can thank God for all who are going elsewhere to seek him in the sincerity of the truth as it has been delivered to them."

Besides Mrs. Howe's work for freedom, for the blind and other unfortunates, her influence on the social life of America has been incalculable. She says, "The general call of society, which once kept our sex within arbitrary limits, now summons it to come forth and start upon a hundred errands of benefit to the race. Women are wanted to Christianize the heathen — let them go! They are wanted to redeem the slums and the prisons — let them go! They are wanted to watch the wicked game in which personal interests are staked against the public welfare. Good and earnest men are saying all the country over, 'Women are wanted to stand for public virtue at the polls — in God's name let them go!'"

At the Woman's Congress in 1891, Mrs. Howe said, "The separate action of men in any community generates something of the element of brute force, so necessary in its use, so dangerous in its abuse. The antidote to this will be found in the combined action of the women of the community, which will tend to uphold order, morality, and good taste. . . . Make it one of your steadfast objects in life," she says to women, "to help other women to overcome grossness with refinement, to replace rude tastes by cultivated ones, and, above all, to represent and uphold everywhere and in all things the charity that suffereth long and is kind."

A student herself, Mrs. Howe has led other women to read and to think. When she began her work, a minister said to her, "I don't like Plato in petticoats." Other people said, "Women want to understand Greek and Latin, do they? How very humorous!" Mrs. Howe's own social position assured, she has shown to her equals the noblest way to live. "Money," she says in the *Forum* for June, 1888, "is neither power, merit, nor happiness. It is, like fire, a good servant, but a bad master. Its legitimate use is not to exaggerate the inequalities of human condition, but to correct and harmonize them. In the training which was familiar to my youth, the religious aspect of this idea was not without a place. The desire to outshine others was held to be unworthy; the attempt to do so by outward display was simply considered mean."

Again she says, "I would, if I could, compel the attendance of our men and women of fashion upon lectures in which the true inwardness of European society should be exposed, and the danger shown of the follies and luxurious pomp which they delight in imitating, and which, however æsthetically adorned and disguised, are for us a lead in the pathway of moral and intellectual deterioration."

Mrs. Howe has shown that a woman may do noble work for the world outside her home, and yet be a devoted and successful wife and mother. Her children are an honor to her, and are following in her footsteps. Florence Howe Hall has written books and lectures. Laura E. Richards has written several books, more especially for young people, but which are delightful to adults as well, "Captain January," "Queen Hildegarde," and others. Maud Howe Elliott, the wife of the artist, John Elliott, has written charming novels, "The San Rosario Ranche," "A Newport Aquarelle," and others, and has lectured successfully. Becoming deeply interested in the work of General Booth in London, she has lectured in Boston and elsewhere on "The Submerged Tenth." Half of the year she usually spends in Rome. Henry Marion Howe has written valuable scientific papers.

Mrs. Howe is past seventy-six in this autumn of 1895, in which I am writing, and one can scarcely believe it as one looks at her cheerful and animated face. Doubtless her love of music and poetry and her bright conversation have helped to keep her young.

When Madame Blanc, the noted French woman, met Mrs. Howe in 1894, she was surprised, for she said, "I expected to see an aged woman. I found a singular youthfulness of complexion, of look, and of smile. She was dressed without any eccentricity, her manners were the perfection of simplicity, and her voice one of the gentlest I ever listened to."

With the opportunity to choose ease, Mrs. Howe has chosen labor.

> "In the house of labor best
> Can I build the house of rest."

With leisure for social life, she has made her time conduce to the highest good of society. With grace and culture she has helped to make unpopular reforms popular. She has never feared to do what she believed to be right. As in her youth, her daughter Laura says, "every one recognized and acknowledged in her 'stately Julia, queen of all,'" so in mature life, she has been ever the dignified, gracious, genial leader whom thousands were glad to follow.

Julia Ward Howe will be long remembered for her work in the anti-slavery cause, for woman, and for literature; but she will be longest remembered and most loved and honored for her inspiring "Battle-Hymn of the Republic."

> "Mine eyes have seen the glory of the coming of the Lord!
> He is trampling out the vintage where the grapes of wrath are stored;
> He hath loosed the fateful lightning of His terrible swift sword:
> His truth is marching on.
>
> I have seen Him in the watch-fires of a hundred circling camps;
> They have builded Him an altar in the evening dews and damps;
> I can read His righteous sentence by the dim and flaring lamps.
> His day is marching on.

I have read a fiery gospel, writ in burnished rows of steel:
'As ye deal with My contemners, so with you My grace shall deal;
Let the Hero, born of woman, crush the serpent with His heel,
    Since God is marching on.'

He has sounded forth the trumpet that shall never call retreat;
He is sifting out the hearts of men before His judgment-seat:
Oh! be swift, my soul, to answer Him! be jubilant, my feet!
    Our God is marching on.

In the beauty of the lilies Christ was born across the sea,
With a glory in His bosom that transfigures you and me:
As He died to make men holy, let us die to make men free,
    While God is marching on."

QUEEN VICTORIA.

ON May 24, 1819, a little girl was born in Kensington Palace, London, who was destined to rule over a vast kingdom and empire. Her father, Edward, Duke of Kent, was the fourth son of George III., who reigned during our Revolutionary War. Edward was the best of the sons, generous, liberal in his ideas of government, which displeased his father and his brothers, and liberal also as far as was possible in pecuniary matters.

When he was eighteen he was sent to Hanover to study to be a soldier, an allowance of a thousand pounds a year being given to his military instructor, Baron Wangenheim, to be used for young Edward. The lad incurred debts, wrote to his father for more money, and finally returned to England. George III., angered at his coming without permission, at once sent him to Gibraltar. Later he was sent to Canada, where he became commander-in-chief of the British forces in British America, and was greatly loved by the people. He was a patron in 1793 of the first Sunday Free School established in Canada, and was active in all benevolent work. In 1802 he became governor of Gibraltar, and with admirable discipline brought the army out of a mutinous condition, and did away with much of the drunkenness and other evils.

QUEEN VICTORIA.

His income, always small for the son of a king, was not sufficient to enable him to pay his debts, which were a source of constant anxiety. He gave bonds to his creditors, and paid as much as he was able.

When he was a little over fifty years of age, in 1818, he married the Princess Louisa Victoria of Saxe-Coburg, who was then thirty-two. She was the widow of Charles, Prince of Leiningen, who had died four years previously, leaving two children, Charles, who succeeded his father, and died in 1859; and Anna Feodora, who married the Prince of Hohenlohe-Langenburg, and died in 1872. The Duchess of Kent was at this time, says Baron Stockmar, "altogether most charming and attractive." She was unselfish, sympathetic, and generous.

The Duke of Kent proved a devoted husband. His younger brother, Adolphus, Duke of Cambridge, was married the same year, 1818, to Princess Augusta of Hesse-Cassel, and became the father of Mary, Duchess of Teck, whose daughter, Princess May, has so recently married George the son of the Prince of Wales, and will herself probably come to the throne. The Duke of Kent and the Duke of Cambridge each received from England a yearly marriage portion of six thousand pounds. The former went with his wife to live in the Castle of Amorbach in Bavaria, which belonged to the little son of the duchess.

The duke believed that he would one day come to the throne. "My brothers," said he "are not so strong as I am, and have not lived so regular a life. I expect to outlive them all; the crown will come to me and my children."

He wished to return to England, that his child might

be Briton-born. He wrote his brothers for money for the journey; but none wished to help provide an heir for the throne they desired to occupy. Finally some friends assisted him. The duchess was taken in the spring of 1819 to Kensington Palace, London; and there, in the latter part of May, her child was born.

The old red-brick palace has an interesting history. It was formerly the suburban residence of the Earl of Nottingham, and was bought for twenty thousand pounds by William of Orange, who married Mary, daughter of James II., and became William III. Sir Christopher Wren enlarged it at the suggestion of Mary, and also built for her successor, Queen Anne, an orangery. George I. added the eastern front of the palace, and George II. built a north-western angle for a nursery for his children. His queen, Caroline of Anspach, beautified the grounds by forming the Serpentine, an artificial lake, seven feet deep in the centre. The Duke of Sussex, Augustus the sixth, son of George III., rebuilt the south-west angle of the palace, died here in 1843, and was buried in Kensal Green. His great library, including one of the finest collections of Bibles in the world, was sold after his death.

Many kings and queens have died in the old palace. Here Queen Mary died of small-pox in 1694, to the great sorrow of William III., who passed away seven years later. On his arm were found bracelets made of the hair of his beloved queen. Here died Queen Anne and her husband, Prince George of Denmark, none of their seventeen children surviving them. Here George II. died suddenly as he sat at breakfast, Oct. 25, 1760.

The poor blind daughter of George III., Sophia, lived

in this old palace, "an example of patient and unmurmuring endurance such as can rarely be met with," says Miss Amelia Murray, in her " Recollections."

Here, too, lived Caroline, the wife of the dissolute George IV., with that beautiful only child, the Princess Charlotte, whose death at twenty-one, Nov. 6, 1817, with her infant son, cast an unparalleled gloom over England. When told that her child was dead, she said, "I am grieved for myself, for the English people; but oh, above all, I feel it for my dear husband!" When she learned that she, too, could not live, she said, "Tell it to my husband, — tell it with caution and tenderness, and be sure to say to him from me, that I am still the happiest wife in England."

Into this old Kensington Palace, full of memories, many of them sad, came the baby queen, Victoria. She was a blue-eyed child, "fair and plump as a partridge," said her happy father. The Dowager Duchess of Coburg, the mother of the Duchess of Kent, wrote to her, "May God's blessing rest on the little stranger and the beloved mother. Again a Charlotte, destined, perhaps, to play a great part one day, if a brother is not born to take it out of her hands. The *English like queens*, and the niece of the ever-lamented, beloved Charlotte will be most dear to them."

When the baby was a month old, a gold font, long unused, was brought from the Tower; and she was baptized by the Archbishop of Canterbury and the Bishop of London. George IV., then prince regent, named her Alexandrina, after Alexander, the Emperor of Russia. The Duke of Kent asked that her mother's name, Victoria, be added. "Give her her mother's also, then," said the prince; "but it cannot precede that of the emperor." The child was usually called "Princess Drina;" but when she came to the throne she commanded that she should be called Victoria only.

The Duke of Kent lived but eight months to enjoy his child. "Take care of her," he used to say, as he showed her to friends, "for she will be queen of England." This did not seem very probable, as there were uncles and cousins who were entitled to the crown before herself.

When she was six months old her parents moved to Sidmouth, on the Devonshire coast, "to cheat the winter." "My little girl thrives," said the father, "and is, I am delighted to say, strong and healthy; too healthy, I fear, in the opinion of some members of my family, by whom she is regarded as an intruder. How largely she contributes to my happiness at this moment, it is needless for me to say."

The winter would not be cheated, however. The duke, taking a long walk with a friend, Captain Conroy, was caught in a storm. He was urged to change his wet boots; but meeting the nurse with his baby, as he went to his room, he was tempted to play with the child until he received a chill. Inflammation of the lungs followed; and he died on the morning of Jan. 23, 1820. George III., his father, blind and insane, died six days later, Jan. 29, and George IV. came to the throne.

The duchess gave up all her husband's property to his creditors. She was enabled to return to Kensington Palace, to bring up the future ruler of the nation, by the aid of her brother Leopold, the husband of the lamented Charlotte, who gave her an allowance of three thousand pounds a year. When Victoria was six years of age Parliament voted six thousand pounds a year for her education. Leopold continued to give the former amount until he became King of the Belgians in 1831. The Duchess of Kent devoted herself to the education and proper training of her child in all that was good and noble. The little girl lived a natural and simple life in the open air. In Kensington Gardens she used to ride on a donkey, "gayly caparisoned with blue ribbons," a soldier, a servant of the late duke, her father, leading the animal. Sometimes the little princess walked between her mother and sister, Princess Feodora, nine years older than herself, and bade a pleasant " Good-morning " or " How do you do?" to those whom she met, or kissed her hand to those who looked through the railing to see royalty.

The soldier servant had two children, a boy and a girl, both delicate. The former died, and the latter was never well. The princess used often to carry her little gifts. When she became queen, she sent to the sick girl a Book of Psalms, marked with her own hand on the days when she had read them, and a bookmark with an embroidered dove upon it, done by herself. The girl wept with joy when she received and showed these gifts to others.

Victoria was devoted to dolls, of which it is said she had one hundred and thirty-two, in a house of their own. She made the daintiest dresses for them, the needlework of which is an astonishment. Baroness Lehzen by means of these beloved dolls taught her royal pupil the forms of court etiquette at receptions and the like.

Lord Albemarle, in his autobiography, speaks of the

"pretty little girl, seven years of age, engaged in watering the plants immediately under the window. It was amusing to see how impartially she divided the contents of the watering-pot between the flowers and her own little feet. Her simple but becoming dress — a large straw hat and a white cotton gown — contrasted favorably with the gorgeous apparel now worn by the little damsels of the rising generation. A colored fichu round the neck was the only ornament she wore."

Sir Walter Scott wrote in his Diary, May 19, 1828: "Dined with the Duchess of Kent. I was very kindly received by Prince Leopold, and presented to the little Victoria, the heir apparent to the crown, as things now stand. The little lady is educated with care, and watched so closely that no busy maid has a moment to whisper, 'You are the heir of England.'"

When Victoria was twelve years old, in 1831, her governess, the Baroness Lehzen, with the consent of the Duchess of Kent, purposely placed in a book the royal genealogical table. When Mr. Davys, afterwards Bishop of Peterborough, the instructor of Victoria, was gone, the princess opened the book, and said, "I see I am nearer the throne than I thought." "So it is, madam," replied the governess.

After some moments the princess said, "Now, many a child would boast; but they don't know the difficulty. There is much splendor, but much responsibility," and giving her right hand to the governess, added, "I will be good, dear Lehzen; I will be good."

George IV. had died in 1830, and been succeeded by his third brother, William IV. The second brother, Frederick, the Duke of York, had died in 1827. During his last illness Victoria brought him a bouquet each day. The two children of William IV. and Queen Adelaide, Charlotte and Elizabeth, each lived but a short time, the former a few hours, the latter, seven months younger than Victoria, about three months. Adelaide wrote to the Duchess of Kent, "My children are dead, but yours lives, and she is mine also."

Victoria was very truthful. "I remember," said Dr. Davys, "when I had been teaching her one day, she was very impatient for the lesson to be over, — once or twice rather refractory. The Duchess of Kent came in, and asked how she had behaved. Lehzen said, 'Oh, once she was rather troublesome.' The princess touched her and said, 'No, Lehzen, twice; don't you remember?'" The Duchess of Kent, too, was a woman of great truth. She used to say to her daughter Victoria, "I am anxious to bring you up as a good woman, and then you will be a good queen also."

The daily life at Kensington Palace was as follows: "Breakfast at eight o'clock, Princess Victoria having her bread and milk and fruit put on a little table at her mother's side. After breakfast there was a walk or drive for an hour; and then, from ten to twelve, she was instructed by her mother, after which she would amuse herself running through the suite of rooms which extended round two sides of the palace. At two came a plain dinner, while the duchess took her luncheon. After this, lessons again till four, then a visit or drive; and after that the princess would ride or walk, or sit out on the lawn under the trees with the rest of the party. At the time of her mother's dinner she had her supper laid at her side; then, after playing with her nurse

(Mrs. Brock — 'dear, dear Boppy'), she would join the party at dessert, and at nine go to her bed, which was placed by the side of her mother's."

The Rev. E. J. Hardy relates, that so simply had the princess been reared, when asked at Maidstone, where her mother stopped to change horses on a journey, what she wished for refreshments, she replied, " A small piece of stale bread."

The princess was taught economy. When she was eight years old, at a bazaar at Tunbridge Wells, having spent all her money in presents for various friends, she bethought her of another cousin, and wished to buy for him a box marked half-a-crown. Of course the patron asked her to take it. The governess said, "No. You see, the princess has not the money, and so, of course, she cannot buy the box." It was laid aside for her; and the next quarter-day, when she received her small allowance, she rode to the bazaar on her donkey, and carried away the precious box.

The first drawing-room which she ever attended was on the birthday of Queen Adelaide, in February, 1831, when she was twelve years old. She stood on the left of the queen, dressed in English blonde, a pretty kind of lace over white, and was, though seemingly unconscious of it, the centre of attraction.

From time to time the princess was taken by her mother to various parts of the kingdom, that her people might see her, as they were eager to do, and to broaden her own education. In Arreton churchyard she sat by the grave of the "Dairyman's Daughter," and read that touching story to her mother. At Plymouth, where she examined the dockyard, as the daughter of the admiral was ill, the princess and the Duchess of Kent went upstairs to see her. The young lady rose from the sofa to get a chair for her future queen.

"Pray do not rise," said the duchess; "you are ill. Victoria will get a chair for herself." A distinguished naval officer related in after years how, as a boy, he had managed to touch the princess's dress with his fingers, as she went out of the dockyard gates.

Grace Greenwood tells an amusing story of these early years. When visiting with her mother at Wentworth House, the home of Earl Fitz-William in Yorkshire, the gardener saw the princess flitting among the shrubberies, about to descend a slippery place on the terrace. He called out, "Be careful, Miss; it's slape!" using a Yorkshire word.

"What's slape?" asked the curious princess, turning her head towards him, while at the same instant her feet slipped and she fell. The old gardener ran to lift her up, saying, "*That's* slape, Miss."

At Malvern, in her childish gayety, she climbed an apple-tree, and could not get down. The gardener, Davis, finally heard her sobbing, and brought her down by means of a ladder. He was rewarded with a guinea, which he had neatly framed, and always preserved.

At Ramsgate, Mr. Montefiore sent a golden key to the little princess, that she might daily enjoy his private grounds. She did not forget it when, years after, she knighted the distinguished philanthropist, making him Sir Moses Montefiore.

At Burghley, when she was sixteen, the mayor and other officers of the town gave her a reception, with much ceremony. Greville says at the great dinner an excited waiter emptied a pail of ice into the lap of the duchess, which, "though she took it coolly, made a great bustle." Lord Exeter gave a magnificent ball in the evening, opening it with the princess in the first dance, after which, at her mother's wish, she left the party and went to bed.

N. P. Willis, the American author, saw the princess at this age. She was dressed in rose-colored satin, with large pink hat and black lace cape. He said, "She is much better looking than any picture of her in the shops, and, for the heir to such a crown as that of England, unnecessarily pretty and interesting."

All these years she was studying regularly. She spoke French, German, and Italian fluently, could translate Vergil and Horace, was especially fond of botany, had much skill in drawing, and was an unusually good musician. Caroline Fox says of her in her "Journals and Letters," "She is a good linguist, an acute foreign politician, and possesses very sound common-sense."

The Duchess of Kent did not allow her daughter to appear often at court, as she feared its corrupting influence. King William IV. was angered at this, as George IV. had been before him, and at a birthday party of a hundred guests, in 1836, which proved his last, said in a speech that "he hoped in God that he might live nine months longer, when the Princess Victoria would be of age, and he could leave the crown to her, not under the authority of a regent who was sitting by him." This was the Duchess of Kent, who sat unruffled at the anger of the king; but Victoria burst into tears. He commanded that in future she should appear at court.

The following May 24, 1837, all England was rejoicing over the eighteenth birthday of Princess Victoria. Bells were rung, schools were closed that children might join in the festivities, cities were illuminated, and a grand state ball was given in her honor at St. James's Palace.

The king was in his last illness, and could not attend, but sent Victoria a piano costing two hundred pounds as his birthday present. The princess for the first time took precedence of her mother, and occupied the central chair of state. She danced first with the Duke of Norfolk, and afterwards with the Austrian Prince Esterhazy, who was so covered with diamonds that they were even on the heels of his boots!

Less than a month after this birthday party William IV. died at Windsor Castle, at twenty minutes past two o'clock on the morning of June 20, 1837. At once the Archbishop of Canterbury and one or two others left the castle and hastened in a carriage to Kensington Palace, arriving about five in the morning. They knocked and rang the bell; but it was some time before they could arouse the porter at the gate. Then they asked an attendant to summon her Royal Highness, as they wished to see her on important business. The attendant stated that "the princess was in such a sweet sleep that she could not venture to disturb her." Then they said, "We are come on business of state to the *queen*, and even her sleep must give way to that."

"To prove that she did not keep them waiting," says Miss Wynn, in her "Diary of a Lady of Quality," "in a few moments she came into the room in a loose white nightgown and shawl, her nightcap thrown off, and her hair falling upon her shoulders, her feet in slippers, tears in her eyes, but perfectly collected and dignified."

Her first words to the archbishop were, " I beg your Grace to pray for me," which he did. She soon wrote a letter of condolence to Queen Adelaide, begging her to remain at Windsor Castle as long as she wished. It was addressed, " To Her Majesty, the Queen." Some one remarked, " Your Majesty, *you* are Queen of England." — " Yes," was the reply; "but the widowed queen is not to be reminded of the fact first by me."

At eleven o'clock the young queen met the Council at Kensington Palace. When asked if she would enter the room accompanied by the great officers of state, she said she would come in alone. "Never," says Greville in his Memoirs, "was anything like the first impression she produced, or the chorus of praise and admiration which is raised about her manner and behavior, and certainly not without justice."

She read her address before the lords, saying that she should " steadily protect the rights, and promote to the utmost of my power the happiness and welfare of all classes of my subjects." Then she signed the oath for the security of the church of Scotland, administered by the Archbishop of Canterbury. The privy councillors were sworn, the two royal dukes, Ernest of Cumberland and Augustus of Sussex, being the first to take the oath. Greville says, "As these old men, her uncles, knelt before her, swearing allegiance and kissing her hand, I saw her blush up to the eyes, as if she felt the contrast between their civil and their natural relations ; and this was the only sign of emotion that she evinced. Her manner to them was very graceful and engaging; she kissed them both, and rose from her chair and moved towards the Duke of Sussex, who was farthest from her, and too infirm to reach her. She seemed rather bewildered at the multitude of men who were sworn, and who came one after the other to kiss her hand. . . . She went through the whole ceremony with perfect calmness and self-possession, but at the same time with a graceful modesty and propriety particularly interesting and ingratiating." Sir Robert Peel was amazed "at her apparent deep sense of her situation, her modesty, and at the same time her firmness. She appeared to be awed, but not daunted." An hour after the meeting of the Privy Council, that of the Cabinet ministers was held.

The next day the ceremony of the Proclamation took place from the open window of St. James's Palace. The queen was in deep mourning, with white collar and cuffs, and white lace under her black bonnet. The Duchess of Kent stood near her daughter, while the king-at-arms read the Proclamation, and the band played " God Save the Queen."

Miss Martineau wrote of this scene: " There stood the young creature, in simplest mourning, her sleek bands of brown hair as plain as her dress. The tears ran down her cheeks as Lord Melbourne, standing by her side, presented her to the people as their sovereign."

A few days later Greville writes in his diary: " Her majesty has continued quietly at Kensington, where she transacts business with her ministers; and everything goes on as if she had been on the throne six years instead of six days."

On July 13 the queen left forever her childhood's home at Kensington Palace, and removed to Buckingham Palace. This stands at the west end of St. James's Park, on the site of the Mulberry Garden, where mulberry-trees were planted by order of James I. to encourage the growth of silk-making. The palace built here by the Duke of Buckingham was sold to George III., where he lived for many years, and was remodelled by George IV. in 1825. Queen Victoria has added greatly to its size and beauty. The east front was added at her accession, and cost about £150,000. The state ballroom, finished in 1856, is said to have cost £300,000. The throne-room is sixty feet long, its walls hung with crimson satin, the ceiling carved and gilded. The yellow drawing-room has its furniture overlaid with burnished gold, and covered with yellow satin. The picture gallery, one hundred and fifty feet long, has many fine paintings. The gardens cover about fifty acres.

Into this luxurious home came the quietly and sensibly reared queen. Four days later, July 17, she went in state to dissolve Parliament. Her carriage was drawn by eight cream-colored horses, and the Horse Guards were her escort. She had on a crimson velvet robe trimmed with gold and ermine over a white silk skirt embroidered with gold. She wore a magnificent tiara of diamonds on her head, with a necklace, stomacher, and bracelets of diamonds. When the queen was seated on her new throne of crimson velvet and gold, the lords-in-waiting placed the royal mantle of purple velvet upon her shoulders. She read her speech in a clear, fine voice, heard all over the great chamber. The Hon. Charles Sumner, who was present from America, wrote to a friend: "I was astonished and delighted.

Her voice is sweet and finely modulated; and she pronounced every word distinctly, and with a just regard to its meaning. I think I never heard anything better read in my life than her speech; and I could but respond to Lord Fitz-William's remark to me when the ceremony was over, 'How beautifully she performs!'"

This year Parliament voted the queen an income of £385,000 a year, nearly two million dollars. She paid the debts of her father, the Duke of Kent, fifty thousand pounds, saying to her prime minister, Lord Melbourne, "I *must* do it. I consider it a sacred duty." She also sent valuable pieces of plate to the largest creditors, in appreciation of their patience in waiting so many years.

Many incidents illustrating the queen's kindness are told. For years a poor man had swept the crossing opposite the avenue leading to Kensington Palace. The princess used to throw him silver from the carriage window. When she became queen she ordered that eight shillings a week should be paid him as long as he lived.

One day she was examining some bracelets sent on approval; but just as she had decided in favor of a pair worth twenty-five pounds, one of her ladies entered with a petition for the widow of an old officer. She replaced the bracelets in the jeweller's case, and gave the twenty-five pounds to the widow.

Early in her reign the Duke of Wellington brought to her a court-martial death-sentence for her signature. Tears filled her eyes as she asked, " Have you nothing to say in behalf of this man ?"

"Nothing; he has deserted three times," replied the duke.

"Oh, your Grace, think again!"

"Well, your Majesty, he certainly is a bad soldier; but there was somebody who spoke as to his good character. He may be a good fellow in private life."

"Oh, thank you!" said the queen, as she wrote "Pardoned" on the paper, and signed it "Victoria R."

The queen had the highest admiration for the aged Duke of Wellington. At his death in 1852 she wrote in her journal, published in her "Life in the Highlands," "In him centred almost every earthly honor a subject could possess. His position was the highest a subject ever had — above party, looked up to by all, revered by the whole nation, the friend of the sovereign; and *how* simply he carried these honors! With what singleness of purpose, what straightforwardness, what courage, were all the motives of his actions guided. The crown never possessed, and I fear never *will*, so *devoted*, loyal, and faithful a subject, so stanch a supporter! To *us* his loss is *irreparable.*"

While the young queen was busy with drawing-rooms and matters incident to her position at the head of the nation, she allowed no time to be wasted. While her hair was dressed, one of her ladies read to her. She rose at six in her morning, and spent considerable time in reading the Bible. While at breakfast her mother talked to her about the books of the day which she was unable to read.

She was thorough in her official duties. When Lord Melbourne said to her that she need not hesitate to sign a certain paper without examination, as it was not a matter of "paramount importance," she replied, "But it is for me a matter of paramount importance whether or not I attach my signature to a document with which I am not thoroughly satisfied." When Melbourne apologized for the great number of wearisome documents to be read, the queen said, "My lord, it is but a change of occupation. I have not lived a life of leisure; and, as you know, it is not long since I left off daily lessons." Lord Palmerston has recorded that in one year (1848) not less than twenty-eight thousand despatches were submitted to the queen, and carefully examined by her.

Her majesty was then, and has been always, extremely punctual. One of her ladies-in-waiting having been late twice when the queen was going to drive, found on the third occasion that Victoria stood with her watch in hand. The lady apologized, fearing she had detained the queen. "Yes; for quite ten minutes," was the grave reply. Perceiving that the lady was so abashed that she could not arrange her shawl, which she had put on hurriedly, the queen helped her with her own hands, saying, "We shall all in time be more perfect, I hope, in our duties."

The queen began her reign, and has never changed, with a strict observance of Sunday; and the effect upon the nation has been marked. One of her ministers arrived at Windsor Castle, one of the royal homes, late one Saturday night. "I have brought for your Majesty's inspection," he said, "some documents of great importance; but as I shall be obliged to trouble you to examine them in detail, I will not encroach on the time of your Majesty to-night, but will request your attendance to-morrow morning."

"To-morrow is Sunday, my lord."

"True, your Majesty; but the business of the state will not admit of delay."

The next morning the queen and court went to church and listened to a sermon on "The Christian Sabbath: its Duties and Obligations," the queen having sent the clergyman the text from which he preached. Not a word was said about the state papers during the day. At night Victoria said, after telling him that she sent the text, "To-morrow morning, my lord, at any hour you please, — as early as seven, if you like, — we will look into those papers."

"I could not think of intruding upon your Majesty at so early an hour," was the reply of the minister; "nine o'clock will be quite soon enough."

A little more than a year after she came to the throne, Victoria was crowned, June 28, 1838, in the midst of the greatest rejoicing from one end of the kingdom to the other. The people were tired of immoral kings. As the Duchess of Coburg had said, "The English like queens;" and now one was to be crowned who had been reared in purity and sweetness by a noble mother.

A new crown had to be made for this fair young head. The old crown weighed seven pounds, and was too large and heavy for the girl-queen. One of half the weight was made, the jewels in it valued at £112,760. There are said to be two thousand, seven hundred and eighty-three diamonds; the large ruby in front was worn by Henry V. at Agincourt. The Kohinoor diamond, "Mountain of Light," had not yet been obtained. The latter, weighing one hundred and sixty-two carats, and variously estimated at from £1,500,000 to £3,000,000, was formerly in the possession of the rajah of Lahore, and came into the hands of the English in 1849, in their conquest of the Punjab.

At ten o'clock on the morning of June 28 the great procession started from Buckingham Palace. The Life Guards, the Scots Fusiliers, and other military bodies, preceded forty magnificent carriages and escorts of the foreign embassadors come to attend the ceremony. Then followed the royal family. The first two state carriages held the Duchess of Kent and her attendants. Then came the queen in the grand state coach, drawn by eight handsome cream-colored horses. In the procession were six saddle horses, richly caparisoned, belonging to the queen, each led by two grooms. In an hour and a half the procession reached Westminster Abbey, through the almost impassable streets. When the queen alighted, cannons were fired and trumpets blown. Opposite the altar, under the central tower of the abbey, on a platform covered with cloth-of-gold, were the new " chair of homage" and the old chair, in which all the sovereigns of England had been crowned since Edward the Confessor, the latter having underneath it the "Stone of Scone," on which the ancient Scottish kings were crowned.

Victoria, only nineteen, wore a robe of crimson velvet, furred with ermine and trimmed with gold lace, her train borne by eight young ladies of noble birth. After the music, prayers, and a sermon, the oath was administered, the queen kneeling, with her hand on the open Bible, saying, "The things which I have here before promised I will perform and keep, so help me God!" She then kissed the book, and still knelt while the choir sang, "Come, Holy Ghost, our souls inspire."

Then, sitting in St. Edward's chair, a cloth of gold

held over her head by four Knights of the Garter, she was anointed on her head and hands with holy oil by the Archbishop of Canterbury. She was then invested with the imperial robe, the sceptre, and the ruby ring, and the beautiful new crown was placed on her head by the Archbishop. At this moment all the peers and peeresses put on their coronets, and all shouted "God save the queen!" while trumpets were sounded, drums beat, and cannon fired.

After the queen was conducted to the chair of homage, the Archbishop of Canterbury and her uncles, the Dukes of Sussex and Cambridge, knelt, saying, "I do become your liege man of life and limb, and of earthly worship and faith and truth I will bear unto you to live and die against all manner of folk, so help me God." The dukes kissed her left cheek, while the other dignitaries kissed her hand. Lord Rolle, who was over eighty, as he attempted to do homage, stumbled and fell down the steps leading to the throne. The queen rose and held out her hand to him, which thoughtful act was cheered by the great assembly.

After this Victoria received the Sacrament, taking off her crown as she did so, and, passing into King Edward's Chapel, changed the imperial for the royal robe of purple velvet, and at four o'clock started homeward in her state carriage, the crowd cheering all the way. On reaching Buckingham Palace, she heard her favorite spaniel barking; and loving dogs then as ever afterwards, she exclaimed, "There's Dash!" and hurried away to greet her little friend.

That night she had a hundred guests at dinner. Feasts were given to the poor, and cities all over Great

Britain were illuminated. The coronation cost the Exchequer £70,000, but the people of London paid £200,000 for seats to see the procession.

With all this elegance of courtly life, the queen's own tastes were simple. James Gordon Bennett, writing home this coronation year, says Grace Greenwood, saw Victoria in the royal box at the opera, "a fair, light-haired little girl, dressed with great simplicity, in white muslin, with hair plain, a blue ribbon at the back." He also saw her riding in the Park, in a barouche with three of her suite, "dressed very simply in white, with a plain straw, or Leghorn bonnet, and her veil was thrown aside. She carried a green parasol."

Of course at this time there were many men quite ready and willing to marry the young Queen of England. King William desired her to wed a prince of the Netherlands. Several were urged; but Victoria, as in other matters, had a mind of her own. The Uncle Leopold, who, since his own beloved wife, Charlotte, did not live to come to the throne, had been especially fond of Victoria, had hoped she would choose his handsome nephew, Albert, son of his eldest brother, Ernest, Duke of Saxe-Coburg-Saalfeld. The Duchess of Kent was also extremely fond of this nephew, whose tastes were refined, and whose habits seemed above reproach.

Albert at seventeen, and his older brother, Ernest, had visited England with their father in May, 1836, to see the Princess Victoria, who was three months older than Albert. They came by invitation of the Duchess of Kent. The round of parties did not especially interest Albert; but he found Victoria, "our cousin, most amiable," and enjoyed most of all the singing of the charity children at St. Paul's. He knew, of course, that he had been thought of by his noble grandmother, the Dowager Duchess of Coburg, as the one to wed Victoria; but how his cousin, the queen, would regard the matter, he could not know.

He used to say, "When he was a child of three years old, his nurse always told him that he should marry the queen, and that when he first thought of marrying at all, he always thought of her."

When Victoria came to the throne, and Albert was at the University of Bonn studying, he wrote her: "My dearest cousin— Now you are queen of the mightiest land of Europe, in your hand lies the happiness of millions. May Heaven assist you and strengthen you with its strength in that high but difficult task. I hope that your reign may be long, happy, and glorious, and that your efforts may be rewarded by the thankfulness and love of your subjects. May I pray you to think likewise sometimes of your cousins in Bonn, and to continue to them that kindness you favored them with till now? Be assured that our minds are always with you."

Three years had gone by since the first visit of Prince Albert. The Uncle Leopold was anxious lest his plans come to naught. Victoria wrote that Albert was "dear to her," but both were too young; she did not wish to marry for four years, and the affair could be considered as broken off. Then the wise uncle, knowing that proximity usually aids love, arranged for another visit in October, 1839.

When Albert and his brother reached Windsor Castle, Thursday evening, October 10, the queen received them at the head of the staircase. The next day she wrote her uncle: "Albert's beauty is most striking, and he is most amiable and unaffected — in short, very *fascinating*. The young men are very amiable, delightful companions, and I am happy to have them here."

Five days after the arrival of the prince, at half-past twelve o'clock, he was sent for by the queen. What happened at that interview is best told in Albert's letter to his grandmother: "The queen sent for me alone to her room a few days ago, and declared to me, in a genuine outburst of love and affection, that I had gained her whole heart, and would make her intensely happy if I would make her the sacrifice of sharing her life with her, for she said she looked on it as a sacrifice; the only thing which troubled her was that she did not think she was worthy of me. The joyous openness of manner in which she told me this quite enchanted me, and I was quite carried away by it. . . . Since that moment Victoria does whatever she fancies I should wish or like, and we talk together a great deal about our future life, which she promises me to make as happy as possible. Oh, the future! does it not bring with it the moment when I shall have to take leave of my dear, dear home, and of you! . . .

"I ask you to give me your grandmotherly blessing in this important and decisive step in my life; it will be a talisman to me against all the storms the future may have in store for me. Good-by, dear grandmamma, and do not take your love from me. Heaven will make all things right."

The same day on which the queen offered herself to Albert, she wrote to her Uncle Leopold: "My mind is quite made up, and I told Albert this morning of it. The warm affection he showed me on learning this, gave me great pleasure. He seems perfection, and I think that I have the prospect of very great happiness before me. I love him MORE than I can say, and shall do everything in my power to render this sacrifice (for such in my opinion it is) as small as I can. He seems to have great tact, a very necessary thing in his position. These last few days have passed like a dream to me; and I am so much bewildered by it all that I know hardly how to write, but I do feel very happy."

The pleased uncle wrote back: "May Albert be able to strew roses without thorns on the pathway of life of our good Victoria. He is well qualified to do so. . . . I had, when I learnt your decision, almost the feeling of old Simeon: 'Now lettest thou thy servant depart in peace.'"

On Nov. 23, the queen communicated to eighty members of her Privy Council, gathered in Buckingham Palace, her intention to marry. "The room was full," records the queen in her journal, "but I hardly knew who was there. Lord Melbourne I saw looking at me with tears in his eyes, but he was not near me. I then read my short declaration. I felt my hands shook, but I did not make one mistake." She wore a bracelet containing Prince Albert's picture; and this, she said, gave her courage.

Jan. 16, 1840, the queen announced her engagement to Parliament; and the next month, Feb. 10, at one o'clock, she was married to the prince of her choice in the Chapel Royal of St. James's Palace. The bride wore a rich white satin dress trimmed with orange-blossoms, a wreath of the same flowers on her head, and a veil of Honiton lace costing £1,000, ordered to encourage the lace-trade in the Devonshire village of Honiton. Her train was borne by twelve noble ladies dressed in white satin. When the ring was placed on her finger, the firing of guns and the ringing of bells announced it to the multitude outside. After the wedding-breakfast at Buckingham Palace, Victoria and Albert drove to Windsor Castle, past twenty-two miles of enthusiastic spectators. All over England there was great rejoicing. Dinners were given to thousands of the poor. After three days the queen and prince returned to London, and began their busy life for the state.

On Feb. 28, the father and brother of Albert returned home, and all were much affected at the parting. The queen writes in her journal: "Oh, how I feel for my dearest, precious husband at this moment. Father, brother, friends, country, — all has he left, and all for me. God grant that I may be the happy person, the *most* happy person, to make this dearest, blessed being happy and contented! What is in my power to make him happy I will do."

For twenty years Victoria and Albert lived a life that has been the admiration of the world. They drew and etched a great deal together; they were both fond of music, and skilled in its execution. Mendelssohn came to Buckingham Palace in July, 1842, to test an organ for the prince, and thus writes to his mother: "I found him alone; and as we were talking the queen came in also alone, in a simple morning-dress. She said she was obliged to leave for Claremont in an hour, and then suddenly interrupting herself, exclaimed, 'But goodness, what a confusion!' for the wind had littered the whole room, and even the pedals of the organ, with leaves of music from a large portfolio which lay open. As she spoke, she knelt down and began picking up the music. Prince Albert helped; and I, too, was not idle. Then Prince Albert proceeded to explain the stops to me, and she said that she would meanwhile make things straight. I begged that the prince would first play over something, so that, as I said, I might boast about it in Germany; and he played a chorale by heart with the pedals, so charmingly and clearly and correctly that it would have done credit to any professional; and the queen, having finished her work, came and sat by him and listened, and looked pleased."

Then Mendelssohn sang, and then the queen, at the request of Albert. "And which did she choose?" writes the composer. "'Schöner und schöner schimmkt sich!' sang it quite charmingly, in strict time and tune, and with very good execution. . . . Then I was obliged to confess that Fanny had written the song (which I found very hard, but pride must have a fall), and to beg her to sing one of my own also. If I would give plenty of help she would gladly try, she said; and then she sang the Pilgerspruch, '*Lass dich nur*,' really quite faultlessly, and with charming feeling and expression. I thought to myself one must not pay too many compliments on such an occasion, so I merely thanked her a great many times, upon which she said, 'Oh! if only I had not been so frightened; generally I have such long breath.'"

Prince Albert, from the first, took the deepest interest in everything which concerned England, as the five volumes of Sir Theodore Martin's "Life of the Prince Consort" fully show. " He was habitually an early riser," says Sir Theodore. "Even in winter he would be up by seven, and dispose of a great deal of work before breakfast, by the light of his green German lamp, the original of which he had brought over with him, and which has since become so familiar an object in our English homes. The queen shared his early habits; but before her majesty joined him in the sitting-room, where their writing-tables stood always side by side, much had, as a rule, been prepared for her consideration."

When years after the Duke of Wellington urged that the prince take the command of the army, he refused because he thought it his duty, as he wrote the duke, to give his life "wholly to the queen's assistance, to sink his own individual existence in that of his wife; . . . continually and anxiously to watch every part of the public business, in order to be able to advise and assist her at any moment in any of the multifarious and difficult questions brought before her — sometimes political, or social, or personal."

The prince wrote his stepmother in 1848: "I must tear myself for a moment from the whirl of business, of emotions, fatigues, etc., to thank you for a long, dear letter. I never remember to have been kept in the stocks to the same extent as I am just now. The mere reading of the English, French, and German papers absorbs nearly all the spare hours of the day; and yet one can let nothing pass without losing the connection and coming in consequence to wrong conclusions."

Sometimes, especially to keep Victoria's birthday,

May 24, they went to Claremont, and enjoyed the country, of which the prince was passionately fond. The Queen writes in her journal: "I told Albert that formerly I was too happy to go to London, and wretched to leave it, and how since the blessed hour of my marriage, and still more since the summer, I dislike and am unhappy to leave the country, and could be content and happy never to go to town. This pleased him. The solid pleasures of a peaceful, quiet, yet merry life in the country, with my inestimable husband and friend, my all in all, are far more durable than the amusements of London, though we don't despise or dislike these sometimes."

To enjoy a rest and have a home which did not belong to the State, Osborne, in the Isle of Wight, was purchased, and a new palace in the midst of several thousand acres made ready for occupancy, Sept. 15, 1846. It is of light stone, with broad piazzas. As the years went by, a Swiss cottage was built, in which the royal daughters had a kitchen and dairy, where they learned to cook and gave the food to the poor, except when the queen and her husband dined with them. There was a carpenter shop for the boys, a museum where they kept specimens in natural history, — the prince was well-read in science, — and nine gardens, where the nine royal children worked and received the exact market price for their labor.

Here Prince Albert built model dwellings for his agricultural laborers, and schools for their children. Here are pretty red brick houses, one story high, built for the aged servants. Some years ago I visited an old thatched-roofed cottage at Osborne, and the humble woman who occupied it told me with pride about her queen. "She has often stood in this very room," she said. "Ah! a grand woman she is. Me and my husband ha' lived together forty-five year, and our eight children is all out to service; but the queen, God bless her, remembers the name of every one o' them, and always asks about them. We always stands when she comes. In the next house she has a little waiting-room, and I go there and gets her a cup o' tea. She never dresses fine. Ah! we all loves her."

Not far from the palace is Whippingham Church, where Victoria and Albert used to worship. It is built in the form of a Greek cross, her beloved Albert having laid the corner-stone. The royal portion is upholstered in blue, with a chair for the queen quite hidden from the other worshippers. In the quiet churchyard are the graves of several of the queen's servants. On one of the new graves, I was told, she had laid the oak metal wreath with her own hands.

The queen never forgets her servants. Her last book is dedicated to "My loyal Highlanders, and especially to the memory of my devoted personal attendant and faithful friend, John Brown." She says later in the book, "His loss to me is irreparable, for he deservedly possessed my entire confidence; and to say that he is daily, nay, hourly, missed by me, whose life-long gratitude he won by his constant care, attention, and devotion, is but a feeble expression of the truth."

When the baby of her wood forester was baptized and named Victoria, she went to the christening and kissed the baby. Also to the christening of a child of William Brown, John Brown's brother, named Albert.

In 1848 a house was purchased in Scotland, as Prince Albert needed the mountain air. The prince wrote, "We have withdrawn for a short time into a complete mountain solitude, where one rarely sees a human face." The queen writes of Balmoral, in her "Life in the Highlands," "It is a pretty little castle in the old Scottish style. There is a picturesque tower and garden in front, with a high wooded hill; at the back there is wood down to the Dee, and the hills rise all around."

Six or seven years later a large palace was built of red granite, and in 1856 the queen writes in her journal, "Every year my heart becomes more fixed in this dear paradise, and so much more so now that *all* has become my dearest Albert's *own* creation, . . . and his great taste and the impress of his dear hand have been stamped everywhere."

A year later the queen records in her journal some visits to the cottages of the poor. Meeting a woman eighty-eight years old, she says, "I gave her a warm petticoat, and the tears rolled down her old cheeks, and she shook my hands, and prayed God to bless me; it was very touching. I went into a small cabin of old Kitty Kear's, who is eighty-six years old, quite erect, and who welcomed us with a great air of dignity. She sat down and spun. I gave her also a warm petticoat." To another she gave a dress and a handkerchief, and the aged woman wept, and said, "You're too kind to me; you're over kind to me."

When the father of her faithful servant, John Brown, died, she says, "I went back to the house, and tried to soothe and comfort dear old Mrs. Brown, and gave her a mourning brooch with a little bit of her husband's hair which had been cut off yesterday, and I shall give a locket to each of the sons."

When a little boy was drowned, the queen went to the house of mourning, took the hand of the poor mother, and said, "how much she felt for her." No wonder the gifted Dr. Norman Macleod wrote: " God bless the queen for all her unwearied goodness! I admire her as a woman, love her as a friend, and reverence her as a queen."

A little incident in the fall of 1869 shows the queen's kind heart. She and some friends were riding among the lakes and mountains of Scotland. Near "Helen's Isle," mentioned in "The Lady of the Lake," she gathered a handful of pebbles; "some of the same white pebbles," she says, "which my dearest Albert picked up and had made into a bracelet for me."

The next day as they drove up the noble Pass of Leny, she says in her journal: "A little boy tried to give me a nosegay which was fixed to a pole, and in trying to catch it, Colonel Ponsonby let it fall. The little boy screamed, 'Stop, stop!' and ran in such an agony of disappointment that I stopped the carriage and took it from him to his mother's great delight."

With all these delightful outings, the cares and duties of both queen and prince increased as the years went by. Nine children were born in the royal homes.

Victoria Adelaide Maria Louisa, born Nov. 21, 1840.
Albert Edward, Prince of Wales, Nov. 9, 1841.
Alice Maud Mary, April 25, 1843.
Alfred Ernest Albert, Duke of Edinburgh, Aug. 6, 1844.
Helena Augusta Victoria, May 25, 1846.

Louise Caroline Alberta, March 18, 1848.

Arthur William Patrick Albert, Duke of Connaught, May 1, 1850.

Leopold George Duncan Albert, Duke of Albany, April 7, 1853.

Beatrice Mary Victoria Feodore, April 14, 1857.

Each of Victoria's children, as well as those of the Prince and Princess of Wales, have been christened in the same gown and cap of Honiton lace.

After the birth of the Prince of Wales, the queen wrote her Uncle Leopold: "I wonder very much whom our little boy will be like. You will understand *how* fervent are my prayers — and I am sure everybody's must be — to see him resemble his father in *every* respect, both in body and mind. Oh, my dearest uncle, I am sure if you knew how happy, how blessed, I feel, and how proud in possessing such a perfect being as my husband, and if you think you have been instrumental in bringing about this union, it must gladden your heart."

Again she wrote: "Albert is indeed looked up to and beloved as I could wish he should be. . . . People are much struck by his great power and energy; by the great self-denial, and constant wish to work for others, which are so striking in his character. But this is the happiest life. Pining for what one cannot have, and trying to run after what is pleasantest, invariably ends in disappointment."

Years later she wrote to the same uncle, after whom she had named her fourth son: "It is a mark of love and affection which I hope you will not disapprove. It is a name which is dearest to me after Albert's, and one

QUEEN VICTORIA. 337

which recalls the almost only happy days of my sad childhood."

This son, though delicate, had a very bright mind. Professor Tyndall, who went to Osborne to talk to the queen's children on science, relates how the little Prince Leopold showed him "his implements of husbandry, wheelbarrows, spades, rakes, and hoes allotted to him, his brothers, and his sisters, by their most noble and wise father. He showed me their museum, and told me to whom each of the objects belonged; and it was a profound comfort to me, for I felt that I was standing, not in the presence of any hollow artificiality, but in the presence of royal persons who had changed hollowness and artificiality for the cultivation of those virtues which lie in the power of every upright, wise man in any grade of society."

The children were reared carefully, yet simply. Their clothes were plain, as well as their food. The queen now and then took time to hear their lessons, and always insisted on their courteous manners toward everybody. The Rev. Mr. Hardy relates this story of the Princess Royal, Victoria, who, at a military review, seemed to be coquettish with some young officers of the escort. "Her majesty gave several reproving looks at her without avail. At length, in flirting her handkerchief over the side of the carriage, she dropped it, *not* accidentally. Instantly two or three young heroes sprang from their saddles to regain it. 'Stop, gentlemen!' exclaimed the queen. 'Leave it just where it lies. Now, my daughter, get down from the carriage and pick up your handkerchief.'"

When younger, the Princess Royal was told that if

she called the family physician "Brown," without prefixing Mr. or Dr., she would be sent to bed. The next day she said, "Good-morning, Brown," and then, looking at her mother, added, "and good-night, Brown, for I am going to bed," and went at once to receive the punishment.

A sailor carried one of the queen's daughters on board the royal yacht, and as he placed her on the deck, said, "There you are, my little lady." The child replied, "I am not a little lady; I'm a princess." The queen said, "You had better tell the kind sailor who carried you that you are not a little lady yet, though you hope to be one some day."

Grace Greenwood relates a story of the prince consort and his son riding across a London toll-bridge, when the keeper saluting them, the prince returned it, while the Prince of Wales dashed on. "My son, go back and return that man's salute," was his father's command; and it was obeyed.

Despite this affectionate home and loyal people, there were trials and dangers. The queen used to say, speaking of the prince, "Trials we must have; but what are they if we are together?" Many times the prince was blamed by the English nation, which did not fully appreciate him till he had gone from them forever. Seven different attempts have been made upon the life of the queen. She has met all bravely, as she wrote to Baron Stockmar, "Great events always make me calm. It is only trifles that irritate my nerves." On June 10, the year of her marriage, while riding with her husband in Hyde Park, she was shot at by a boy of seventeen, named Edward Oxford.

He was a bar-tender; and out of a situation. He was sent to Australia. Two years after, as Victoria and the prince were returning from church, a man named John Francis fired at her, and the day following again, as she was driving. When found guilty and sentenced to death, he fainted and was carried out of the court insensible. The queen commuted the sentence to imprisonment for life. Soon after a hunchback, Bean, fired at her as she was driving to the chapel of St. James's Palace. The pistol contained powder and pieces of a clay pipe. July 19, 1849, an Irish bricklayer, Hamilton, fired upon the queen and her three children as she was returning from a drawing-room. She stood up for a moment, and told the coachman to drive on. The pistol contained powder only. The man was sentenced to seven years' transportation.

In June, 1850, as she was leaving Cambridge House, where her uncle was dying, a captain of Hussars, named Pate, struck the queen on the face with a stick, crushing her bonnet, and inflicting quite a severe wound. He, too, was banished for seven years. In 1872 and in 1882 her majesty was fired at, and in both cases the men were believed to be insane.

In 1847 Prince Albert, then only twenty-eight years old, was made Chancellor of the University of Cambridge. Seated on the throne in the great hall of Trinity, the queen received the new chancellor, who read to her his speech. "I cannot say," wrote the queen, "how it agitated and embarrassed me to have to receive this address, and hear it read by my beloved Albert, who walked in at the head of the University, and who looked dear and beautiful in his robes."

The prince advocated increased study of science and literature at Cambridge, rather than so large a part of the course given to classics and mathematics. The London *Times* said, "The nation owes a debt of gratitude to the prince consort, the Chancellor of the University, for having been the first to suggest, and the most determined to carry out, the alteration in the Cambridge system."

In 1849 the prince planned and began to work for the Great Exhibition, which proved a wonderful stimulus to English industry and art, and indeed to the whole world. He met with opposition on every hand; but with great energy, persistency, and good-nature he at last overcame all difficulties. The exhibition was opened by the queen in the great Crystal Palace, May 1, 1851. London was crowded to repletion. The queen records in her journal: "The glimpse of the transept through the iron gates, the waving palms, flowers, statues, myriads of people filling the galleries and seats around, with the flourish of trumpets as we entered, gave us a sensation which I can never forget, and I felt much moved." And then the queen's heart is glad and proud of her "beloved husband, the author of this 'Peace-Festival,' which invited the industry of all nations of the earth. God bless my dearest Albert; God bless my dearest country, which has shown itself so great to-day!"

One poor woman, ninety-eight years old, walked from Cornwall, nearly three hundred miles, to see the exhibition and the queen.

For the next ten years, which passed all too quickly, the heart and hands of both queen and prince were full. Distinguished visitors, like Nicholas of Russia, and Napoleon and Eugénie, came to England, and were cordially received. There was no end of institutions to be opened, or great public works to be dedicated, where the queen or prince was called to preside and speak.

The prince was ever planning with Lord Shaftesbury for the betterment of the poor; improved dwellings, more education, provident societies, and the like. He was ever ready, as he said in one of his speeches, to show " his sympathy and interest for that class of our community which has most of the toil, and least of the enjoyments, of this world." He was first called Albert the Good by the ballast-heavers of London.

In 1854 the dreadful Crimean War began, between England and France against Russia, in aid of Turkey. The queen and her daughters made woollen comforters, mittens, and other warm coverings for the soldiers. The prince sent fur great-coats to all his brother officers of the Brigade of Guards. Victoria desired Florence Nightingale to tell the sick and the wounded that "day and night the queen thinks of her beloved troops." She wrote Lord Raglan: "The sad privations of the army, the bad weather, and the constant sickness are causes of the deepest concern and anxiety to the queen and prince. The braver her noble troops are, the more patiently and heroically they bear all the trials and sufferings, the more miserable we feel at their long continuance."

When Lord Cardigan went to Windsor on leave of absence, holding the royal children on his knees, they said, " You must hurry back to Sebastopol, and take it, else it will kill mama!"

The queen went to the hospitals at Chatham, where there were a large number of the wounded from the Crimea, and personally inspected them. She found the buildings bad, and "the windows so high that no one could look out of them." " The proposition to have hulks prepared for their reception," wrote the queen to Lord Panmure, "will do very well at first, but it would not, the queen thinks, do for any length of time. A hulk is a very gloomy place; and these poor men require their spirits to be cheered, as much as to have their physical sufferings attended to." These suggestions resulted in the great military hospital at Netley, one of the best equipped in the world. Victoria and Albert laid the corner-stone of the hospital in 1856. One of the first places to which she went after her husband's death was to this hospital. An Irish soldier, sent back from India, was near death. After the queen had spoken to him he said, "I thank God that he has allowed me to live long enough to see your Majesty with my own eyes." When she had passed through one long corridor, it was suggested that another would tire her; but she went, saying, " The poor men would be disappointed if I did not go to see them." In 1868 she laid the foundation stone of the great St. Thomas's Hospital.

On May 18, 1855, the queen gave medals to the officers and soldiers who had returned from the Crimean battle-fields. The ceremony took place on the Parade between the Horse Guards and St. James's Park. Thousands witnessed it with eyes dimmed with tears.

The queen wrote to her uncle Leopold concerning it: "Noble fellows! I own I feel as if they were my own children — my heart beats for them as for my nearest and dearest! They were so touched, so pleased, — many, I hear, cried; and they won't hear of giving up their medals to have their names engraved upon them, for fear they should not receive the identical one put into their hands by me! Several came by in a sadly mutilated state. None created more interest, or is more gallant, that young Sir Thomas Troubridge, who had at Inkermann one leg and the foot of the other carried away by a round shot, and continued commanding his battery till the battle was over, refusing to be carried away, only desiring his shattered limbs to be raised, in order to prevent too great a hemorrhage. He was dragged by in a bath-chair; and when I gave him his medal, I told him I should made him one of my aides-de-camp for his very gallant conduct; to which he replied, 'I am amply repaid for everything.' One must revere and love such soldiers as those."

A private who had lost his right arm in the trenches was asked by the queen if he still felt pain. He replied, "The time was that I had an arm with which to wield a weapon in your Majesty's service, and had I had fifty arms I would have devoted them all to serve your Majesty and my country; but now I have lost that arm — and it gives me a pain *here*," pointing to his heart. The queen replied feelingly, "I thank you for that!"

In 1857 the queen, before a great concourse of people in Hyde Park, bestowed the Victoria Cross on those distinguished for the highest and most unselfish valor. It is a Maltese cross made from the iron of the cannon taken at Sebastopol. Below the crown in the centre, is a scroll with the words, "For valour." The cross carries with it a pension of ten pounds a year. Victoria, on a roan horse, rode into the Park wearing a scarlet jacket and a blue skirt. Leaning from her horse, she pinned the cross on the breast of each hero.

This year, 1857, occurred the dreadful mutiny of the Sepoys in India, the massacre of two hundred and fifty English women and children at Cawnpore, through the treachery of Nana Sahib, and the relief of Lucknow by the immortal Havelock.

The following year, Jan. 25, 1858, the queen's eldest daughter, Victoria, was married to the Crown Prince of Germany, afterwards Emperor Frederick William. The queen writes in her journal: "The second most eventful day in my life as regards feelings. I felt as if I were being married over again myself, only much more nervous; for I had not that blessed feeling which I had then, which raises and supports one, of giving myself up for life to him whom I loved and worshipped — then and ever! . . . It was beautiful to see her kneeling with Fritz, their hands joined, and the train borne by the eight young ladies. . . . Dearest Albert took her by the hand to give her away — my beloved Albert (who, I saw, felt so strongly), which reminded me vividly of having in the same way, proudly, tenderly, confidently, most lovingly, knelt by him on this very same spot, and having our hands joined there. . . . Fritz spoke very plainly, Vicky too."

The good-byes were sad for all. "I think it will kill me to take leave of dear papa!" said Princess Victoria. A month later her father wrote her, glad of the cordial welcome she had received in Germany: "Let me express my fullest admiration of the way in which . . . you have kept down and overcome your own little personal troubles, perhaps also many feelings of sorrow not yet healed. This is the way to success, and the *only* way. If you have succeeded in winning people's hearts by friendliness, simplicity, and courtesy, the secret lay in this, that you were not thinking of yourself. Hold fast this mystic power, it is a spark from heaven."

In February, 1861, the queen writes to her Uncle Leopold: " On Sunday we celebrated, with feelings of deep gratitude and love, the twenty-first anniversary of our blessed marriage. . . . Very few can say with me, that their husband at the end of twenty-one years is not only full of the friendship, kindness, and affection which a truly happy marriage brings with it, but of the same tender love as in the very first days of our marriage ! "

A month later she wrote him again of the death of the Duchess of Kent: " *She* is gone, that precious dearly beloved, tender mother, whom I never parted from but for a few months, — without whom I cannot imagine life, — has been taken from us ! . . . I held her hand in mine to the very last, which I am truly thankful for ! But the watching that precious life going out was fearful ! Alas ! She never knew me ; but she was spared the pang of parting ! " The people of England loved and mourned the duchess, for she had reared for them a noble queen.

The queen wrote in her journal eleven years later : " Beloved mama's birthday ! That dear, dear mother ! So loving and tender, so full of kindness ! How often I long for that love ! "

This year, 1861, was to bring a double calamity to the queen. Prince Albert had become broken in health from overwork. Nov. 22, he drove in the rain from Windsor to Sandhurst to inspect the new Royal Military College. From that time he complained of "being tired," and did not regain his strength. Four days later, Nov. 28, the facts of the Trent affair becoming known in England, there was great excitement. That English vessel had been stopped early in our Civil War, and Messrs. Mason and Slidell, sent by the Confederates to represent the South at London and Paris, were taken from her and put on board an American ship-of-war, the San Jacinto. Palmerston, too often leaning towards a war policy, prepared at once for war, and demanded the liberation of the envoys. William H. Seward told Lord Lyons, so intense was the feeling at the North at that time, that "everything depended upon the wording" of the despatch sent to America. Prince Albert, ill as he was, with a wisdom and prudence that Americans can never forget, not approving the despatch of Lords Russell and Palmerston, submitted another of kindly tone to the queen, telling her that "he could scarcely hold his pen while writing it." The courteous despatch was sent and well received in America, and Messrs. Mason and Slidell were liberated.

The queen wrote: "Lord Palmerston cannot but look on this peaceful issue of the American quarrel as greatly owing to her beloved prince. . . . It was the last thing he ever wrote."

Through two weeks the good prince grew more tired and weak day by day. He talked with his beloved daughter Alice about dying, but the queen could not listen to it. "I seem to live in a dreadful dream," she writes in her diary, Dec. 7. "Later in the day my angel lay in bed, and I sat by him, watching the tears fall fast as I thought of the days of anxiety, even if not of alarm, which were in store for us."

Dec. 8, for the first time since his illness, Albert asked for music; and a piano was brought into the next room. His daughter Alice played, " *Ein' feste Burg ist unser Gott*," and he listened with tears in his eyes. Later in the day, the queen read " Peveril of the Peak " to him. After dinner " He stroked my face," the queen writes, " and smiled, and called me '*liebes Frauchen*' (dear little wife)."

Dec. 11, the queen writes in the morning: " I supported him; and he laid his dear head (his beautiful face, more beautiful than ever, is grown so thin) on my shoulder, and remained a little while, saying, ' It is very comfortable so, dear child!' which made me so happy."

During the evening of Dec. 12, although the fever had increased, he reminded the queen of business matters. " You have not forgotten the important communication to Nemours?" he asked. The prince seemed to improve; alas! it was only the gleam of light before the darkness. Dec. 14, as evening came on, she whispered, "*Es ist kleines Frauchen!*" ('T is your own little wife!); and he bowed his head and kissed her. Later she knelt by his side, and took his left hand " already cold." Two or three long breaths, and at forty-five minutes past ten the queen was a widow. Next morning, when she awoke after a troubled sleep, in her utter loneliness she said, " There is no one to call me Victoria now!" At Frogmore, near Windsor Castle, where Prince Albert died, she built a beautiful and costly mausoleum; and there, on every anniversary of her husband's death, a memorial service is held. The building is in the form of a cross, seventy feet broad, eighty feet long, and eighty-three feet high. Within, over the granite sarcophagus, is the recumbent statue of the prince in white marble by Baron Marochetti.

The beautiful Albert memorial, costing £120,000, erected by the queen and the nation, stands near the site of the Exhibition of 1851. It is one hundred and seventy-five feet high; a Gothic canopy and spire over a colossal bronze-gilt figure of the prince.

Over thirty years have passed since the death of the prince at forty-two. The queen is now (1895) seventy-six years old. Her life since his death has been a comparatively quiet one, and yet she has kept her resolution "never to shrink from duty." In her public life she has been as earnest and careful as ever. Lord Beaconsfield, through whose efforts the queen was proclaimed Empress of India, Jan. 1, 1877, said in a public address, "There is not a despatch received from abroad, or sent from this country abroad, which is not submitted to the queen. . . . At this moment there is probably no person living who has such complete control over the political condition of England as the sovereign herself."

In 1866, five years after the death of her husband, her majesty once more opened Parliament in person. She did not wear the robes of state. They were laid upon the throne, and the lord chancellor read her speech. Her robe was dark purple, with a Marie Stuart cap of white lace. Her only ornaments were a collar of brilliants and the blue ribbon of the Order of the Garter.

Through these thirty years, or indeed the last fifty,

the prosperity of England under Victoria has been wonderful, as is shown in "The Reign of Queen Victoria," edited by Thomas Humphrey Ward. In England and Wales population has increased ninety per cent; the deposits in the savings banks have increased from fourteen million pounds to over ninety million pounds. Penny postage was introduced soon after the queen came to the throne. The number of letters have increased from over eighty millions to nearly two thousand millions yearly.

Suffrage has been extended to millions; India, Africa, China, Egypt, and other countries have become more or less subject to Great Britain. Wealth has increased from four thousand million pounds to over nine thousand million pounds. While there is much poverty, good legislation has worked great reforms in shorter hours for labor and under better conditions. The wars under the queen in China, Egypt, Afghanistan, and Africa, which have shown England's bravery and power, the great advance along the line of education, the humane work done by Shaftesbury aided by Prince Albert, and other public events under her majesty, I have tried to show in a former book, "Famous English Statesmen of Queen Victoria's Reign."

Her domestic life has been as full of incident as her public. July 1, 1862, seven months after the death of the prince, Alice was married to Louis, Grand Duke of Hesse-Darmstadt. Prince Albert had written Baron Stockmar: "We like Louis better every day, because of his unaffectedly genial and cordial temper, his great modesty, and a very childlike nature, united with strict morality and genuine goodness and dignity." The next year, March 10, 1863, the Prince of Wales was married to the beautiful Alexandra, daughter of Christian IX. of Denmark. London, and indeed all England, gave itself up to rejoicing. Three years later, July 5, 1866, Helena married Prince Christian of Schleswig-Holstein, the queen herself giving away the bride. Louise married the Marquis of Lorne, eldest son of the Duke of Argyl, March 21, 1871. Alfred, Duke of Edinburgh, married the Grand Duchess Marie Alexandrovna, daughter of Alexander II. of Russia, Jan. 23, 1874. They made a state entry into London, after a grand wedding in St. Petersburg. The Duke of Connaught married, March 13, 1879, Princess Louise Margaret of Pussia.

The duke has shown himself brave in war. At Tel-el-Kebir, September, 1882, under Sir Garnet Wolseley, he led his brigade to the attack. Of his letters home the queen writes: "The description of his and the officers' sufferings and privations, as well as those of the poor men, made me miserable." When there was an explosion at the railway station, the duke put his shoulder to the wheel, and helped to push the trucks out of danger. The London *Times* said: "He worked like a navvy, not only leading, but physically helping, his men." When, on the return of the duke, the queen gave him and the officers medals for bravery, as she pinned on her son's medal, she bent forward and kissed him affectionately. The final reward of his gallant services has recently been conferred through his appointment as commander-in-chief of the British army.

Leopold married Helen, daughter of the Prince of Waldeck, Thursday, April 27, 1882. Beatrice married Prince Henry of Battenburg, third son of Alexander of

Hesse, July 23, 1885, at Whippingham Church, Osborne, wearing the veil of Honiton lace worn by her mother forty-five years before. Prince Alexander of Hesse's only sister was the mother of Alexander III. of Russia; so that Prince Henry of Battenburg is cousin to the reigning Tsar. The eldest brother of Prince Henry married Victoria, eldest daughter of Princess Alice. The second brother is Alexander, Prince of Bulgaria.

Being in Europe at the time of Prince Leopold's marriage, I went to Windsor to see the magnificent wedding procession. The state carriages were gorgeous. The queen, in black satin trimmed with pearls, and the Honiton lace worn at her marriage, with the Kohinoor at her throat, and her brilliant orders on her breast, looked kindly and noble. In the carriage with the queen were Beatrice, in satin and lace, and Victoria, the pretty eldest daughter of the Princess Alice. The carriage of the queen was drawn by four cream-colored horses, a man in white pantaloons and blue and red coat sitting on each right-hand horse, with two drivers in red coats and white pantaloons, and two footmen, one of them, John Brown, in his Scotch cap, her devoted servant for more than thirty years. Two of her bodyguard rode beside the carriage; and her trumpeter, in clothes of gold and crimson, rode before her with a large number of her Horse Guards.

In the procession were the Prince and Princess of Wales and their three daughters, the princess looking almost as young as they, and cheered as heartily as the queen and the bride herself. The Duke and Duchess of Connaught, the Duke and Duchess of Edinburgh, Helena and Prince Christian, Princess Louise, the King of the

Netherlands and his wife, Emma, the sister of the bride, and other royal persons, were in the procession.

The bride, eight years younger than Prince Leopold, looked innocent and pretty in her white satin embroidered in silver, the veil and dress-trimmings of point d'Alençon lace, the gift of Queen Emma, her sister. Queen Victoria gave her new daughter two necklaces of diamonds, pearls, and amethysts; shawls, dresses, laces, and brooches.

After the wedding Leopold and his bride went to Claremont for their home, where Victoria had loved to be when a child. The happy marriage was ended in two years by the sudden death of Leopold, Duke of Albany, at Cannes, where he had gone to avoid the harsh winds of spring. He was buried in St. George's Chapel, Windsor. The queen, who had learned to bear sorrow, greatly comforted the young wife.

Another death in the royal family had been extremely touching. Princess Alice, who had shown herself so strong and helpful when her father died, had proved herself a noble woman in both the Austro-Prussian and Franco-Prussian wars. During the latter she had four hospitals under her care at Mayence, till her health failed from overtasking herself. She told her mother that "she saw and smelt nothing but wounds." The queen sent many comforts to the wounded. One lad received a cape of her own making, and insisted on keeping it with him till he died.

At Darmstadt, making the acquaintance of Strauss, author of the "Life of Jesus," Princess Alice was for a time influenced by his teaching. The death of a child brought her back to her Christian faith. "The whole edifice of philosophical conclusion," said the princess, "which I had built up for myself, I find to have no foundation whatever: nothing of it is left; it has crumbled away like dust. What should we be, and what would become of us, if we did not believe there is a God who rules the world and each one of us? I feel the necessity of prayer; I love to sing hymns with my children."

In the autumn of 1878 the children of Princess Alice were ill with diphtheria, — Victoria, Alix, now empress of Russia, Irene, and Marie. Princess May, four years old, died. The only son, ten years old was dangerously ill. He had said, when his little brother died from falling out of a window while reaching after a toy, " When I die, you must die too, and all the others. Why can't we all die together? I don't like to die alone, like Frittie." When May died he wept sadly for her. Princess Alice, comforting him, kissed him, and took the fatal disease.

A few days before this she wrote her last letter to her mother: " Gratitude for those left is *so* strong, and indeed resignation entire and complete to the higher will; and so all feel together and encourage each other. Life is *not* endless in this world. God be praised! *There* is truth and joy — but, here, oh! so much trial and pain; and as the number of those one loves increases in heaven, it makes our passage easier — and *home* is there!"

She was ill only a week. The day before she died she said, "I am sorry to cause my mother so much anxiety," and asked that the Union Jack be laid over her coffin, hoping "that no one in the country of her adoption would object to her wish to be borne to her rest with the old English colors above her."

On the morning of Dec. 14, 1878, the anniversary of her father's death, she died, murmuring towards the last, "From Friday to Saturday — May — dear papa!" At Balmoral the queen has erected to her memory a cross twelve feet three inches high, of Aberdeenshire granite, with the words: "Her name shall live, though now she is no more."

Less than a year later, June 1, 1879, the prince imperial, the son of Napoleon III., was killed by the Zulus in South Africa. The queen records in her last book, "More Leaves from the Journal of a Life in the Highlands," published in 1883, that when told the dreadful tidings, she put her hands to her head, and cried out, "No, no! it cannot, cannot be true! . . . Poor, poor, dear empress! her only, only child — her all — gone!" Victoria erected a white marble cross to his memory in Zululand, on the spot where "he fell with his face to the foe."

The queen has sorrowed with others in their sorrow. More than once the American nation has experienced and appreciated her sympathy. When Lincoln and Garfield were assassinated, and when General Grant died, her words were cordial and heartfelt. To Mrs. Garfield she sent an autograph letter: "Words cannot express the deep sympathy I feel with you at this terrible moment. May God support and comfort you, as he alone can." She sent a wreath of white roses and other choice flowers for the coffin of the dead president.

The queen has ever encouraged literature. Of Tennyson and his works, both she and the prince were very fond. She desired to meet Browning and Carlyle informally, and did so at the deanery of Westminster Abbey, introduced by Dean Stanley. She asked Charles Dickens to accept a copy of her "Journal in the Highlands," with her autograph in it, remarking, as she handed it to him, "that she felt considerable hesitation in presenting so humble a literary effort to one of the foremost writers of the age."

When she visited the home of Sir Walter Scott, at Abbotsford, and took tea in his dining-room, in which room he died, she writes in her journal: "In the study we saw his journal, in which Mr. Hope Scott asked me to write my name (which I felt it to be a presumption in me to do), as also in others."

Both the queen and prince were as kind to animals as to persons. When "Dear Eos" died, as the queen called her, a black greyhound which the prince had brought with him from Germany, the latter wrote his grandmother, "You will share my sorrow at this loss. She was a singularly clever creature, and had been for eleven years faithfully devoted to me. How many recollections are linked with her!" The queen has photographs of her collies, Sharp and Noble, in her second book of "Life in the Highlands." "Dear good Sharp was with us, and out each day, and so affectionate.... My favorite collie Noble is always down-stairs when we take our meals, and was so good, Brown making him lie on a chair or couch; and he never attempted to come down without permission, and even held a piece of cake in his mouth without eating it till told he might. He is the most 'biddable' dog I ever saw, and so affectionate and kind; if he thinks you are not pleased with him, he puts out his paws, and begs in such an affectionate way."

After the prince died the queen used to visit his dumb

animals on his model farm, thinking the poor creatures would miss the voice of their humane master.

Queen Victoria has reigned fifty-eight years. Her Jubilee, 1887, when she had reigned fifty years, made great rejoicing in England. Thirty thousand children celebrated the event in Hyde Park. The great procession to Westminster Abbey, June 21, was a sight never to be forgotten. The Archbishop of Canterbury said, "The queen has identified herself with almost every great movement for the social, moral, and religious progress of the time."

The queen has been a lover of morality, of the Sabbath, of the Bible, of all that makes a nation good as well as great. When an African chief sent her a present of native cloth, and expressed his admiration of England's commerce, she replied, "Commerce alone will not make a nation great and happy like England. England has become great and happy by the knowledge of the true God and Jesus Christ."

As a mother, a wife, and a sovereign, Queen Victoria has been an illustrious example. May the kings who succeed her be as upright in character, and rule as wisely and well!